Journal of a Psychic

Thursday, January 29, 1976:

"I'm crazy, absolutely crazy," I told myself for the hundredth time this afternoon. "I should be on my way to see a psychiatrist instead of a parapsychologist. What do I know about this man anyway? He's probably crazier than I am!"

Thursday, February 26, 1976:

...I'm beginning to feel a bit more comfortable with my experiences. But the more comfortable I feel, the more experiences I have...

Sunday, February 29, 1976:

I want to quit these sessions. My fears are being realized; my psychic centers are being opened. And it's happening so fast that I feel like I'm on a rollercoaster...

Sunday, May 16, 1976:

I went to bed last night feeling great peace. Then I awoke with the impression that I would have some experiences with trance mediumship. I found that thought frightening. If I'd been possessed before, I could be possessed again...

BEYOND THE BODY

Wilma Wake, Ph. D.

LEISURE BOOKS ❧ NEW YORK CITY

to Burt

A LEISURE BOOK

Published by

Dorchester Publishing Co., Inc.
6 East 39th Street
New York City

Printed in the United States of America

ACKNOWLEDGMENTS

This book would not have been possible without the support of Dick Smith and the Prana Foundation. I'm especially grateful to Dick for his permission to quote freely from our sessions together.

Special thanks to those who read early versions of the manuscript and gave me helpful comments. Some of these people are: John White, Joe Hebert, John Hebert, Sue Kelley, Cindy Bevan, William Vogel, Pat Ferguson, David Pastor, Jim Stearns, Justine Wolf, Rick Miller, Lynn Guardiani, Rene Gemmell, Sandy Krot, Denny Rodie, Nancy Christensen, Gary Christensen.

I owe a special debt to my friend who is called Judy in this book for the hours she spent listening to my confusions and searchings.

I'm also grateful to my mother, father, and brother for their help and support.

Special thanks as well to my friend Barbara Jepson for not only editing my material, but also teaching me to be my own editor; and to my typist, Marge Hiller, for her attention to detail and her numerous helpful comments.

I can't put into words my gratitude to my husband Burt. His love, gentleness, humor, and intellectual integrity have been a constant source of strength to me.

PREFACE

It's been seven years now since I began the journey I wrote about in Beyond the Body and Beyond the Mind. When Beyond the Body was first released in 1979, I was afraid that the public would reject anyone involved with past life regression, automatic writing, and trance communication. I chose the pen name "Sandra Gibson" so that no one would know that I, Wilma Wake, was really the author. I was surprised and delighted to receive hundreds of warm letters from readers who were also struggling to understand the psychic. I realized that my journey is not unique, but rather reflects a universal struggle to grasp the mystical dimension of life.

After my second book was released in 1981, I had only one problem: my health. I went to a holistic physician who treated me for severe food allergies. My health improved markedly, but some serious allergies remained. I meditated, and felt guided to begin therapy with a Certified Pastoral Counselor in Concord. (Certified Pastoral Counselors are ministers who have become trained as psychotherapists.) In my work with him, it emerged that I was not expressing all aspects of myself. I discovered that I wanted to be trained for the ministry and to study pastoral psychology. After making the decision to begin seminary studies, my health improved considerably.

When I entered seminary this past January, I discovered Christianity's long mystical tradition, and found in the mystics a common link with my own meditative experiences. I learned that a national organization—the Spiritual Frontiers Fellowship*—strives to integrate psychic phenomena and mystical experiences within the traditional churches. Its academic affiliate—the Academy of Religion and Psychical

*10819 Winner Rd., Independence, MO 64052

Research**—encourages dialogue between clergy and academics. I realized that I wanted to be part of the efforts to join together the religious, the psychic, and the mystical.

I found myself drawn frequently to the Episcopal Church, where I experienced the deepest meditative states and the most profound love I had ever known. In my sense of meditative union with Christ, I felt I was re-connecting with a vital part of my being.

I joined the Episcopal Church, and plan to continue my seminary education. I don't know whether or not I will someday be ordained, but I do know that by integrating my psychic side with my religious nature, I have regained my health.

When my books were scheduled to be reissued this fall, I knew I had to give up my pen name and use my real name on the covers ("Sandra Gibson" is still used in the text). I could not be "Wilma Wake" as I pursued my academic/religious studies in seminary and "Sandra Gibson" as I wrote about my psychic/mystical self. The seminary student and the mystic are the same person, though I've grown and matured through more years of living, meditating, and seeking. I now have more experience and more knowledge than I did then, but I also have more questions and fewer answers. I'm less certain than ever that I understand the psychic or how it relates to the mystical, the religious, and the psychological.

I only know that each of these realities does exist. The same journey that led me into the psychic has led me into awe-inspiring mystical encounters with Christ and is now leading me on a search to understand it all. It is a search that engages all of the dimensions of my being: the mystical, psychic, religious, academic, and psychological.

I invite you now on a journey to a period of my life that radically altered my conception of reality, not because my books are likely to give you the answers to life's mysteries,

---

**PO Box 614, Bloomfield, CT 06002

but because they may raise questions in your mind. If so, I hope you will join me in striving to understand these many dimensions of human existence.

Wilma Wake
June, 1983

PART I

THURSDAY, JANUARY 29, 1976

"I'm crazy; absolutely crazy," I told myself for the hundredth time this afternoon as I maneuvered my way through the New Haven rush-hour traffic. "I should be on my way to see a psychiatrist instead of a parapsychologist. What do I know about this man Dick Smith anyway? He's probably crazier than I am!"

All I knew about Dick Smith at 5:00 p.m. this afternoon was that he is a hypnotherapist who maintains a private practice three days a week and works two days a week at a psychic research center called the Prana Foundation. I first heard about him last November when I saw his name in the paper announcing a lecture he was giving on psychic research.

I wasn't interested in research, but I attended the lecture anyway for another reason. I was seeking help. I've been troubled for a long time by a series of frightening psychic experiences that have me doubting my sanity. When I saw a notice for that lecture, I thought that perhaps Dick Smith was someone who could help me.

So I wandered into a Yale lecture hall on a chilly evening last November and nestled into a chair in the back. I liked Dick Smith right away. He was objective and scientific, yet also open to the occult. And he seemed very knowledgeable about the psychic. That's the kind of person I had been looking for.

My resistance to facing my experiences was so strong, however, that it took me months to find the courage to call this man. I even joined the Prana Foundation, but never attended a function. Many days I picked up the telephone to call for a private appointment, but then hung up before I dialed. Then today, something different

9

happened. It was a slow day at the office. A light drizzle and grey January sky made me more depressed than usual. For whatever reason, I completed the phone call.

"Prana Foundation. Dick Smith speaking."

I panicked, and almost hung up. But I found my voice and spoke. "This is Sandy Gibson. I'm a member of the Foundation and I heard you speak in November."

"Yes, I recognize your name. What can I do for you?"

I paused. Perhaps I could just request information on yoga classes. "I'd like to make an appointment to see you for a consultation." I had said it. It was too late to back out.

"Fine. I'll be working late today. Would you like to come in around 5:00? 5:00 to 7:00. I like the initial appointment to be for two hours."

Initial appointment? That implied others in the future. I wasn't sure I could handle even one. "O.K. I'll see you then."

Several hours later, I drove into a quiet residential neighborhood and pulled up in front of a Tudor office building. I sat in the car for a few minutes to rehearse what I would say. I could try expressing what I felt: "I don't want to be here, and I don't know why I came. I've been having psychic experiences, and they frighten me. I'm afraid they're not real, which means I'm crazy. I'm afraid that they *are* real, and I'm in danger of being possessed. I don't know you and I don't trust you enough to talk to you about these experiences, so my being here is completely pointless."

I sighed and opened the car door. I doubted that I would say what I felt.

The drizzle had turned to snow. I buried my chin in my coat collar as I made my way across the quiet side street to a two-story office building. I'm not sure what I expected a psychic foundation to look like, but I was mildly surprised at the modern, efficient-looking suite of offices I found. The only person I could see was Dick Smith, typing at the desk in the reception room. He looked up as I entered.

"Hi! You must be Sandy." I nodded. "I'm working on

our newsletter." He glanced at his watch. "You're early."

"I'm sorry," I mumbled, taking his remark as a criticism.

"Don't apologize! It's good to be early. An Arien trait, you know." I looked startled. "Of course I know you're an Aries; your birthdate is on your membership application. You'd be surprised how many Prana members are Aries. I'm one myself. Aries is a pioneer in new fields." I didn't know how to respond to his statements. I don't believe in astrology.

"Come on into my office, Sandy." He led the way to a spacious, comfortable room. I noted the blue-green shag rug on the floor, a desk with a large black swivel chair, and a big green recliner chair. He motioned me to the recliner. I paused and eyed it suspiciously. I didn't want that stranger to use his powers as a hypnotist on me. I sat down uneasily.

Dick made himself comfortable in the swivel chair and lit up a cigarette. "I knew you'd be calling for an appointment ever since I saw you in the audience at my lecture."

"How did you know that?" I asked, surprised.

Dick shrugged. "I just knew. What can I help you with?"

This was it. I wished I had rehearsed something. I looked intently at the man, wondering if I could trust him. He appeared to be in his early forties, and had greying hair, mustache, and very clear, intense eyes—a hypnotist's eyes. He was dressed conservatively in slacks and a shirt. He could be an average businessman, instead of a researcher on the occult.

"Well, actually, I don't know if my problem is revelant to what you do here. I remember that in your lecture you talked about the work the Prana Foundation is doing in the area of psychic healing, but I don't have any interest in that."

"Our focus is on healing in all its aspects—spiritual, psychological, and physical. We have a variety of ways that our clients can use to help themselves grow and become healthier. One of the purposes of this first consultation is to discuss which aspect of Prana would be best suited for you. That's why I said this first session would be for two hours. We have an excellent astrologer on the staff. You might want to begin with a reading from her."

"Absolutely not. I don't believe in astrology." His eyebrows puckered; he didn't seem pleased with my answer. "I hope you'll keep an open mind on that."

"Sure, my mind's always open. Maybe someday I'll be into that, but not now."

"That's fine. Just so you stay open. Prana also offers a series of classes. I offer one in self-development, and we have others in meditation, yoga, and astrology."

"No, not now. I'm too uptight about the psychic to keep up with a class."

"And then we offer counseling, on a one-to-one basis."

"That's what I'm interested in. That's the only thing that could help me right now."

"O.K.," Dick said, getting up. "I'll get you the necessary forms." Forms? That seemed committal; I wasn't sure I was ever coming back.

"Let's see," he said, returning to the room. "I've already got your name and address. Age?"

"28."

"Occupation?"

"I'm a full-time research interviewer, and a part-time graduate student. I'm writing my dissertation for a Ph.D. in education. I taught high school for a year and college for several years. But then we moved to New Haven and this job was the only one I could find. I really want to be a family therapist, though, and I hope to find a counseling job when my research contract runs out in May."

"Married?"

"Yes. Burt is 30. He's a social psychologist. He's just finishing his doctoral work, too. We moved to New Haven nine months ago when Burt got his job offer. Before that, we were in graduate school together for several years outside of D.C."

"O.K., now I have a statement we ask clients to sign. I'll read it to you: 'It is my understanding that Prana is a

12

non-profit, charitable psychic research foundation and all information offered is at my request. The information given will be used as a guideline in personal matters and is not to be accepted as "fact." I shall, if possible, offer an honest evaluation of all data received.' Do you understand that?"

"Yes, it's clear. But I'm not sure I'll be back. I want to think about it first, especially before I sign anything. I'm not even sure that my problem is relevant to the kind of counseling you do. And I'm not sure that I want to commit myself to counseling. This first session is exploratory for me—to give me a chance to decide if I want to go ahead with it or not."

"Good. You can take all the time you want to decide. You might leave here tonight and never come back—or come back in a year or six months. The door will always be open to you. And we'll love you just as much whether you ever come back or not."

Was this talk about love sincere or was this man a phoney? It was hard to tell. "Look, you still don't know if my problem is relevant to what you do here."

"I can't tell you that until you tell me something about your problem."

I paused, wondering how far I could trust this stranger. I said softly, "I think I've been having psychic experiences. They're frightening and confusing, and I'd like them to go away."

"Keep talking. You're in the ball park. This is the type of problem we specialize in working with."

"How do you help people understand the psychic?" I wanted Dick to talk so that I wouldn't have to reveal anymore.

"You're an individual. I trust you don't doubt that at all?" I shook my head. Individuality is something I understand. "We deal with everyone as an individual. My approach to each client is different." After a pause, he added, "I can only give the most general responses to your questions, because you've given me only the most general idea of your problem."

"O.K., I'll tell you more specifics. Basically, these

13

psychic experiences fall into three areas. First, there are the pre-cognitive experiences. There are times when I know that something is going to happen. When the event comes to pass, I get very upset, not understanding how I could have known, and wishing I didn't have to see things in advance. I don't know how to deal with it. And the other problem is that—well—I sometimes feel that I've lived before. Sometimes, when I'm falling asleep at night, I see myself in a different body in a different time. Usually, I'm seeing some traumatic event. I have very strong emotional reactions to these scenes, and I'm not sure what to do with those feelings. I wish the scenes would go away and leave me alone."

I had been looking off into space, but now glanced up. Dick Smith was watching me with full concentration, while puffing absently on a cigarette. "And the third?"

"The what?" My mind had wandered.

"The third type of psychic experience you've had."

"I'm sorry. I can't discuss it. Not yet."

"Look, Sandy," Dick's voice was gentle. "I need to know more about what you've experienced if I'm going to help you. But I won't pry things out of you. It's up to you to bring out what you want to talk about."

I felt depressed. I just couldn't tell him about that third area. I didn't want to discuss my problem and I didn't want to come back. But yet, I felt that I would return and pour out my heart to this stranger with the hypnotic eyes. How could I reconcile my desire to forget all this with my gut feeling that I'd be back soon?

"Something heavy going through?"

I started. I must have been staring into space for several minutes. "I'm thinking about whether or not I want to continue with these sessions."

"I don't want an answer from you tonight. Wait until you're sure. Often, clients expect me to tell them whether or not they need to come back, but I refuse to make that decision for them. Only you know what you need, and how you want to meet that need. Something inside of you got you in here for this session tonight. That same thing in you will either bring you back here or lead you elsewhere for help. Listen to your inner voice. As I said, the door here is always open."

"O.K. I don't want to discuss anything else tonight."

"That's fine. Do you have any questions you'd like to ask while you're here?"

"Yes. What do you use hypnosis for?"

His answer was vague; perhaps he could sense my fear of hypnosis. "It's just a tool we sometimes use to explore past lives."

That sounded safe. I have no intention of exploring past lives. I want those so-called "memories" to go away; I don't want to explore them further.

Dick glanced at his watch, and said, "I'll just charge you for one hour tonight." He made out a bill and handed it to me. "We charge $25 an hour, but you can adjust the bill according to your willingness or ability to pay."

"Well," I said, "if I don't come back, I'll send you a check."

"If you want. It's up to you."

We walked out to the reception area, and Dick gave me a big smile. "It's been a real pleasure talking to you, Sandy. Whether you come back or not—take care. And thanks for coming tonight."

"Good-night, Mr. Smith."

"'Dick,' please. I much prefer being called Dick."

"Good-night, Dick."

For the first time in months, I felt that maybe everything would work out all right. Maybe—just maybe—I'm not crazy. But if I'm not crazy, I may be on the road to possession. I shivered from much more than the cold as I pulled away from the curb. I tried to put the whole thing out of my mind. Burt would be home, and I hoped he'd have dinner ready when I arrived.

He did. I could smell the soup as I walked up the stairs.

He gave me a big hug as I walked into the kitchen. I love the feel of his soft, curly beard against my cheeks. Burt is just the right size for me—5'6" to my 5'2". Tonight his hug was especially warm and supportive.

We had a long talk over dinner. He surprised me. I thought he would consider my visit to Prana foolish. Burt is much more intellectual than I am. I tend toward the intuitive, and Burt toward the logical. He sometimes scoffs at my intuitive and generalized approach to situations, in contrast to his very precise, scientific mind. But I keep forgetting that Burt has been changing. One night last year he tuned in telepathically on a friend of ours, and the two of them transmitted mental images to each other all evening. Burt was amazed and has been interested in ESP ever since. He's also been involved this past year with yoga, meditation, and T'ai Ch'i.

*   *   *   *

"So that's what happened in my session, Burt. What do you think? Should I go back or just quit now and forget the whole thing?"

"I think that's a decision you'll have to make for yourself," he responded, putting the kettle on for tea. Burt doesn't like to give advice to people, yet I'm always asking for his opinion.

"I know, but what do you *think*?"

"Well, I think you've got to have help. This has been going on for a long time. And maybe this man can help you. In your position, I'd give it a chance."

I was disappointed in Burt's support. I wanted him to talk me out of going back. "Yes, but what if all this is my imagination? Or what if I'm going crazy? Maybe it'll just get worse at the Prana Foundation."

"There's only one way to find out. I don't think you're crazy, and I don't think your experiences have been your imagination. There've been too many over too many years for it to be all coincidence. Looking at it logically, something's going on. And you're depressed about it. So in your situation, I'd go back. But that's got to be your decision, honey."

I left the table glumly and cleared up the dishes. Then I made a cup of peppermint tea, and came in here to my study to write out these experiences. So it's up to me. And I don't know what to do. I can't shake this feeling, from deep down inside, that I'm going back. I resent that. Where's my free will?

I don't know if I'll go back or not. But I am going to start keeping this journal so I can write out my feelings and experiences. Maybe, in this way, I can come to understand them.

TUESDAY, FEBRUARY 3, 1976

Today I called Dick and told him that I want to continue with counseling. It was hard to work up the courage to do that; I've been struggling with myself for several days. I'm not sure why I decided to go back. I guess I'm too depressed not to.

Dick asked me to write out a description of the kinds of psychic experiences I've had. That was a stroke of genius on his part; I'll be freer in what I write than I would be speaking to him in his office.

It all started when I was 13. Our eighth-grade science class was studying hypnosis, and the teacher casually mentioned a book called *The Search for Bridey Murphy*, in which a woman under hypnosis recalled a previous life. I was intrigued and raced to the public library that evening. I was a fast reader, and had finished most of the book before I went to sleep that night. It was the most fascinating, yet also most frightening, book I'd ever read. The concept of reincarnation was appealing to me, but the thought of disembodied spirits floating around was scary. For many years after that, I was afraid of the dark.

It was a few months after reading that book that my own experiences started at night after I went to bed. As I sit here, trying to compose the next sentence, I find myself shaking. I can't write about it; I still don't want Dick to know about this "third area." I'll just skip it for now and go on to other things.

Those night-time experiences tapered off in a couple of years. Between my 15th and 23rd years, I had very few psychic experiences—just little things, like sensing in advance what the school cafeteria would serve for lunch. I was both fascinated by and repelled by the occult. I'd read a book or two on reincarnation, and then the old fears would set in. Those scary night experiences would start again, so I'd give up my interest for months or years at a time.

During those years I was busy going to school, and, from my 19th year, dating Burt. Then Burt and I got married in June of 1970 when I was 23 and he was 24. We spent the summer touring Europe in a leased Renault, sleeping at night in our pup tent. Our travels were quite an adventure, but I learned a strange new fact about myself. I was terribly afraid of heights. It posed a problem because Burt loved climbing every tower or castle we passed. I found it increasingly difficult to accompany him on these climbs. My fears reached a climax when we visited an old Spanish castle. We wandered around inside, then ended up on a lovely balcony over-looking a valley. Suddenly I turned pale and began to shake. I ran inside the castle and sat on a stone step. Burt ran after me, and sat down.

"What's the matter? You look like you've seen a ghost."

"I had the strangest, craziest feeling on that balcony."

"Tell me about it." Burt was trying his best to be patient, but he was getting tired of my acrophobia and was eager to return to the panoramic view outside.

I looked around. No tourists in earshot. "Well, it's absurd, but I had a feeling that we had been on that balcony before."

"That's crazy. We've never been to Europe before." Burt's impatience was growing.

"I know. That's what's so weird. I felt that we were there in a different time—maybe centuries ago. And we had a fight, and..." my voice started quivering and I could feel tears welling up in my eyes "...and we had a fight, and you pushed me off!" The tears were rolling down my cheeks.

Burt was thoughtful as he put an arm around my shoulder. "You're talking about reincarnation."

"I guess I am."

"Well, it's possible, of course. Anything's possible. But we don't have any evidence. I doubt that we ever will. Let's forget it, and finish exploring the castle. Whatever I may have done centuries ago, I'm not going to push you off the balcony now, so come and enjoy the view."

I didn't think Burt was taking me seriously, which was understandable under the circumstances. I was struggling with my *thought* that the entire incident was absolutely absurd, but yet with my undeniable *feeling* that I had been there before and pushed to my death. I refused to go back out to the balcony, so I went down to buy some postcards while Burt enjoyed his view.

After our trip, Burt and I moved to the Washington, D. C. area where he started his graduate work in psychology and I began mine in education. Our lives were absorbed with the daily routines of graduate school, making new friends, and exploring the area. But the terror of that Spanish castle scene kept plaguing me.

Usually, the memories came as I was falling asleep. Just as I had given up conscious control of my thoughts, but before I had entered the sleep state, I would often find myself jerked fully awake with another upsetting "memory." A number of times, I saw the scene enacted in my mind; a panoramic scene, in living color. I could see a young woman, whom I knew to be of noble birth, and a young man, perhaps a prince. I knew the two of them were in love, probably engaged to be married. I saw them wearing clothing of hundreds of years ago. I also knew that I was the young woman and the young man was Burt. Then an argument would break out and something would be hurled by the young man. I could see and feel the young woman falling, screaming, to her death. I would find myself wide awake, gasping, and afraid to sleep again.

By the next morning, with the sun streaming into the bedroom window, it would all seem like nonsense. But the feelings aroused by those scenes continued to impose themselves at the strangest times. There were times when that scene would suddenly pop into mind while Burt and I were making love, and I couldn't dispel the feeling that I was making love with my murderer. I felt that he had no right to touch me. We finally realized that, no matter how bizarre that scene was, its emotional impact on me was undeniable, and we had to discuss it. We handled it like any other trauma. Burt encouraged me to talk about it over and over until I began to accept it. But the process produced some absurd discussions.

"What's wrong, honey?"

"That Spanish castle scene just appeared to me," I would confess in an agonized voice, feeling guilty that I couldn't continue with our lovemaking.

"O.K. Tell me what you're feeling."

I would again pour out the story. "I was just standing there. I was so in love with you, and so pleased when we were engaged. You were of a higher rank than me, and you were quite a catch. But more than that, I was desperately in love with you. I wanted so much to marry you and live in that castle. It would have been such a great life." At that point, I would start to sob. "How could you have done it? How could you have killed me?"

Burt would come up with reassurances that sounded as weird as the entire scene. "Look, honey, I'm sure I was miserable the rest of my life. I probably felt guilty and lonely that entire lifetime."

I would feel better, the sobs would cease, and we would return to our caresses. That pattern was repeated a number of times before the pain of the scene dulled and we could joke about it freely.

That's when the scenes from England started imping-ing upon my consciousness. I would see myself as a young, upper-class Englishman around the turn of the century. And Burt's image would pop into mind again and again, but as a beautiful Englishwoman, extremely feminine, with long blond hair. As I fell asleep, I would feel myself transported again and again to an England that had existed long before my birth, and I would be hit with a rush of impressions about the relationship be-tween Burt and me. Or actually between "Sylvia" and "Edward."

"Burt, I feel awful," I would say.

"Why, honey?"

"I was a playboy in that life, and I think that you were terribly in love with me although I rejected you. Or Sylvia, actually."

"Well that's understandable, considering I had pushed you off a castle wall just 300 years before that! Whatever Edward did to Sylvia is over now. I forgive you completely."

"Are you sure, Burt? Really sure? I feel that I treated you pretty shabbily and never did marry you."

"Well, you married me this time, and that's all that counts." With that, Burt would return to his paper or book. These conversations were extremely strange since neither of us believed in reincarnation.

It was during the second year of our marriage that I became aware of pre-cognitive impressions. They started the year we planned a summer vacation trip to Mexico. I dearly loved Mexico, ever since I had spent a summer there before our marriage. I wanted very much to take Burt there and share with him the places, food, and people I had come to love. I was very excited when we agreed on a summer camping trip into Mexico. But, as the date for departure grew close, I realized that I had lost my desire to go. I couldn't understand it.

"It's weird, Burt," I said. "I just don't want to go anymore. I feel uneasy about something."

"That's crazy. Everything's all planned and you've looked forward to it for months," Burt responded sensibly.

"Well, I know. That's why I can't understand why I don't want to go now."

The trip was a disaster. Less than a week after leaving, on the 4th of July no less, our car's engine broke down and had to be replaced. Hoping to save money, we hired a mechanic to rebuild the engine. He estimated three or four days for the job, but it took him ten.

But at least we had some money, some time and a functioning car. We proceeded towards Mexico. Against my better judgment.

"I feel that we ought to turn around and go home," I confessed.

"Look, that's crazy." Burt's common sense again. "Your previous feeling about not coming may have been an intuition that we should have listened to. But whatever you sensed has now happened. So we can continue and still have a nice trip."

It made sense. But didn't explain my feelings of uneasiness. Several days later, as we approached the border, our car broke down again. This time we took it to a VW dealer, who took a week and another $200 to repair it. The trip was completely ruined, but it convinced Burt that I had sound intuitions, and ever since then, he's respectfully asked my feelings about any trip or major project he undertook. I feel very uneasy about being consulted, and don't take my own intuitions seriously.

A few months later, I had a terrifying dream. I saw a fire on our wooden kitchen table. It was burning in a perfect circle in one corner, but it never consumed the table or tablecloth. When I woke up, I wanted to dash into the kitchen to make sure our table was O.K. But I talked myself out of it and soon fell asleep again. By the next morning, I had completely forgotten it.

Until the next week, that is. I came home from the campus early one afternoon, and was alarmed when I smelled smoke after opening our apartment door. I ran inside, and discovered a pile of ashes, in a circle, on our table. I sank weakly into the nearest chair. It couldn't be—it just couldn't be! There was no sign of how it might have started. Or, more strangely, why it stopped instead of spreading. I made sure the ashes were cool, and then flew out of the apartment and back to school.

I found Burt in the psychology lab getting ready to run a subject for his master's thesis. Breathlessly, I spilled out the story.

"It's not the fire that's so scary—it's the dream. I saw it all before it happened. And it seemed so real in that dream!"

Burt was concerned and curious, but not frightened. "As soon as I run this subject, I'll be ready to go. Just sit down and relax, honey."

Burt, too, was puzzled when he saw the ashes later. We never did find the cause for the fire, or any reason for it to mysteriously stop after burning a circle.

About that time, I had an auto accident. It was very

minor, on the surface. I was fully stopped when a woman hit me from the rear. I've heard jokes about people claiming whiplash injuries from such accidents, but I never understood what dreadful pain they could entail. After a few months of medical treatment, the doctor said everything was fine, and the pain would eventually subside. It never did. So, discouraged, I took up hatha yoga. I was immediately impressed at the improvement in my back, and in my general sense of well-being. Gradually, I became interested in meditation. As I meditated, I felt myself grow spiritually. As I grew spiritually, the psychic experiences increased. I had more of the horrible night experiences that started at 13. I "remembered" more past lives. I had more pre-cognitive feelings.

On New Year's Eve last year, Burt asked me to make some predictions for the coming year. I wrote some out, and we went over them together. I predicted that Burt would receive a job offer the coming spring from a New England state—most likely Connecticut. That was hopeful, since Burt had just started looking for jobs as his graduate work neared completion. But he had sent very few applications to any New England states. I predicted that the job would be academically-oriented, but that Burt would soon become discouraged with it. I also wrote that I would have trouble adjusting to the move and would become depressed. But by the fall, I would have a job, too. It would not be ideal, but would likely be a stepping-stone to a better job in the spring. I also felt very strongly that I was rapidly reaching a point where my psychic experiences would become so frightening that I would not be able to cope alone. And at that time, I felt, someone would come into my life to serve as a teacher or guide to help me understand the psychic and overcome my fears.

I was shaken up, of course, when my predictions came to pass. The job offer from New Haven was totally unexpected because Burt hadn't applied for it; he knew nothing about the job. An old friend, now affiliated with Yale, had called and invited him to apply. I became

24

depressed when we moved, as I missed my friends and my job opportunities in the D.C. area. But I have felt better since I started my research job in September.

The weird experiences continued, however, and have been getting more frightening. Like the experience of hunting for an apartment in New Haven. When we were shown the apartment we eventually rented, Burt was ecstatic. It was spacious, charming, furnished, and cheaper than anything comparable we'd seen. But I was uneasy. The landlord was out of town for the week-end, so we drove up to Cape Cod to rest and talk it over.

"Can you be more specific about your feelings on this apartment?" Burt queried as we plopped onto a gorgeous beach, on a gorgeous day.

"Well, my feelings center specifically towards the back of the place. I guess around the back door." The feelings seemed so far away in this paradise.

"O.K. Keep trying to get in touch with what you feel about the back door."

"What I feel is vague, but I'll try and translate it into words. It's a feeling of a break-in. On a day when I'm in the apartment, and scared out of my mind. But not hurt."

"Do you feel this break-in could be prevented?"

"Not the attempt, but maybe its successful completion."

"How soon?"

"Oh, maybe within two to six months. This is silly, Burt, just absurd. It's a nice apartment; let's get it."

It *was* a nice apartment, and we rented it that Monday. But Burt spent considerable time making it very difficult to break in our back door. Three months later, alone in the apartment, I was taking a shower when I heard a knock at the back door. By the time I got there, no one was around, so I forgot about it—until later that day. The other tenants reported that someone had broken into several other apartments, but hadn't been able to get into ours. The broken window above the lock was proof he had tried. I was scared. Not from the attempted burglary, but because I had sensed it in advance.

One of the most unsettling experiences was my

airplane flight last summer. After we got settled in New Haven I decided to fly to Illinois for a week with my parents. As I was musing over what day to leave, a thought popped unbidden into my mind: "Don't take American Airlines out of New York on Monday." I paused a moment to try and interpret the feelings that had come with that thought. They weren't feelings of disaster, but of mishap or accident. I couldn't be sure they even applied to any plane I might be on, but just to some American Airlines jet leaving New York on that Monday. I decided the feelings were absurd, and to prove it, I booked a Monday flight on A.A. I felt jittery afterwards, but was determined to prove the foolishness of my wild imaginings.

My flight was smooth and uneventful, so I arrived feeling rather smug. I had outsmarted whatever force seemed to be pursuing me with unwanted psychic adventures. After landing, I phoned my Mom to let her know I had arrived.

"Thank goodness you're safe!" she blurted out. I started feeling uneasy.

"What do you mean?" I asked tentatively.

"Didn't you hear about the accident?" she asked. "An American Airlines jet leaving New York had an accident. That's all that was on the news, and I didn't know if it was your plane or not."

Coincidence! Complete coincidence, I convinced myself. Until I saw the evening news on TV. There was something about seeing the story reported in living color that was unnerving. An A. A. plane heading West had had an accident on the runway, and there had been some minor injuries. That was the first time I had ever seen an intuition of mine come true and be reported in the news. I raced upstairs to be alone for awhile. I felt weak and faint. For the first time, I knew that it had not been coincidence. I really had known about that accident in advance. And it scared the hell out of me. I had to have help.

As the days went by, I lost my conviction that any of my experiences were genuine psychic experiences, and instead started to suspect I might be crazy.

Well, I guess I can summarize those incidents for Dick. I wonder if he's the teacher I predicted would come into my life to help me understand the psychic? Perhaps. But right now he's a stranger to me, and I don't trust him enough to tell him about the third type of psychic experience I've had. I'm afraid to reveal it. I'm afraid of being thought crazy. I'm afraid of being possessed.

MONDAY, FEBRUARY 9, 1976

I've finally started the counseling, but I'm seriously considering quitting. Dick talked about nonsense during my first session. I had mailed him a summary of my experiences, with a note, saying "I have good feelings about our sessions, and look forward to getting started." But those good feelings disappeared on Friday afternoon, a few hours before my session. I felt nauseous and had a headache. I was restless and withdrawn at work, wishing I had never made the appointment.

My uneasiness increased when I arrived at the Foundation, and found Dick poring over some books on astrology.

"Hi, come on in!" he called to me in a friendly voice. "I'm no astrologer, but I'm looking over some of the things in your horoscope. You're rather secretive, aren't you? Not revealing your inner self easily to others, assuming they won't understand?"

I sat down with resignation. What a waste of a busy person's time, going over astrological charts! But I had a feeling this wouldn't be the last time I'd hear about the subject from Dick Smith. "No, I don't think I'm a secretive person. I'm very open, but only with a few close friends. I don't reveal my inner self easily to casual friends." That should disprove the accuracy of anything in my chart, I thought.

"Yes, that's what I mean. And something else very interesting here. You know a lot of things without knowing *how* you know them. You learn almost by osmosis. That's a blessing in many ways, but also confusing when you don't understand the source of your knowledge."

"That does sound like me," I admitted reluctantly.

Dick swiveled his chair away from his desk to face me. "I got your letter. It was very interesting. But I'd like to wait a few weeks before giving you my impressions about what's going on. I don't want to lead you. And you're not here to get your ego fed."

That sounded very strange. Did he think that it would feed my ego if he told me he thought the experiences were real? Didn't he understand the real terror I felt about the possibility of their reality?

"Have you ever had any other counseling along these lines?"

That question startled me; it was unexpected. "Well, I did have one session about a year ago with a friend, visiting from California. He's a reincarnation therapist— specializing in helping people get in touch with their past lives and relive the traumas back there. I was curious and asked him a lot of questions about his work. Then he offered to give me a sample free session to give me a better idea of what was involved."

"And what happened at that session?" Dick seemed interested.

"I don't want to talk about it."

"It's important that you do. Let me explain why. You can say 'I don't want to talk about it' as much as you want. But the more you say it, the longer it's going to take to work through your present problem. The only way you'll ever work through your fears and resistance is by talking about them."

I sighed, and while formulating the words to explain that I didn't care how long it took, in no way could I talk about it today, I found myself pouring out a story that I thought I didn't want to reveal.

"Two days before the scheduled session with him I woke up screaming from the most terrifying dream I've ever had. I knew that in that dream I had seen whatever it was that made me so afraid of the psychic. But after awakening, I couldn't remember a thing. Except a name: 'Mr. Rock' or 'Mr. Stone.' But I felt the terror. When I met my friend for the session, I told him about the dream.

He had me lie down and relax and then recount the dream over and over, until I could feel myself actually getting into it again. I felt myself falling through a black pit and then suddenly landing on a rocky, alien planet. I was in a different body, I think long ago." My voice started cracking, and my eyes were filling up with tears. The pain from that experience was still terribly real. "I was apparently on an enemy planet, and I was taken to a room and brutally tortured, and then left to die near the rocks, under the hot sun." I started crying, but composed myself quickly and changed the subject. I was relieved to see that Dick let me get away with it. "My main concern right now is that fear that I have. How can I get rid of it?"

"Before you leave today, I'm going to teach you an exercise that will help."

"What kind of exercise?" My curiosity was aroused.

"It involves mentally projecting a protective white light around yourself." That sounded weird. "Do you understand the concept of auras?" I looked confused, so Dick went on. "We all emanate colored lights from our bodies that give indications of our emotional state and personality. White is the presence of all color, and contains the finest and highest vibrations."

The man really was crazy! I blocked him out and didn't hear another word for ten minutes. I was trying to figure out what had possessed me to tell him about that planet experience. Suddenly I was aware that Dick was talking about how to do this exercise. I let bits and pieces of his words filter into my consciousness. Something about visualizing a symbol above my head—any symbol of my choice that had a spiritual significance to me—and picturing a bright, pure white light coming out of that symbol into my head and penetrating my entire body. I tuned out again for awhile, and then in again just in time to hear... "...and then you recite the 23rd Psalm or some similar protective prayer."

That did it. I don't believe in prayer or in the Bible. I seriously considered never returning.

"You should do that twice a day, for just a few minutes each time. And one more thing I'd like you to start doing.

30

Keep a notebook. Write down anything you'd like in it—experiences, dreams, questions for me. It's to help you."

"O.K., I'll keep a notebook, but I'm not at all certain I'll do that white light exercise."

"Why not?" Dick seemed surprised.

"It sounds weird and I don't feel comfortable with it."

"There's not much I can do to help you unless you begin white-lighting yourself. It's the only way you're going to feel secure and safe."

"I'll think about it." I gathered up my things to leave. I had had enough for one day, and wanted to go home and consider whether I should ever come back. I said good-bye quickly.

Burt and I talked that night at dinner, and I tried to explain why I didn't want to try the exercise.

"For one thing, it sounds religious, and I'm an agnostic, as you well know." Burt considers himself an atheist, and we've had many arguments over the years on the virtues of our respective positions. Burt delights in quoting Walter Kaufmann, saying that an agnostic is really an atheist who doesn't want to offend people. I then counter with the argument that an atheist is as bad as a theist, because there is no way to either prove or disprove the existence of God. Then Burt starts drawing analogies to Santa Claus and the Tooth Fairy, and I change the subject.

"And in addition, I'm suspicious of the exercise. I'm afraid that in some way it will increase my psychic experiences instead of halting them." Burt was a practical man. I felt certain he would agree with me on the absurdity of the exercise, and encourage me to drop out of the therapy.

"If I were in your position, I'd certainly give it a try." Burt's response surprised me. "You've been troubled for a long time, and you've finally met someone who may be able to help. It only makes sense to give his advice a try. I can't see how it could possibly hurt you."

"I'll think about it." I knew I absolutely did not want to try it. On the other hand, I had that uncomfortable feeling

31

deep down inside that I would get into it, sooner or later. That night I slept fitfully.

I woke up Saturday morning with a strange sense of peace. On a very deep level, I felt I was finally getting the help I needed and that everything would be O.K. I slept well that night.

But any security I obtained on Saturday crumbled yesterday. Burt and I seemed to be plugged into each other telepathically and I'm quite unsettled by the experience. During the afternoon, I was contemplating the 200 records in our collection trying to pick one that matched my mood when I had a sudden impulse to put on a particular Chopin nocturne. I was rather surprised at my choice, since I had just been thinking I was in a Rolling Stones mood. Burt walked into the room, delighted at my choice. "I was just thinking about that Chopin nocturne before you put it on!" he reported gleefully. I found the incident extremely disturbing. If I was acting on Burt's thoughts instead of my own, where was my free will? How did I know if I did what I did because I wanted to do it, or because I was picking up thoughts telepathically from others? I lay awake a long time last night trying to understand.

I'm very troubled about this white light exercise. I really do want to give the counseling a chance, and feel that I *should* try what Dick suggested. But I don't *want* to. I'm afraid of opening my psychic senses even further, and encouraging these experiences. I'm not sure that Dick understands that I want to *stop* my experiences from happening; I don't want to encourage them in any way. I don't trust Dick; I'm afraid he won't help me stop the experiences. I don't think he can stop them. And if he can't stop them, why am I going? My thoughts are very muddled.

THURSDAY, FEBRUARY 12, 1976

Tomorrow I see Dick again, and I'm going to let him know that I want to stop these experiences. I've written out a list of questions for him, so that I can understand what this white light nonsense is all about. I already tried it yesterday, and, just as I feared, it produced another strange experience.

I refused to pray beforehand, and instead read a poem I like from the *Tao Te Ching*. I'm more comfortable with Eastern religions than I am with Christianity. I tried it first thing in the morning, and nothing at all happened. So I felt a bit more relaxed, and confident when I tried it in the evening. But as soon as I put that white light around myself, I had a strong sense of several presences in the room. They radiated a sense of protection. So I stopped the white-lighting at once. I don't want any "presences" around for any reason whatsoever!

SUNDAY, FEBRUARY 15, 1976

I went into Friday's session prepared to tell Dick that unless he could stop my experiences, I was quitting. But I never got around to saying that. Instead, we covered a lot of areas—some scary, some fascinating. I took my tape recorder because last time I had blocked out most of what he said, and for $25, I want to remember every word.

I went in with a list of questions, which Dick asked to read. I settled into the big green chair with a cup of tea and switched my recorder on as we began.

"O.K. 'On the white light exercise—What does it do and why?'" He read off my first question. "Now some of this I'm saying, of course, is redundant."

"That's O.K.; I remember almost nothing from last week."

"There are clairvoyants who are able to see colors around people—or auras. They can tell what an individual is drawing in terms of colors or energies."

"So the color is like an energy?" I found myself more curious and less resistant than last week.

"It's a form of energy; yes. The color indicates what kind of energy you as an individual are drawing. Your color indicates your mood, your state of health, your personality, your spiritual growth. White respresents the purest form of all colors. Call it a cloak of protection, if you will. All right, now—anyone, absolutely anyone, who is searching psychically, is sensitive. They're opening their sensitivities to psychic things. This is common sense. So what you're doing is trying to protect yourself from the thoughts and feelings and attitudes of others, so that you can find your own identity, your own feelings, your own thoughts—"

34

"So I'm less likely to, say, be telepathic with the white light?" I was thinking of last Sunday's experience and hoping Dick was pointing out a way to avoid such experiences in the future.

"Oh, you'll still be telepathic, but you'll be picking up only the finest of vibrations. But these you won't mind receiving, because they obviously bring *your* vibrations up, and when yours go up, you start transmitting them, too."

"I'm afraid of it sensitizing me to more scary experiences."

"It's the opposite. You are doing it to attune yourself to the higher vibrations."

"But it won't necessarily eliminate my own psychic experiences?"

"No. If anything, it'll filter them."

"But I don't want to have any at all."

Dick cleared his throat. "This is something that, in all fairness to you, Sandy, you're not going to turn off. You are having them because obviously it's time for you to have them. There is a need for you to know."

"But I feel a need to shut them off at least long enough to figure out what's happening—if it's psychic, or my imagination, or whatever. I want to understand it and get hold of it."

"Have you been using the white light every day?"

Time for true confession. "I started on Wednesday. I was afraid to try so I decided to wait until a couple of days before the session, so if it was a frightening experience, I could talk about it with you right away."

"You could have called." I hadn't thought of that. "You can call in the middle of the night if it's an emergency."

"I'm afraid that these sessions will increase my psychic experiences," I said.

"Well, whether you come here or anywhere, Sandy, I will say this, and it's meant to be encouraging, and not discouraging, all right? You must be able to appreciate that you the soul—*you the soul*—have selected a very specific path to walk. And you brought tools to work with

35

to accomplish your mission on earth. Now for years there has been a great attempt on the part of the soul to awaken you to the reality that you've got something to do. When you think about it *in context* nothing has happened to you to blow your mind. You've been upset, depressed, moody. But nothing, absolutely nothing, has happened to hurt you. You follow me? What you're running away from is the fear of fear. No matter how far you run, no matter how fast you run it's still *you*; you're going to bring your soul with you. And your soul apparently has already resigned itself to the fact that Sandy has chosen a path and Sandy's got a lesson to learn, so she'd better settle down to listen."

"Well, if I could be convinced that everything that's happening is by my own choice, it'd be a lot easier to handle. For example, I had a spontaneous urge to put a particular record on the stereo. And then I found out that Burt in the next room had just been thinking about that particular record. Now that may have been a telepathic experience."

"Sure."

"Well, it seemed to me at the time that I had a spontaneous urge to do something. But maybe it wasn't my own desire. Maybe I was picking up Burt's desire in the other room."

"But, so what? Look at it objectively. Does it matter whether you were transmitting to him or he was transmitting to you? It was something you both enjoyed. It was a higher vibration."

"But what I'm asking is 'How do I know?' Say I feel a spontaneous urge to do something. How do I know I'm not actually picking up what somebody else wants me to do?"

"This is one of the reasons for the white light. We could sit here for many hours relaying perfect examples of telepathy as higher vibrations. Like thinking: 'Gee, I think I'll turn right instead of left' while driving down the road. And your friend is down the road stranded, thinking, 'Boy, I wish somebody would come by and pick me up.' Normally you never go home that way. All right, this was a charitable thing that was transmitted to you, a desire to do a charitable act. It was a higher vibration. Now your objective, obviously, with this ability is to serve. If it's realistic, if no one's going to get hurt by it, then do it. Putting on a record isn't going to hurt a soul; so you put on a record. You follow me?" I did and didn't. It was a lot to absorb all at once. "You've got to use common sense in this. Have you ever worked with a psychic before? I mean a real honest-to-goodness psychic? Not one who just thinks he or she is—there're all types."

"No."

"An honest-to-goodness psychic is almost 100% self-less. Their lives are truly dedicated to serving. When they go into 'trances' or altered-states-of-consciousness, whatever you want to call it, these individuals almost totally set aside their own ego, and they become super-conscious. The information that flows through them is really beautiful. But when we sit down and *try* to do this we get very little. It has to be *so natural*—you cannot force it. We all have potential psychic ability but either it's your time to work with it or it just isn't. Am I getting away from your questions?"

A million miles away. I couldn't understand why he was telling me all of that. "Well, let me make sure I understand the exercise. I picture a spiritual symbol above my head..."

"In gold."

"Oh, I forgot that. Why gold?"

"Gold in auras is symbolic of wisdom—great knowledge on a spiritual level. You're using the gold symbol because it represents a cosmic consciousness—God. Your God. The God. Whatever you relate to. So you're requesting a shield of white light from that golden object which is, in essence, saying that you request that only truth come through."

"All right, now out of this gold symbol comes a white light which is supposed to go into my head . . ."

"Into the crown chakra. The body contains seven chakras or points where energy enters. You don't need to know the specifics on chakras right now, only that there is a crown chakra on the top of the head. The object is above your head, and the light's pouring down through a funnel-shaped dome into your head. When you do it right, you'll feel a protective warmth, you'll *feel* secure. Nothing freaky about it. If you ever feel anything freaky, that's you; it's not the white light. It's your own imagination getting carried away. Now it goes into your spine, fills your whole body—imagine a shell being formed around your body. The more you do it, the greater the shell becomes. You only have to do it for about a minute."

I told Dick I had selected a poem to use instead of the 23rd Psalm, and he emphasized the importance of my being comfortable with whatever I chose.

"We raise our vibrations in many ways—with color, with sound, with smell, O.K.? When an individual says a meditation, a mantra, a prayer, it's got to be from the heart. Sandy, if you don't feel it, forget it."

"Well, I don't feel comfortable with the 23rd Psalm."

"O.K., that's fine. It was a suggestion because it's very emcompassing and very profound. It could be just a simple: 'Dear God, use me as a tool, thank you,' and that's it. Regardless of what you think on a conscious level, if your gut says to say it, and you feel you're being a hypocrite—don't worry about the conscious mind. You've got to follow what's inside."

"I wouldn't want to say 'Dear God' because I don't believe in a personal god." It had to come out sometime. All this god talk was making me very uncomfortable.

"This may be one of the areas where you're having great conflict. Perhaps the fact that you're not fully grasping the fact that *you* are God might be giving you trouble."

That was a relief. I had heard the theory before that "God" was actually the combined total of all living things, the life force in us all. I was comfortable with that. "That's O.K., I can deal with that."

"All right, let's talk about that. You *are* God—in the *becoming*. You are in the process of becoming perfect."

"I don't like to use the word 'God' because of the connotations it has in most religions."

"That's unfair—to you. What you're discussing now is religious philosophy, not spiritual truth. There is a spiritual truth. There is one God, regardless of what you call that one God. God is universal consciousness consisting of all souls. So all souls *collectively* are God. Now, if you can relate to that, what's wrong with God?"

"Nothing, if that's the way you're using the term."

"Sure."

"But people are always praying to God as though he were somebody outside; and that's something I don't like."

"Again, you must hear this in context. I'm really glad you brought this little machine; you can study this, if you wish. All right now, we are all striving very, very hard to establish an identity. When we understand who we are, we realize that we are God in the becoming. There is energy contained in every cell of our bodies that we call God. Now when you say a prayer, what you're really trying to do is attain a state of harmony with cosmic consciousness, with all souls. Prayer is an exchange of the higher vibrations. So when you say 'God in heaven,' if you can understand that in context, God is within. God is a state of consciousness. It's knowing without really being able to grasp or understand. And, of course, you have Mercury in Pisces."

"Mercury in Pisces?" He was talking gibberish again.

"It's a blessing in many, many ways, because you learn by osmosis. It's like knowing, but not knowing why you know what you know. It sometimes causes us a great deal of confusion."

"Well, sometimes I may have an intuition about something. And maybe it's a very valid intuition which I should follow. On the other hand, maybe it's not. Maybe it's imagination. How do I know which it is?"

"All right. For instance?"

I paused. "Well, how about that experience with American Airlines—when I sensed an accident in advance?"

"O.K., I'll tell you what I would have done. Again, you have to follow *your* gut feelings. I would have made a phone call and I would have said: 'My name is Dick

Smith, and I'm very much involved in a study of the occult and metaphysics. For what it's worth, you people do whatever you want with it, I got a very strong impression that something may happen to one of your flights. I don't know whether it's a defective engine, a defective landing device, but I'm telling you...'"

"I think you'd get on the FBI list, with all the scare about airport bombings..."

"Fine; so what? My life is completely open. I've nothing to hide. I don't say very much unless I'm asked, but I don't go around hiding my life. It's there: if you want to see it, look at it. If I were to concern myself with what other people think, I'd dig a hole and bury myself. That makes us self-conscious, bringing that ego back into play again. It's the very thing we're here to pull out of. 'What are they going to think about me.' Who cares? A lot of people think I'm nuts. So what? That's their bag. I would have made the phone call." Dick paused for a moment then continued. "Now, let's assume that with all these things you've been experiencing, hit or miss, that it is possible that you may get a message, a feeling, a thought, a vibration, that's going to be heavy. It is possible that all of these years, you've been trained for the sole purpose of preventing *one* thing. You see, our guides, spirits, guardian angels—what do *you* call them?"

This *was* heavy; I was starting to feel depressed. "I don't even know if they exist, much less have a name for them."

"They exist, whatever you want to call them. They're energies functioning on a higher vibration; they're kind of like college grads doing post-graduate work by helping us. A lot of people have gone through the earthly cycle and they know what we're going through. They have an empathy for the human race, so they're going to try their very best to help as many as ask for it. So they gather around us and feed us bits of information when we ask for it, or they feed us gut feelings. Some people call them guides, some people call them spirit energies; it's irrelevant. It's beautiful, whatever it is. And these little energies will feed something into you, and they'll say

40

'Hey, Sandy, there's something going to happen over here. Get on the horn and correct it or do something about it.' And you do. You may save one life. You may save hundreds of lives. The mere fact that you were used as a tool to perform a function, to prevent a disaster, is the important thing. The whole trip was worth it."

I was close to tears. The very idea that I might be put in a position to prevent an accident was overwhelming. Undoubtedly, I'd get the message wrong and blow the whole thing.

Dick's voice became soft and gentle. "In time. We'll work it out. How're you doing?"

"I'm scared," I blurted out, starting to cry.

"Of what?" Dick seemed surprised, as though he couldn't imagine anything to be scared of.

"I'm scared of the whole thing." I felt that should explain it adequately. In case it didn't, I elaborated. "I'm scared to be alone, I'm scared to go to bed at night. I'm afraid of something happening."

"O.K., what could possibly happen? Let's take it to the extreme."

I didn't want to talk about it, but I was crying, and again found myself blurting out information I didn't think I wanted to share. "Well, the thing I'm really scared of is tappings."

"Tappings? What kind of tappings?"

"That's the third type of psychic experience I've had. I often hear tappings in my room at night, and I sense a presence around." Tears were rolling down my cheeks. It was too late to back out. I continued. "They started when I was thirteen. I heard them at night on my alarm clock. Now when it happens, I hear a ticking in my room—then these code-like taps."

"Fine, I believe you; you hear tappings and tickings. But in my mind, I ask: 'Does it hurt you?' You've got to look at things in context. What's the worst thing that could happen?"

"Well, the kind of thing that happened in the *Exorcist*. I think that would be the most frightening thing that could happen." It was out; my fear of possession.

"All right. Let me explain something to you. The odds against being possessed are *horrendously* high. Did you read the book?" I nodded. "OK, that's good because the movie cheated the book. They left out the most important part of the whole damned book, and that was how she got involved. In the movie she was talking with Captain Jack, or whatever his name was—her friend from the Ouija board. The book went into great detail about how this young teen-aged gal got involved with the Ouija board—no white light, no previous training, and totally opened her mind to the occult. She was sensitive to begin with, and this 'thing' moved in. OK?" Again I nodded. "The odds against this occurring are very high! Now, in my mind, it was a karmic thing. Are you aware of the true story?"

"I just heard it was based on a newspaper account."

"It was a twelve or thirteen year-old boy. And the priest didn't die; he's in an asylum. Other than that, it's based on an accurate story. My feeling is that this child, in a past life, consciously, knowingly, and willingly, conjured up some really heavy vibrations and started sending them out after people. He was consciously aware, and did it on purpose for selfish reasons. The universal law of karma dictates: 'Whatever you sow, so shall you reap.' How else is this little kid going to know what it's like to have a weird thing floating around in your aura doing a number on everybody unless he lived through it? Bet you a nickel that next time around he's not going to zap anybody. He's going to think twice. You follow me?"

"Um hmm."

"OK, so this is one of your fears—becoming possessed. All right, my immediate reaction again, looking at it logically, is 'Why the hell are you here if you're going to be possessed?' Obviously you're here for the reassurance that, number one, there's no way you're about to be possessed; number two, why would you begin to hear about the white light and mantras, and prayers, and why would you even begin to explore the higher forms of vibrations if you were being prepared to be possessed? Common sense, now."

"I'm afraid, too, of the possibility that somebody's trying to communicate with me." My deepest fears were coming out.

"OK, suppose somebody is?"

"Well, how would I know how to deal with it?"

"The white light. Now I know you're afraid to use the white light for fear of opening your psychic senses, and yet I'm trying to relay to you the importance of it. Absolutely, positively, to the best of my knowledge nobody's ever been hurt by the white light. Not one single, solitary person. Now, by using the white light, you may make contact. Maybe your grandmother or your grandfather or your great aunt or somebody is trying to say: 'Hey, Sandy, keep an eyeball out for Suzy Glutz. Keep her home Saturday.' And you'd respond: 'Oh, all right. I'll talk to her about it.'"

"Well, when I did the white light yesterday, I had the feeling somebody was in the room with me. It was a protective feeling, but . . ."

"Fine. This is what you'll attract."

"But it's hard to deal with this feeling that somebody's there when there's *nobody* there."

"Nobody's there that you're able to see, granted. But what you sense is the frequency that the energy is transmitting to you. Warmth, benevolence, love, caring— it's like a big mother's around you, and she's saying 'Sandy, honey, we're not going to bite you.' Follow me? 'Relax, kiddo, there's nobody after you, take it easy. We're here to help, we're here to serve. Nobody's out to get you.' And you can almost feel this." That was quite an insight. It really hadn't occurred to me that this presence I felt might be there to help rather than to try to possess. "Look, Sandy, nothing I say is thought out; it's spontaneous. In other words, I don't try to talk with you. I just open my mouth and let the words come out, and figure you can do whatever you want with them. At least I'm a tangible source of information; I'm flesh, I bleed when I get cuts and scrapes. I'm really mortal. I have to shave once in awhile—the whole scene! So to you I'm tangible; someone to relate with. These little energies that

43

are around you are saying, 'Hey, Sandy, go see Dick Smith, he's a kook and he'll really get into this stuff with you.'"

"One of the things hard for me to deal with is decision making. Like, coming here. I felt that on one level the decision was already made. And on another level I felt I was trying to make it."

Dick smiled. "It was already made."

"But it's very hard to deal with. I feel that I don't have any free will."

"Oh, but you do. Absolutely, you do. You didn't have to be here today. You made the decision many years ago that *in time* you were really going to nail this thing down. Years ago you made that decision. But it wasn't time. Now it is."

Dick glanced down at the page of questions again. "Have I answered all of these?"

"I think you hit most of them."

"Now your writing is a confirmation of your chart. You have a tendency to let your heart rule your head. It's called 'Heart-Ruling-Head-Disease,'" he added with a smile. "It's fine, but you're a little bit too emotional."

"You read handwriting, too?" Light was dawning. Now I understood why he had asked to read from my questions directly—they were handwritten!

"Yes, I've been a graphologist for many years. It's a little hobby, and a very good one. I do a little bit of everything—a typical Aries—jack of all trades, master of none!" He laughed heartily. "I'm into a lot of things—herbology, numerology, astrology. Everything everybody throws out, I go around with my dust pan and sweep up!"

I left the session feeling very relieved. I didn't understand it intellectually, but I felt marvelous. I didn't have time to talk to Burt until late that evening, however. He had recently heard of a vegetarian co-operative dinner held every Friday evening, and we decided to try it out that night.

We were both quite impressed with the dinner. The food was good, plentiful, and cheap and the vibes were warm and relaxing. We sat at long tables, which

44

facilitated discussion, but I found myself answering perfunctorily when addressed. My mind was still back at the Prana Foundation. Many of Dick's comments kept floating through my mind: "Obviously, you're here for the assurances that there's no way you're about to be possessed . . . it's like a big mother's around you, and she's saying 'Sandy, honey, we're not going to bite you. . . . Relax, kiddo, there's nobody after you, take it easy. We're here to help, we're here to serve. Nobody's out to get you.'"

It was late that night before Burt and I had a chance to talk, and I summarized the session for him. "You know," I said, "intellectually, I feel I'm a fool to have wasted $25 and an hour of my time today to listen to that nonsense. On the other hand I can't deny how much better I feel. It's like my subconscious mind got reassurances that I'm not aware of consciously."

I feel so much better since that session, that I'm considering trying yoga and meditation again.

WEDNESDAY, FEBRUARY 18, 1976

Outside of my sessions with Dick, life has been rather boring lately. I'm tired of my job. I interview people, which in itself is interesting, but most of the time, I'm tabulating data and helping to write research reports. I'm not very interested in that kind of work. And I end up having large blocks of free time to chit-chat with co-workers or read books.

I recently signed up to do some volunteer work in family therapy. I'll be working one evening a week with a very experienced family therapist. That starts next week, and I'm really excited about it.

That's the kind of work I want to do. I had a year of training in family therapy while we were in graduate school. I worked as a co-therapist once a week, attending seminars and lectures, and working with families. I want to continue that training, which is one reason it was so hard for me to leave the D.C. area and come to New Haven. I felt I was giving up some career opportunities for myself for the sake of Burt's career. And since we strive to have an equalitarian marriage, I resented it. We do agree that both of our jobs are equally important, but it can be very difficult to put that concept into practice!

However, after a couple of months in New Haven, Burt's boss called me. He told me there was a job opening in his department for a research interviewer that I might like to apply for. It could possibly entail some counseling, but in any case would enable me to make contacts with people in the counseling field. I would only have to make a commitment to stay until May. So I applied, was offered the job, and immediately accepted. I started the first of September.

The job was interesting and challenging for a couple of months. But the counseling opportunities never worked out. And now it's just boring.

FRIDAY, FEBRUARY 20, 1976

We just got back from this evening's co-op dinner, and I have to put down my feelings about what happened today. I saw Dick again. I decided in advance that I was going to discuss my tappings with him.

I started by telling him I was meditating again; he was pleased. Then I confided in him the incident that had led me to give up meditation.

"It happened several months ago. I had been meditating deeply when I had a sudden, virtually uncontrollable impulse to race to the closet and drag out my old Ouija board. I had had it for years, but never found the courage to use it. But during this meditation, the urge was over-powering. I felt a presence in the room, and almost felt that I was in communication with that force. I found myself pleading mentally with this unseen intruder: 'Please go away. I can't use the Ouija board. I'm scared.' I felt a rush of thoughts and emotions, as if in answer. 'I'm friendly. I won't hurt you. We need to communicate.' 'No,' I found myself screaming mentally. 'I'm all alone in the house right now, and anything could happen. Maybe it's safe to communicate with you, but I don't know how to ensure my safety.' Again, I felt a rush of thoughts in answer: 'Do what you need to do to feel safe. I've waited for a long time, and can continue to wait. But for your sake, don't waste time. There is much to be done.' With that, the presence vanished. I was so shaken that I gave up meditation. About a month later, I heard about the Prana Foundation, and realized I needed counseling." I paused to collect my thoughts, and then continued. "I want to discuss those tappings some more. At first, they were always from the area of my alarm clock. It was like somebody took a pencil and tapped on the clock. And it sounded like a code."

"If tappings show some sign of intelligence, as opposed to a very rhythmic pattern, we pay more attention to them," Dick commented.

"Well, being thirteen, and being fairly open, I thought it might be somebody trying to contact me. So I figured if I was receiving a code, the best thing would be to write it down and try to decipher it. So I did that for a long time, but could never decipher it. Part of the problem was that I had to be passive and quiet to hear them at all; trying to write them down often broke the contact. Then I tried to communicate with the taps. I said mentally: 'Look, let's work out a system: 3 taps for yes; 2 taps for no.' And then I'd ask questions, and I'd get these yes-no answers for awhile. But then the tappings would just take off again and give out a whole series of code-like taps."

"Is it like you weren't asking the right questions?" Dick queried.

"Something like that. I got frustrated after awhile and gave up. I stopped paying any attention to them, and they went away for a number of years. And then they started coming back. It's been getting more and more frequent. I have this feeling that it keeps coming back asking if I'm ready to try and communicate yet."

"Has anyone else ever heard these tappings?"

"No. When I was a kid, I had my Mom come in and listen, but she never heard anything. And Burt's never heard them."

"So they're meant just for you." Dick pointed out that it was possible that a guardian angel was trying to "wake me up" to spiritual and psychic growth, and perhaps only through the kinds of unsettling experiences I had had, would I have been sufficiently motivated to seek help. He then advised me how to handle any future contact. "Mentally project a white light around yourself, and then put a white light around the area where the tappings are coming from. And then a pink light. It represents love."

"Is it possible that someone's trying to contact me?"

"For what it's worth, my very first gut feeling when you

started talking about this was that a 'guardian angel' is trying to communicate with you."

"But isn't it possible that it's unfriendly?"

"Well, I doubt it, Sandy. I don't really get negative vibrations from you. I don't get hostile vibrations from you. I get confused, frightened vibrations from you—or I did. I don't today. So I would say the odds are immensely in your favor that it's someone trying to help you, or love you. Ask direct questions. You've got to establish contact. If it happens, fine . . ."

"What about using a Ouija board?"

"I wouldn't try anything like that yet. In time, when we both feel you're ready, and confident, we'll work together with auto writing. But we've got to feel it together."

"So it's possible to do this safely?"

"Oh, sure." Dick's voice radiated confidence. "Absolutely. We must have total rapport on the conscious level. You have to be convinced that I'm not going to bite you. But first you've got to build confidence and security through using the white light. You've got to feel safe on a gut level. Then we'll do it together. You'll white light yourself, you'll white light the paper, you'll white light the pencil, and while you're doing it, I will white light you. And I'll pink light you. We'll have an energy field that's unreal by the time we get through."

As I left that session, I felt I was flying. I felt fantastic! Absolutely, utterly, completely fantastic! When I got home, Burt was in the living room doing T'ai Ch'i exercises, so I quietly slipped into my study for yoga and white light/meditation. I had the most intense experience I could remember in months. My white-lighting seemed to charge the whole room with high energy, and I felt the high vibrations being fed back into my body. The white light was brighter than it had ever been before.

I was far more talkative this time at the co-operative dinner. I was laughing, high, getting into the vibes there. Then about halfway through the evening, something hit me. The reason I felt so good, was that Dick said he could help me make contact through automatic writing. Suddenly I knew that I had been waiting to hear that. It caused something to click on a very deep level. I hadn't realized it consciously, but unconsciously, I had apparently expected that when I met the "guru" I had been awaiting for a year, that he/she would help me make contact with my tapper. I realized how often I had thought, "If only there were someone I could trust, who could help me figure out a safe way to find out what this tapper wants." And I've finally met such a person. I know now that Dick is the person I've been expecting, and that the main reason I'm consulting him is to learn how to make contact with my tapper. It's a sobering thought.

THURSDAY, FEBRUARY 26, 1976

I'm glad that I'm seeing Dick tomorrow. So much has happened this week; so many confusing things. I've been carrying around a small notebook to jot down questions to discuss with him. At first, I didn't want to tell him anything; now I want to discuss everything with him. I'm beginning to feel a bit more comfortable with my experiences. But the more comfortable I feel, the more experiences I have.

Last Saturday, I woke up feeling full of energy. I was still excited by the realization that I had met the person who would help me contact my tapper safely. I spent Saturday morning cleaning up the apartment, while mulling over the things Dick had said in Friday's session. Then, in the late afternoon, I went into my study to do hatha yoga and to white-light myself while I meditated.

I was just finishing my final asana, when I felt a sudden and unexpected "invasion" of my mind. I had an incredibly strong and vivid image of my grandmother, who had been dead for nearly a year. I found myself utilizing my usual approach; blocking it. But then I remembered the things Dick had been saying, and reminded myself that I could run and call him if this thing got out of hand. So, slightly apprehensive, I lay down on my mat and began the white-lighting process. The image grew stronger and I could swear I felt my grandmother's presence in the room. It was a strange feeling because it was different from the presence I normally felt with the tappings. Something about it seemed distinctly character-istic of Grandma. I started to pick up emotional impressions from her "presence" and image. She was troubled—very unhappy and confused. She wanted to talk. I felt myself saying mentally: "Gee, Grams, I wish I could help. I'd like to talk, but I don't know how to communicate with you, or what to say." Her image took on a very sad look and then faded away.

I was both shaken and touched. Touched because I had been close to Grandma in her life, even though we had many differences. She was a fundamentalist who expected harps and streets of gold after death. I felt shaken because the experience had been so real at the time. But within minutes, I was again doubting my sanity. "Hallucination," I thought. "I should be seeing a psychiatrist to get to the bottom of this instead of going to Prana where my delusions get encouragement."

I lay awake for quite awhile that night, trying to assimilate all that has been happening to me. At last, I began drifting comfortably into a sleep state. Just before sleep, however, I suddenly heard tappings. "Oh, no," I thought. "Why can't I be left in peace? It's been a difficult week—I just want to sleep." As if in answer, I felt a rush of sensations in my mind, as though I were being told:

"Relax, just relax, you won't be hurt. But you must be prepared, and the preparation must be done slowly, so that when you finally begin auto writing, the experience won't be traumatic. You are now about to experience sensations in your right arm that are similar to those experienced in auto writing. You are perfectly safe. However, we can't proceed without your conscious consent."

I sighed, wanting to just roll over and go to sleep. But I did want eventually to learn who my tapper was and what he/she wanted. And Dick's number, after all, was next to the phone, just a few feet away. So I white-lighted myself and then pink-lighted myself, focusing on my arm. I did the same thing for the corner from which the tappings seemed to come.

"All right, now, notice the increasing sensation in the right arm." It was like being on a tour and having a guide point out sights of interest. I couldn't swear to it, but I felt I was picking up a distinct sense of humor coming from my "tour guide," as though a deliberate attempt was being made to make the situation casual and light-hearted. "Notice, if you will, the distinct difference between the right and left arms. The left arm continues to feel perfectly normal, but the right arm feels warm, tingly, and full of energy."

I lay there thinking, "This can't be happening. It just can't be. Everything is perfectly normal—Burt's sound asleep next to me, I hear a dog barking outside. But yet I have the strangest sensations in my right arm, and these crazy thoughts flowing through my mind. They could so easily be imagination. So easily. How can I know?"

The lecture was continuing: "Now pay attention to this sensation. It is but a small sample of the changes your arm will undergo during auto writing. We will go through this procedure a number of times, as a dry run, to prepare you for the real thing. Now good-night!"

The sensations disappeared as suddenly as they had appeared. The room was quiet with no disturbing tapping. My mind was disturbed, however. But being exhausted I fell quickly asleep.

I've reached the point where I feel I must know what's happening to me. Dick said that he would give me his impressions after a few sessions. I'm going to ask him tomorrow.

SUNDAY, FEBRUARY 29, 1976

I want to quit these sessions. My fears are being realized; my psychic centers are being opened. And it's happening so fast that I feel like I'm on a roller coaster. I'm terribly depressed this evening. My week-end has been over-whelming.

I went to my Friday session feeling relaxed and confident, and determined to ask Dick what he felt was going on in my life.

I began by telling him how much better I had felt since he told me it was possible to make safe contact with my tapper.

"Do you know what faith is?" he asked me as I was turning on my recorder.

"Not really." Actually, I didn't believe in it, seeing it only as a blind acceptance of something that couldn't be proven.

"Faith is knowing that you're a tool. Every soul selects very specific tasks to accomplish while in the physical. We struggle and fumble through life, and quite often we don't awaken until somewhere between twenty-eight and thirty-five years old. The first part of life is like a prelude. Now something inside of you is always pushing, and guiding and shoving and poking and prodding, always trying to make you line up again on the path you've selected." I wasn't sure why Dick was telling me that, and I felt even more confused by his next remarks. "Whenever information is fed to you, it is for you to work with. Suppose you sense that your cousin Nellie is going to die. Now that doesn't mean you run and tell her husband that she's about to pass over. You let it be known in a very subtle way that you're there as needed. One of the most

55

difficult things for psychics to do is to shut up. They're beautiful people but quite often they offer information that should be very discreetly handled. Or without much thought as to *how* it should be handled. Or they volunteer information prematurely, without being asked. It's possible that you may get a very srong impression, and you have to weigh it. Use good old common sense."

This seemed a good opening for the question weighing on my mind. "You said that after a few sessions you'd share with me more of your impressions about what's going on. Do you feel ready to tell any more yet?"

"I'm spoon feeding it to you as we go along." Dick paused and lit a cigarette. He watched the smoke curling up towards the ceiling as he considered his next remarks. "I'll give you the biggest one, OK? Basically, my gut feeling is that you are quite psychic, quite clairvoyant. And I feel it's free will as to whether or not you develop this ability."

His words hit me hard. I thought I was prepared to hear whatever he had to say about the subject, but I was wrong. I wished I had never heard his words. I don't want to be psychic!

"You can totally deny your ability. Things may still come through once in a while, but you don't have to do anything with it. You can close your senses just by choosing to spend this life getting into the mortal scene. You can close them by abusing your ability or by using it for materialistic gain. Now, if you continue on this path, it is possible that someday you'll get into doing professional readings. Not professionally, but of professional quality."

I couldn't believe Dick had suggested I might actually give readings someday. So maybe I had had a few psychic experiences, but that was a far cry from giving readings. I was feeling increasingly depressed by his comments and decided to turn the conversation to the experiences I had had during the week. I started by asking about the incident where I sensed my grandmother's presence. I asked if it could have been real.

"What you're saying is a possible reality." Of course. Knowing Dick, what did I expect him to say, after all?

"Well, is there any way I can be of help to Grandma?"

"Yes, absolutely. When you meditate, use the white light, and prayer. Make sure you feel confident, because she's capable of receiving what you transmit. If you feel her presence again, say mentally, 'Hey Grams, we've got to talk. Are you aware that your body is no longer functional?' She may say, 'I don't know what happened. I'm kind of confused.' 'You're a mortal with a body. The body ceased functioning, and you died. Look, Grams, what you should do is sit down and pray for guidance. If you wish, I'll help you pray.' If she agrees, you pray with her for guidance for her soul. Picture an evolved soul coming towards her. It may be somebody she knows."

"Aren't there evolved souls around to help anyway?"

"Oh, definitely. But the vibrations have to be emitted before they're attracted. They'll come there to help, and be denied otherwise. They're not going to force anything. But they've got more patience than Carter's got little liver pills. She'll be back. She may be gone a day, a month, a year, but she'll be back."

I didn't feel comfortable about playing the role of messenger between this world and a spirit dimension. "Something else happened this week—Sunday night." I explained about the tappings and the "tour guide" sending sensations into my arm. "I had the distinct impression that the tappings were there not to be communicated with, but rather to demonstrate to me that a force, an energy, a presence was in the room." I described the sensations.

"I haven't told you about this, have I?" Dick asked. "Or have you read anything about it?"

"I don't think so. If I have, I don't remember." Actually, I felt quite certain that I hadn't, but I wanted to be scrupulously fair.

"Well, that's exactly what happens."

"You mean the sensations in my arm?"

"Yes. To do automatic writing, you do not have to be 'possessed.' Take that in context. It's a *form* of possession, but not the way you've used the term. It's an interaction of energies—physical energies, spiritual energies. They use

57

the electrical impulses of the muscles and the tendons. It's like putting my arm on your arm and guiding it. You will find that you feel a warmth around your body. It doesn't mean it's a form of possession. It's like a mother cuddling a child to her breast. Now in order for us to develop a faith that this energy has a mission for you to do, any message has to be evaluated carefully. If it's logical, if it's practical, if no one will be hurt by it, fine. A true spiritual source is not demeaned in any way by questioning and evaluating. In the beginning you will probably receive something which I'll verify later; I don't want to consciously influence you." I was intrigued. What could possibly come through that could be verified? Would it ever come through me? "In the meantime, you can practice in a very effective way through white-lighting yourself, and closing your eyes so that you are receptive to any visual images."

"There have been two Sunday nights in a row now that I've heard tappings. Maybe I'm going to be contacted every Sunday night. Should I continue to be receptive to that?"

"Definitely. If you like, ask Burt if he'd be interested in also white-lighting you and white-lighting the room. But he shouldn't do it unless he really wants to."

"If these energies are friendly, why have they given me heavy experiences—things that I've found frightening?"

"You can almost rest assured they're not doing anything to frighten you. Not on purpose. But at times you have had to be scared out of your britches to wake up, so to speak. If the mission's important enough, they're going to do what they have to to get you to pay attention."

"That makes sense. It's primarily because of all the scary things that happened that I came here in the first place. I'd just as soon have forgotten the whole thing."

"Sure. Let's put it this way. Energies have been proven to take on some pretty negative vibes—in terms of blowing your mind. They're capable of psychokinesis, moving objects, and those energies are just fooling around. I don't think you've had that at all. Everything you've mentioned so far seems to point to attention-getters for you."

"But why would some spirit energy spend fifteen years trying to make contact with me?"

"There is no time for them, remember. Fifteen years are nothing. We all are assigned guardian angels whose sole purpose is to lead us, to guide us. And the fact that they volunteered for this is a way of growing spiritually from the other side. So these souls—these spirits—are doing their job with love, not out of an attempt to frighten. They're working very patiently and with great love. I get the feeling they're trying to tell you that . . ." Dick paused.

"Tell me what?"

"I don't want to lead you. I promise, in time, we'll compare notes. Fair enough? And I'm really not trying to be secretive, but I'd like you to be you, OK? Not Dick Smith. And the Moon's in Aquarius. Theoretically, I'm hyper-psychic when the Moon's in Aquarius. I start picking up a lot of vibrations, tuning in on things, making profound statements. I never noticed it before until an astrologer pointed it out to me. But take advantage of that little exercise. They are—" Again Dick paused, as though he were listening carefully to something far away. "Yeah, it's 'they.' More than one. I feel quite certain of it. They are working very patiently and with tremendous love."

"What would be the purpose?" I just could not understand why a bunch of spirits would spend half of my lifetime trying to communicate something to me.

"It's to help you help others, spiritually. What I'd like to say—but I'm not sure if I'm supposed to or not." Again Dick paused. "But maybe I got it so I'd share it." He was quiet for several minutes and looked very far away. I squirmed uneasily in the chair. Maybe Dick wasn't trying to be secretive, but I hated his withholding feelings from me. I wanted so desperately to understand these past fifteen years, and if he had any answers I wanted to hear them. I might not believe his answers, but I'd at least have something to think about. Those were my thoughts as I waited for what Dick had to say next. After I heard his next statement, I was sorry I had wanted him to tell me anything. His words hit me like a thunderbolt.

"I think you abused psychic powers."

"You mean in a past life?" I had tried to ignore them all this life; I didn't see how I could possibly have abused them.

"Yeah, I think you really did a number on some people." I was quiet. It sounded so awful. The thought of anyone abusing psychic powers was scary, but the thought that I might have done it was overwhelming. "But what you have to understand is that it's ancient history. And you also have to understand that you were very mortal then, too."

"Do you think it's possible I'm being prepared to be possessed as punishment for that?"

"No, I don't. I was a warlock back in Atlantis. I really did a number on a lot of people. I had psychic powers but used them to satisfy greed and lust. I'm not proud of it, but it's nice to *know* that I know so that I can accept it in context. OK, so I was a mortal. These are things I've grown out of. And I think that perhaps subconsciously and super-consciously you fear that if all of these doors open up, you might get greedy and selfish and blow it again."

"And that could be the basis for my fears?"

"Yes. You don't want to put yourself through the same trip as last time. If you really did a number on some people, you probably already went through those lives where you had your mind blown open a few times. It's karma. Now you're in a cross-roads life, where you can develop these abilities to be of help to others. But it's free will. You have a right to choose. Now, of course, none of this could be true. I'm giving you some impressions, and you have to decide what to do with them. Now, you may well have already worked out these lives. Now, in this life, you have a choice to open the doors and grow spiritually helping others, or open the doors for greedy and selfish purposes."

Enough of that. "OK, so for now, you're saying the best way to prepare myself for auto writing is white light and following these exercises that come on Sunday nights."

"Yeah. You may well find that the tappings will cease

soon. They've got your attention—they served their function. And you are now preparing for a much more sophisticated means of communication."

I drove home feeling despondent. First Dick had said I was quite psychic and then he had said I abused my abilities in a past life. This would be a good evening, I mused, to go to a light movie. But, I thought with resentment, we were entertaining all evening. We had invited two couples over for dinner, neither of whom we knew very well. The last thing I felt like doing was preparing a meal for six people and then trying to be sociable for several hours. These thoughts were on my mind as I pulled into the graveled area behind the house and parked. I glanced over at the garages that some of the tenants rented, and stared in amazement. Lurking around my friend Judy's garage was a distinct vision of an evil-looking man. I couldn't make out any features, but felt the vibes and saw his outline. I shivered as I made my way up the back stairs.

Judy lives in the third floor apartment, and we've become good friends. She's twenty-nine, attractive, single, and a social worker by profession. She also wants to become a family therapist and is very interested in the occult. She is the only person besides Burt who knows about my sessions with Dick.

I let in our guests two hours later and tried to look happy and relaxed. We all sat for a long time around our dining room table after dinner, sipping wine and coffee and talking. I did my best to follow the conversations and even contribute now and then. Suddenly, it really hit me. I remembered the words: "I think you abused psychic powers ... I think you really did a number on some people." I had heard the words before; I had reacted to them before. But suddenly I understood them. I felt the room swaying, my mind spinning. I feared I was about to pass out, or maybe let go of my mind and never again regain it. I was terrified. I excused myself, ran to the bathroom, and locked myself in. "I've got to get hold of myself. I've just got to. I can't lose my mind! I can't!" I sat on the floor and white-lighted myself. I tried to meditate.

61

After a few minutes, I felt myself pulling together. At least, I didn't feel in any immediate danger of losing control. So, tentatively, I made my way back to the dining room, and rejoined our guests and Burt. I somehow managed to hold together for the rest of the evening. Our guests left fairly early, but not as early as I'd hoped.

"I'm pooped," Burt reported. "I'm going on to bed."

I suddenly realized I was tired, too, and eagerly anticipated falling into a nice, deep sleep.

"Well, at least I made it through the evening, and I still seem to have my sanity," I thought as I nestled under the covers. But as I was drifting off to sleep, I started hearing tappings. And I felt a strong sense of the presence of the tapper. Dick's words still kept drifting through my mind: "You abused psychic powers... you abused psychic powers." Then suddenly I saw before me a long dark tunnel. It terrified me, and I tried to shut the image out of my mind. As I did so, I received a rush of impressions, sensations, thoughts flowing into my head. "That long dark tunnel you're facing is something you must go through in order to come out on the other side. Before you can fully develop your abilities you must face and accept your past lives, and in no way is it going to be easy. In many ways it will be terrifying. But there is something that will sustain you throughout your journey through that tunnel: you are not alone." As I mentally heard the words, I felt my hands come alive with energy. It was as though my hands were being held by very high energy forces. I felt myself surrounded with love and caring. "We will be with you throughout your journey. Only you can choose to make the journey. Just remember, you cannot get to the other side without first traveling through the tunnel. But you will never be alone."

After a few minutes the tingling in my hands subsided and the tappings ceased. Relieved, I turned over and started drifting into sleep. Just before reaching the sleep state, but just after giving up control of my conscious mind, I was jerked awake by a very vivid image of my dead grandmother. As before, I sensed sadness, confusion. "O, God," I thought. "Not again! I just want peace. I just want to sleep." But I remembered Dick's words. Suppose, just suppose, my grandmother's spirit really were there with me. If I could know for certain that she were really there, I would have thought nothing of giving up a night's sleep to talk with her. If this were even a possibility, wasn't it worth it?

I white-lighted myself and started sending mental thoughts out. "Look, Grams, you've passed over. Technically, you're dead. But 'death' means just passing into a different form. You left your body behind. It was old and you didn't need it anymore. Now you're in the spirit world with a spirit body." I still sensed a lot of confusion coming from her. "I know, Grams, that it's not like you thought it would be. A lot of people are wrong about that. Actually, it's better than you imagined. There's no hell unless you create it for yourself. You can create your own heaven, too. If you just open yourself to help, you'll receive it from the many advanced souls that are around your spirit world."

I picked up some vibrations that could be interpreted loosely as "stuff and nonsense" and her vision disappeared. My mind was full of all that had been happening, and it was half an hour before I felt tired. But, alas, just before drifting off, again Grandma's presence became vivid. She had a questioning countenance this time. "Explain all that again, please," is what it seemed to say. I started again, explaining slowly and patiently. "You have such great opportunities for growth on your side, Grams, if you can accept where you are and open yourself up for help. There are lots of helpful spirits over there." And just where are they now, I wondered. Why doesn't somebody come by and explain this to her? I don't know anything about life on the other side, I could be totally wrong about everything I'm saying. What if I blow it and make things worse for Grams?

"Well, I'll think about it," Grams seemed to say, as her image drifted off again. Again, it was nearly a half hour before I could quiet my mind enough for sleep. As I was drifting off, her image returned again.

"One more time, please." She looked less confused, but

pained, as though many difficult and painful truths were registering in her consciousness. Again, I white-lighted myself and repeated the explanation. As I was doing so, I was suddenly conscious of Burt's arms around me. He was awake.

"Honey, could you white-light me?" I asked. I hadn't told him a thing yet about my session, so he didn't know about Dick's suggestion that he white-light me during times of contact. I wasn't sure he'd understand what I was talking about.

"I already am. I have been for the last ten minutes."

On and on I talked mentally, explaining all I had ever heard about "the other side" and the experience of death. I didn't know if I talked for two minutes or several hours. At last, I sensed her features relax as she seemed to finally comprehend my words. At that instant, another spirit appeared, took her hand, and they walked off together. I knew instinctively that it was the spirit of my Grandpa, who had died many years ago.

I breathed a sigh of relief. Whether it was imagination or reality, it was at least over. Burt had long since drifted off to sleep again and the first rays of daylight were sifting through the window shades. For what I hoped would be the final time that night, I let myself drift towards sleep. But the room came alive with tappings once again, and I felt the same familiar presence that always accompanied them. I suddenly felt a strong energy force just outside my arm, and I sensed that permission was being sought to enter. "Oh, hell!" I thought. "I thought we were going to have these preparation lessons on Sunday nights, but this is only Friday night. Or technically Saturday morning now. What the hell are you doing here?"

The answer I got back in terms of mental words rushed in with a definite tinge of humor and warmth: "Because, my friend, you happen to be in an extremely receptive mood at this moment. And receptivity is far more important than what day of the week it is."

So I resigned myself and allowed the energy to enter. Again, I experienced the warmth, the tingling, the numbness in my arm and felt it vibrating with energy.

This time the energy was stronger, and there was another startling difference. As soon as the energy nestled comfortably in my arm, I felt the arm shoot up into the air. I could swear I hadn't consciously directed it, but there it was. The arm started making small, circular movements, as though trying to draw circles in the air. After a few moments, the energy ceased and my arm dropped heavily to the bed. The tappings and presence vanished. I glanced over at the clock. 700 a.m. "My, God," I thought, "I haven't slept a wink this entire night!" My eyelids felt heavy, and I was totally exhausted. Just before sleep, Grams appeared. I was wondering what more I could possibly say this time, when I noticed the glow emanating from her image. "Thanks," she said and her image disappeared. Within minutes, I was in a deep sleep state.

I slept soundly until late that afternoon. I sleepily made my way to the kitchen, and heated the water for tea. Burt sauntered in from the living room. "Well, good afternoon! How'd you sleep?"

"Just fine, after 7 a.m. when I finally fell asleep." As I started my breakfast, I relayed to Burt all that had happened during the night.

"That's weird, really weird."

I was quiet for a few minutes while sliding my fried egg onto my plate and pouring a glass of juice. "Honey, do you think I might be crazy? Last night was awfully strange. It could have all been hallucination. Maybe I belong in a mental institution."

"I really don't think you're crazy. I think you're psychic. And there *is* a difference, you know." I wondered about that.

I've been depressed all week-end, and now I think I'm coming down with the flu. I can't stand to be sick and have to lie around in bed feeling helpless.

I'm very disturbed about Friday night's experiences. *Very* disturbed. What do they mean? Will they happen again? I wish I had fewer questions and more answers.

WEDNESDAY, MARCH 3, 1976

I was home from work today with the flu, but feeling
better, so I called Dick for a special session this afternoon
to discuss my experiences of Friday night. I'm still upset
and depressed about them.

When I arrived, I told Dick about Friday night and my
fear that it was all imagination. He responded: "Let's
suppose it is imagination. So what?"

"I don't want to live my life carrying on imaginary
conversations in my head with dead people."

"Look, Sandy, the possibility of the reality of your
experiences is there. You have not hurt anyone. You
haven't even hurt yourself. You did get to sleep eventually
that night. You haven't hurt one single solitary person,
consciously or unconsciously. What I'm trying to do,
Sandy, is get you to look at these things pragmatically."
That's something I'm not sure I'll ever be able to do.

When Dick heard I'd been sick, he started talking
about green lights. "When you're sick, change the white
light to a green light. There are a limitless number of
shades of green on the astral plane. Close your eyes, and
let the light come in whatever shade of green best matches
your body's needs. It will be something close to what we
call an emerald green. I could not possibly describe it to
you. There is a luminescence to it that cannot possibly be
seen physically."

I left the session in a thoughtful mood. I was trying very
hard to look at my experiences pragmatically, but it
wasn't easy. That evening, Judy came down from her
apartment for tea and we chatted. "There's something I
guess I should mention to you," I said, "although it seems
really silly and I feel I should forget the whole thing. But

I'm trying hard to accept that there could be a reality to at least some of my experiences."

"What is it?" Judy looked concerned.

"I saw the image of an evil-looking man around your garage."

Judy really looked startled, and was quiet for a few minutes. "The last few days, I've had the strongest urge to board up the windows of my garage so that nobody could get in."

It was sobering that we both had similar feelings at about the same time. "Well, if I were you, I'd be extra careful for awhile—especially when you come in at night."

"OK, I will. By the way, how are your sessions at Prana going?"

"Well, OK, I guess. I suppose I'm making some sort of progress, but lately the sessions have been making me feel depressed. And I'm having a terrible conflict between my head and my emotions. Intellectually, I think all my experiences must be imagination or hallucination. And that I'm crazy to spend money and time exploring them further instead of doing something worthwhile and useful."

"That sounds like a tough position to be in." Judy was a very sympathetic listener and easy to talk to. Perhaps it was a combination of her own intuitive sense about people and her professional background.

"It is. But my intellect is starting to accept the fact that I feel such a strong impulse to explore the psychic that I just can't turn back now. Despite all the depression and conflict, I feel terribly drawn to continue this path."

THURSDAY, MARCH 4, 1976

I was still running a fever this morning, so called in sick again. But I'm tired of lying around, so I'll try to sort out some of my thoughts.

I wonder why my resistance to the psychic is so strong. If anyone else had had these experiences I could easily accept them as genuine psychic experiences. Why can't I accept my own? I honestly don't believe that any of my experiences have been more than coincidence or imagination. Yet I have an inner compulsion to continue my sessions with Dick. To continue investing time in something I don't believe is putting me in great conflict with myself. I'm getting more depressed all the time.

I remember something William James wrote about psychic experiences. He said that a mystic can't expect others to accept the validity of his mystical experiences. But he does have to accept and live by them himself. Why can't I do that?

I've had an intellectual interest in reincarnation and ESP for many years. I was raised in a religious home, first as a Baptist and then later as a Presbyterian. But I gave up religion at eighteen when I became an agnostic. So I no longer automatically accept a life after death. But I know there are verified accounts of people leaving their bodies, sometimes at will. I know researchers such as Ian Stevenson have uncovered many cases of people recalling past lives. I'm also impressed by stories of mediums. Edgar Cayce, of course, is the all-time great in that realm. His readings, from a trance state, provided medical information that was verified time and again. Other mediums have provided similarly impressive evidence. Jane Roberts goes into trance and her spirit control, Seth, produced an excellent book, *Seth Speaks*.

I wish I could dispassionately consider the possibility of the reality of my own experiences instead of investing so much energy in resisting them. A thought just occurred to me. Someday, I'm going to break. Someday, a barrier in my mind is going to crumble, and for the first time, I will really face the possible reality of my experiences. And that realization will be mind-blowing. I'll burst into tears and sob as a wall of resistance melts away. Maybe it'll happen next week; maybe in ten years. But I feel sure that it's going to happen.

I wonder if my resistance might be related, as Dick suggested, to a past life. I don't want to go back to the past; the thought frightens me. But I do want to get to the bottom of this. Perhaps I'll ask him about past life work during tomorrow's session.

FRIDAY, MARCH 5, 1976

I had quite a session with Dick today. We covered material that will take me years to understand. Burt came along this time. Dick says it is very difficult to grow spiritually if one's spouse is resistant to the process, so he's encouraged me to invite Burt to our sessions. Since his schedule is different from mine, he normally can't attend. But Dick offered to schedule a session at 5:00 instead of 4:00 today, so we gathered in Dick's office with a tape recorder and a long list of questions.

I started right off. "OK, question number one, out of about 100. Could you define 'psychic' for me?" If I was going to be accused of being psychic, I could at least be given a definition of the term.

"It's one who has an ability to develop rapport with their super-conscious mind. We are all psychic; we all have the rapport. Some have it more than others. The label 'psychic' on a person means one has a little bit more talent than another person in utilizing the powers of the super-conscious mind. They're not weird; they're not strange. They just have more rapport with their super-conscious mind."

"What's the super-conscious mind?"

"Conscious: you're here communicating, your eyes are open, you walked in here out of free will. That's all conscious. Unconscious: sounds off in the background, maybe the radio's on, maybe some friends are talking. Even while involved in things on a conscious level, you may unconsciously be receiving sounds, impressions, vibrations, all the time. Everything that goes through the conscious and unconscious computer goes into the subconscious computer. The subconscious mind is the level of our mortal side that records everything since birth and in some cases, prenatal impressions. The super-conscious mind is the level of consciousness that is the soul level. It is the portion of our composition that is cosmic consciousness and has recorded all our experiences since time pertaining to our soul."

"So the conscious and unconscious pick up things during this lifetime, but the super-conscious has memory of all lifetimes? Like the soul?"

"It *is* the soul."

"Well, how do psychics know what's going to happen in the future?"

"Now, you'll never, ever understand this intellectually, but intuitively you'll know what I mean. Super-consciously, on the soul level, there is no time. There's no beginning and no ending. If there's no beginning and no ending, everything is now. When you contact a ripple or a vibration it's difficult for even very gifted psychics to know if it is happening, it's going to happen, or it did happen. Because you're not in a time zone as we know it."

I changed the subject. "How do I know that it will be beneficial for me to explore past lives?"

Dick turned to Burt. "Maybe you and Sandy had many lifetimes together before this. Maybe you were the female before, or her mother or father. The details don't matter. What does matter is that you're two souls learning together. You have a task to perform here on earth, and you've chosen to do it together. And that's more important to me than the details of the past. If you go into past lives, you've got to do it with that attitude. Why ask if it's accurate? Who cares? What I want to know is: Does it make sense? Does it fit into a pattern which forms you today? Does is symbolize where you're supposed to be going? That to me is far more important than whether it was really 1771 or 1770. It would be nice for research purposes to have dates. But it's not necessary for your understanding of the emotional forces of the past that still impinge upon you today."

"You know," I said thoughtfully, "I've been considering your comments that my resistance to the psychic comes from my past lives. That theory makes sense. I can't think of any other reason for my resistance. But I'm not ready to look into the past. It's scary. I may have experienced great tragedy. I may have done awful things. I don't think I can face it."

"What we consider to be tragic things in our lives were merely reference books that we didn't enjoy. I have to look at this very matter-of-factly. If you came in and said 'Dick, I was once a witch, and I toasted people and I fried them and I pulled their nails out,' I would react by saying, 'OK, fine.' If I got the vibrations from you to support it, I'd probably believe it. It was a part of your earth experience that you had to live through to grow." After a pause, Dick continued very gently, "I can understand your hesitancy to explore the past, Sandy. It may be very traumatic. But sometimes we have to face pain and trauma to grow. I'll say again—the decision is yours. I won't push you into anything. You may come in here sometime and say, 'Dick, let's spend today's session trying to explore the past.' Or you may never feel ready to do it. It's up to you."

Suddenly the tape clicked off, and I realized we were already over the allotted session time. Although, to Dick, session time is very loosely interpreted. An hour isn't the traditional therapeutic 50 minutes. It's an hour and 10 minutes. Or longer if the client had something important going on that needed to be discussed. His appointments are always scheduled at least 1½ hours apart so that going over time never interferes with the next client's time. The few times I finished up in less than an hour, I was charged less.

We left in thoughtful moods.

WEDNESDAY, MARCH 10, 1976

Something very startling just happened; I'm shaking as I write. While I was meditating, I felt a presence in the room. Then I felt my arm surrounded with energy. It seemed that the energy wanted to enter my arm, but was seeking permission to do so. I was very uneasy. I white-lighted myself, then pink-lighted myself. I tried to tune into the vibrations of the presence. It seemed to be warm, loving and protective. I took a deep breath and muttered, "OK, whoever or whatever you are, I give you permission to enter my arm." Then I found myself praying: "Dear God, please protect me."

My arm filled with warm, tingling energy and then became still and numb. It rose into the air and started making circular motions, as a child first learning to write might do. Then something totally unexpected happened: I sensed words flowing into my mind that I wasn't consciously producing. The words "Dear Sandy..." came through, and as they did so, I felt my arm slowly writing out each letter in the air. Then "I am a..." came into my mind as my arm wrote it out. "Friend" came through to complete the sentence. I felt the energy drain out of my arm, and normal sensations return. I let my arm drop. Could this be the first message from my tapper? I doubt that it is. The fact that the words were in my mind first seems a strong argument for imagination. Obviously, the words drifted up from my sub-conscious, as a reflection of what I really wanted to hear. And then in some subtle way, I sent messages to my arm to write out those words.

But the experience was very profound. I actually felt love and caring surround me. I felt energy in the room. I felt energy in my arm. I felt all that five minutes ago but can't believe it now.

THURSDAY, MARCH 11, 1976

I had another strange experience this evening in meditation. Again, I felt the energy and granted it permission to enter. Again, my arm rose into the air. Then a word flowed into my mind while my arm wrote it out: "Love." I felt surrounded with love and caring. Then another word came through: "Paper."

I think I understand the significance of that word. It's a message to start auto-writing. Perhaps in tomorrow's session I'll tell Dick I'm ready to begin.

WEDNESDAY, MARCH 17, 1976

I'm going to try and do some writing this evening, but it won't be easy. Burt is sitting on the guest bed in my study reading and keeps interrupting me every few minutes to read me a passage. He just started Le Shan's little book, *How to Meditate*. It contains a fascinating selection of meditation techniques; I just finished it myself. It's nice having Burt's company while I write. I'm going to write fast so we can be together this evening. We've had so little time to spend with each other lately. I've been taking a Spanish class on Tuesday evenings, and just started doing family therapy on alternate Wednesday evenings. Burt's been taking T'ai Ch'i lessons on Monday evenings. And I have a job interview tomorrow evening. I'm wasting part of this evening by sitting at this darned typewriter to record more of my experiences. I don't know why I bother. But I have a strong urge to do it. I think it helps me sort out my thoughts to write them.

I had planned to begin auto-writing last Friday in my session with Dick, but when I got there, I chickened out, and just went over a few questions I had.

I've noticed that in the past week or so my experiences with meditation have become much deeper. I've given up the poem and now pray for protection. Dick's explanation of God and prayer have broken down my original resistance to prayer, and I find myself praying daily. Afterwards, I meditate. I'm slipping into deeper and deeper states. I often feel in touch with a universal energy, and feel myself vibrating in frequency with the rest of the universe. I come out of such experiences feeling very peaceful.

Other things have been happening in my life the past

couple of weeks. I've become friends with Pete, a man from another agency who comes into our office every week. He told me recently that there's a counseling job opening up in his agency on April 1st. It will involve individual and family counseling, both of which I'd love to do. It will also involve some counseling, teaching, and leading discussion groups in various high schools in the area. He felt that my qualifications for the job were excellent, and encouraged me to apply for it.

I have a lot of mixed feelings about this job. If I were offered it and accepted it, then I would have to leave my present job before my May commitment is up. I'd feel bad about letting down our friend who hired us both.

On the other hand, this other job sounds ideal for me—just the kind of opportunity I've been looking for.

From the beginning, I've had a very strong feeling that I would be offered this job. I was one of ten out of eighty applicants called for an interview last week. Afterwards I felt I had done well, and Pete told me that I was in the top two for the job. Three other applicants and myself are coming in tomorrow night for a final interview.

Hearing that I'm so close to getting this job makes me uneasy. Although I think that I will get the job, I have a feeling that I'm not ready for it. The time isn't right. In perhaps another six months I will be ready. If I'm offered the job, I might even turn it down. I know that sounds crazy when this job is just what I'm looking for. But if I'm not learning anything else from Dick, I'm learning to trust my feelings.

THURSDAY, MARCH 18, 1976

Well, the decision is made for me. I ended up in second place for the job. I don't think I did as well at the interview this time. Did something in me keep me back from sounding more impressive? Did I unconsciously "blow it" so that I wouldn't have to deal with making the decision? Or is this the way, as Dick would say, it's supposed to be?

I felt a little disappointed when Pete called me with the decision. It's more ego-boosting to be in first place than to be in second. But I also felt a great deal of relief. I don't have to make a decision. And it feels right to continue in my present job for now. I talked with Pete about the possibility of doing some volunteer work at his agency, especially involving family counseling. He was enthusiastic about the idea, and suggested that I contact Vanessa, the woman they're hiring.

I'm going to begin auto-writing in tomorrow's session. I think I've achieved the conscious rapport with Dick that he says I need. I want to find out what my tapper wants. Perhaps tomorrow I'll get some answers.

SUNDAY, MARCH 21, 1976

So many strange things have happened the past few days, that I'm confused and depressed.

I saw Dick on Friday, and asked about auto-writing.

"I've been sensing messages mentally while my arm writes them out in the air. Is that a sign that it's my imagination?"

"No," Dick responded. "Anyone who does auto-writing is capable of receiving the messages telepathically. A good test of whether it's imagination is the logic behind the message. It doesn't matter where information comes from, as long as it rings true to you."

"Well, that leads to what I'd like to do for the rest of the session. I'd like to try doing auto-writing with paper and pencil."

His answer was highly unexpected. "The Moon's in Scorpio."

"What does that mean?"

Dick gave a hearty laugh. "It's the time to do it. Pluto rules the occult. It's one of those 'coincidences' that you picked today. What do you think will happen when we try it?"

"Maybe nothing. I feel rather tense about it."

"Well, it doesn't matter. I don't have any expectations: whatever happens, happens. Today will be kind of a walk-through, just to get you used to the procedure. Sit back, relax. Now we'll both white-light you."

I had never been white lighted by anyone besides Burt, and had no idea how I would react to the experience. I felt a heavy grogginess come over me. "Now a purple light. This is for extra assurance. It's like an egg: you are the yolk, the white is the white light, and the purple is the shell."

The grogginess deepened, and I felt my eyeballs moving rapidly, even though the lids were closed. I hadn't consciously caused it, and I couldn't stop it. But I wasn't concerned, I was too relaxed. "My eyes!" I mumbled, with effort.

"That's REM—rapid eye movement. It means your body is sound asleep. But your mind is alert and able to hear everything I say." I felt surrounded by energy; I felt it moving into my body. My hands were especially alive with energy. Dick kept talking. "To whoever is here in the room with us, we're open to receive any communication you have." I felt the now-familiar energy enter my arm. It became numb and slowly rose into the air. But I wasn't as preoccupied as usual with the process. Actually, I felt detached from the entire proceeding. "Can you identify yourself?" I heard Dick ask. "Sandy, is any name coming to mind?"

I hesitated. "Well, yes, there is a name. But it may be my imagination." I found it hard to talk, and was mumbling my words.

"What's the name?"

I hesitated, not wanting to give it. But it was being written in the air by my arm and the name kept coming into my mind with greater force. "Joey."

"Does that name mean anything to you?"

"Yes, that's the name of my little brother who died when he was only a few days old. I was nine."

"Sandy, are you seeing any visions or colors?"

"Colors, yes." I managed to say, although I was feeling increasingly disoriented. "Gold, purple."

"How do you feel?"

It was difficult to answer. I had to search hard for my voice. "I'm dizzy. I feel far away."

"OK, let your arm drop now, and sit back and relax. Just relax and listen to what I say. You will find that you can hear me clearly and you will respond to any suggestion I give you as long as it doesn't violate your morals or principles."

I sat back groggily and tried to listen, but it was a strain. I was surprised at the words Dick was speaking and the soft, soothing tone of voice he had adopted. I thought to myself: "He's talking to me like he thinks I'm hypnotized. But I'm not, I'm just deeply relaxed. Actually, I wish he'd be quiet and let me drift off to sleep."

But he kept talking. "Now, you've had contact with some very high energies here today. But these energies will not in any way disturb your sleep pattern tonight. You'll find that when you go to bed tonight, you'll slip immediately into a deep sleep, and rest peacefully all night. You'll also find, over the coming days, that any information you need at this time to understand your past lives will come to you. You will find yourself able to remember any dreams that contain past life information that you need to know. Now, I'm going to count slowly from 1 to 10. At each number, you'll find yourself a little more alert, a little closer to a normal, functional state of consciousness. When I reach 10, you'll be fully awake, alert, and functional . . . you'll feel peaceful and relaxed."

"Darn," I thought. "I'd just as soon stay in this state awhile longer." But Dick started counting, and I felt myself gain clarity and alertness with each number. He reached 10.

"Now, Sandy, let your eyes open all by themselves. Don't rush it."

My eyes opened slowly, facing a yellow, abstract painting on the opposite wall. I felt I was awakening in the morning to the sunrise.

"Good morning!" Dick's cheerful voice called out.

I glanced over, and smiled.

"How do you feel?"

"Like I just slept for several hours."

"Your eyes look clear, as if you just had a good nap."

I glanced at my watch. "My God! That lasted for twenty minutes! I thought it was only five or ten minutes! Just what was it that happened?"

"You were in a trance state. In an altered state of consciousness."

"Was I hypnotized?"

"Well, of course, hypnosis doesn't really exist. Not the way people use the term. But the way I use it, yes, you were most definitely hypnotized." I was quiet, trying to absorb that fact. "Now one thing that very possibly might have happened, was an out-of-body experience. I could give you a lot of interpretations of what happened. But, again, I'll try not to lead you. After you experience something, I'll verify it. But I don't want to put ideas in your head. I have a lot of ideas as to what's going on. And it's nice."

"Are you concerned about my imagination?"

"Right. Not because you're you, but because you're mortal, and all mortals have a problem with imagination. That's why I prefer to verify things after they happen. Like you saw gold. So now I can tell you that gold is one of the colors you see when in touch with higher vibrations."

"Did you white-light yourself during that?"

"No, and I'll tell you why. I like to leave myself open to feel the vibrations of whatever's around. If there's something around that we don't want to be in touch with, I'll get these prickly feelings on my skin, and I want to be open to that. But today I felt very secure with whatever was here."

"How come I felt so dizzy?"

"That's something you'll feel when you're moving through higher vibrations. I had you relax shortly after you started feeling it, because you've got to get used to it, and it takes time. You were raising your vibrations quite high, and that was enough energy for today. I don't want to push you. Take a little at a time. As you get used to it, we go a little further. And when you get used to *that*, a little further. I'm in no hurry."

"Is it safe to do this on my own?"

"If you feel it, sure. Use the white light."

"OK, that's all the questions I have for now. We're going to New York next week for a convention, so I won't be here on Friday. I'll see you again in two weeks."

"Fine, but if anything comes up and you want to talk sooner, don't hesitate to call."

I doubted that anything would come up because I felt so good as I left. I felt relaxed and peaceful. I had a good time that eveing at the co-op dinner, enjoying the company and the food. Until about 8:00 p.m. Suddenly, the full reality of the afternoon's experiences hit me. I became extremely depressed. I wandered over to the big windows and looked down at the cars passing on the street below. I needed to be alone for awhile. How had I managed to let myself be hypnotized? I wasn't ready for it. I hadn't decided for sure that I even wanted it. Was this another one of those "decisions" that managed to get made without my conscious involvement? I knew people couldn't be hypnotized without their consent, but when had I given my consent? I had just wanted to do some auto-writing. And we never did get around to that.

My depression deepened on Saturday. I got up early and, as usual, started my day with meditation. Instead of drifting into my usual, familiar meditative state, I felt my eyes moving wildly and felt myself again enter the depth of the state I had been in Dick's office. Was that damn Moon still in Scorpio? I wondered how long it would be there. I jerked myself out of meditation, and suffered some dizziness for a few minutes. But in no way was I going to get into that strange state alone.

This morning, Sunday, I woke up before Burt, so I padded into my study to start my morning meditation. Again, my eyes started their movements, and I jerked out of it. I lay down on the guest bed in my study feeling extremely dejected. Things were getting worse instead of better. Now I couldn't even meditate anymore; I kept slipping into that weird state. My eye movements were beyond my control. And I had no desire to slip into a state that might well be beyond my control, too. After all, how did I know if I could get out of it by myself? I felt I had reached rock bottom. "I can't meditate anymore; I'm harassed by weird experiences I never asked for, never wanted, and don't understand," I thought, feeling very sorry for myself. Burt was still asleep, so I decided to try and sleep some more, too. I stayed on the guest bed. Just before falling asleep, however, I felt the presence, and I felt that I was being told that there was a message for me if I chose to be receptive to it. I thought, "Oh, hell, go away and leave me alone! Can't you ever leave a poor tortured soul in peace?" The vibes I picked up in response seemed to say, "But this message will be of a reassuring nature."

"Oh, hell," I thought again. "Well, why not? Things can't get any worse. Go ahead with your message." I white-lighted myself and gave a quick prayer for protection.

Immediately, energy diffused throughout my right arm, and it shot into the air. The name "Joey" again popped into mind, and the word was written out in the air. Then an entire sentence appeared in my head: "I will be with you." As before, vivid emotions accompanied the words. I felt completely surrounded by protective and loving energy. "Bullshit," I thought. "This is obviously all my imagination." But the warm feelings were so real that I felt very comforted. I started drifting into a deeply relaxed state, and felt my eyes again moving rapidly beyond my control, but I felt so peaceful that I didn't care. I was thoroughly relaxed and enjoying myself when the ring of the telephone brought me back to every-day reality.

After coming out of that state, my depression again returned. "What the hell is going on?" I wondered. I didn't think I liked it. This afternoon, I saw Dick at the Foundation's membership meeting, and I stayed a few moments afterwards to request an appointment. He scheduled me for Tuesday afternoon. Until then, I won't meditate again. I'm scared. I wish I could crawl into a warm, dark, protective womb and escape the world altogether. I want to escape my uncertainty, confusion, and conflict.

TUESDAY, MARCH 23, 1976

I saw Dick this afternoon, but it didn't make me feel any better. We're leaving tomorrow for a few days in New York. Our office is sending us to a conference, and paying for the hotel and food. I hope it will be a chance to get away from all this for awhile; I'm very depressed right now. Today's session was discouraging. I started by discussing my feelings.

"I've been depressed since Friday, and I think the reason is my confusion about what's been happening. I didn't expect it to happen and it took me by surprise. I have a list of all my questions."

"Beautiful."

"What were those eye movements called again?"

"The REM sleep. When the body actually goes to sleep, and reaches a state of low productive alpha level, you enter what is known as REM state of relaxation, or rapid eye movement. This usually occurs during a dream state. If you were watching someone sleep, you could wait until the eye movements stopped, and then wake them up, and they could recount what they'd just been dreaming. So what you experienced here with me, although it seemed strange to you, is something you experience every night when you go to sleep."

"I have a need to label things. At that point, was I in a hypnotic state?"

"Yes, you could say that you were very, very much hypnotized."

"Well, how did I get into that state when we were just doing white lights?"

"You were open and receptive to it. It's a state of consciousness that you will not enter unless you're

84

willing. Consciously, you may question. But subconsciously, if you feel secure, you'll enter quite rapidly."

"Well, I didn't realize I was so secure with it. I didn't think I was."

"I had no idea either. But you were a lot more receptive than I expected."

"I'm still confused by the word 'trance,' and I think you've used it different ways different times. When I first came out of it and you said I'd been in a trance, were you using the term synonymously with hypnosis?"

"Yes."

"Is that different from Edgar Cayce type trances?"

"Yes, he was a trance medium. It's a state of consciousness where you set aside the ego to allow yourself to become a channel."

"OK, now is there any particular reason why my hands felt so full of energy at that point?" Dick hesitated. I had a feeling he didn't want to answer the question. "Look, if this is one of the things you don't want me to know yet . . ."

"No, you've asked. You have a right to understand what's happening. It is possible that that energy indicated an ability to do hands-on healing. Everybody has the ability to do it, but few people recognize it or develop it. It is possible that that is one direction you may choose to move towards." I was feeling extremely upset as I heard Dick's words, but I couldn't understand why. All I could think of was that if I ever tried hands-on healing I would undoubtedly hurt someone. I knew that if we continued this subject, I'd start to cry.

"Well, then, what about the name 'Joey'? How do I know if I was really making contact with the spirit of my dead brother or if it was imagaination?"

"Are you still thinking of Joey as a baby?" I nodded. Dick smiled. "Joey's a soul. And perhaps a very old, mature soul. He's no longer in a baby's body. As to the name, it will probably change in time."

"What do you mean?"

"'Joey' was just the name he had in a particular life-time for a few days. He has another name, a soul name. Perhaps in time that name will be revealed to you."

"Was there actually an entity in the room at the time?"

"A spirit, let's say. I felt a presence, but I felt very secure. I get tingly goose-bumps if something undesirable is around. That's because I used to pray, saying, 'Look, you've got to give me the ability to know when something spooky's around. I've got to have that in the kind of work I do.' When it happens, I send it a pink light, send it on its way, and we try again another day. That's what you've always got to do if there's something around you don't want to get involved with—send it pink, love, and send it on its way. So, yes, I felt something here, and felt completely secure with it."

"I don't feel comfortable with the state I was in. I keep going into it now when I try and meditate. How can I prevent it from happening so I can go back to normal meditation? Instead, I go through REM each time."

"That's great if you're doing it on your own. You've got to realize that that's not common. Some people work for years to achieve what is so very natural for you. I can't give you any suggestions on avoiding it; I could only advise you on how to continue to develop from here."

"I'd gladly give it to someone who really wanted it. I don't."

"You will in time, when you fully understand it. In fact, when you fully understand it, you may not have it any more because you'll try so hard!" Dick chuckled.

"Well, can I always get out of it OK on my own? That's what I'm most uneasy about."

"Always; you're in complete control. It's best to bring yourself out gradually, otherwise you'll get a headache. But that's the worst thing that can happen, a headache for a few minutes."

"How come you didn't have me use paper and pencil during that?"

"It was premature. You did plenty for one day. Next time, we'll go a little further."

"Where should I go from here? I see two directions. One is to continue this kind of contact, which I don't want to do on my own—only during these sessions. And the other is to start the past life work. Should I pursue one or both?"

"The decision is yours, but it seems to me that you'll need to get involved in them both."

"I think in my next session I'd like to start on past lives."

"OK, good. Do you have any questions about it?"

"Just regarding the tape recorder. Does it matter if I use it or not?"

"Not to me—that's up to you. Clients often forget some of the material that they reveal under hypnosis because I always give the suggestion that you will remember only what you're supposed to remember. If you use a recorder only that which you're prepared to deal with consciously will come through."

I left feeling depressed and upset. Dick's answers weren't reassuring. I just want all the weird nonsense to go away and leave me alone. Perhaps our trip to New York will be a chance to forget the psychic for a few days.

SUNDAY, MARCH 28, 1976

It's good to be back home again. Our long week-end in New York was hectic rather than relaxing. I had anticipated getting away completely from the psychic but I can't seem to escape it.

It started on the train into New York Friday morning, as I stared moodily at the landscape.

Burt interrupted my thoughts. "Thinking about your sessions with Dick?"

"Umhmm. But I'd like to try and forget the whole thing for a few days."

"Well, in case you change your mind I packed the Le Shan book." Burt had read Lawrence LeShan's *The Medium, the Mystic, and the Physicist* some months ago and had highly recommended it to me. I had just gotten around to starting it. "How do you like it, by the way?"

"I'm really enjoying it. He's put into words a lot of things I've thought and felt. Like in the introduction where he explains why so many people are afraid of the psychic. Do you have the book handy? I'll read you the part I like." Burt reached into his brief case and produced the paperback. I thumbed through the introductory pages. "Here it is:

> *The occurrence of an "impossible" event makes us anxious and frightened, and when people are anxious they behave in irrational ways. The paranormal raises deep hidden fantasies, and our anxiety level goes up with them. "After all," we unconsciously conclude, "if this is possible, then anything is possible and nothing is impossible. I may find myself living in a universe in which I understand nothing and can predict nothing. A world gone mad.*

I think that's the way I feel a lot."

"A lot of scientists do, too. Have you gotten to the part on healing yet?" Burt pulled out his pipe, and began stuffing it with tobacco; I knew he was gearing up for a long discussion.

"Can't do that here, hon. Remember this is a non-smoking car." Burt nodded absently, and stuck his pipe back in his pocket. I continued, "Yes, I've just been getting into it. It's fascinating. I never understood it before—thinking of it as either a complete fraud on the part of 'healers' or just another variation on the theme of 'the power of positive thinking.' But Le Shan's come up with some impressive evidence for the existence of actual energy that can be channeled for healing."

Burt nodded. "Le Shan seems to be a good researcher and his own experiences have been fascinating. What do you think of his two types?"

"Interesting. The first type where you go into a meditational state and try to unify your being with that of the healee is fascinating. I've experienced the sense of unity many times in meditation, but I never thought of utilizing that state for healing. And I'm also intrigued by the other type—hands-on healing. I've always thought of laying-on-of-hands as being a hoax."

"Umhmm. I was especially interested in how Le Shan compares the views of the world held by physicists and mystics. I've always considered myself a scientist, and been especially fascinated with physics. Then William James got me interested in the mystical. Now Le Shan suggests they may be one and the same."

"Yes, it's interesting, but I'm tired of the whole subject. Let's discuss something else—like this weekend. How many sessions do you think we can avoid going to? I'd rather go out and see New York or just relax in our room."

"Well, I want to go to a few, but I'm sure we can find some free time. I just wish I weren't presenting a paper. I'm not nervous yet, but I'm sure I will be on Sunday."

"Well, I don't envy you. I'm glad I don't have to present the paper I worked on."

Before we knew it, the train was pulling into Grand Central Station, and we made our way through the crowds to the taxi stand in front. It was a beautiful spring day. The streets were teeming with people, and I remembered it was already lunch time; we had left much later than we had planned that morning, deciding not to bother with the opening sessions.

We checked into the Americana, and were shown to a small room. Almost as soon as we walked into it, Burt collapsed on the bed. "Are you OK?" I asked, suddenly noticing that he looked pale.

"No, I have a terrible headache. An excruciating headache."

"I'll get you a couple of aspirin."

"Don't bother. I took three awhile ago in the lobby."

"Well, just lie there and relax. I'll go register us for the conference."

I returned awhile later, to find Burt still sprawled on the bed looking pained and pale. His eyes were closed.

"Honey?" I said softly. His eyes opened. They were filled with pain. "Oh, honey, is it worse?"

"I can't stand it. It's the worse headache I've ever had in my life. It's moving into my chest now; it's getting hard to breathe." Tears started trickling down Burt's cheeks; I knew he must be in terrible pain.

"Oh, honey, if there were anything I could do..." Suddenly I remembered Le Shan's book. "Look, just lie there and relax; I'll sit on the next bed and see if I can help in any way." I didn't think about what I was doing; I just did it. I sat on the next bed, closed my eyes, and white-lighted myself. Immediately, my eyes began moving rapidly. When they stopped, I green-lighted Burt. I let myself drift into a state in which I unified with the universe, and concentrated on merging myself with Burt, and seeing him without pain. After a few minutes, I felt my hands becoming alive with energy, so I sat next to him, and gently massaged his forehead. The energy in my hands gradually subsided, and I felt I had done all I could do. "How do you feel?" I asked tentatively, fearing he might be worse. Burt's eyes slowly opened and he smiled.

"It's all gone. It disappeared soon after you started."

"Maybe the aspirin finally took effect."

"Maybe. And maybe you just did your first psychic healing. We'll never know what caused the pain to go away. All that matters is that it's gone. Now I'm going down to join a session. Bye!" Burt kissed me briefly and then was gone. I sat for a long time staring out the window at the New York City scene below. I should never have attempted to work with energies I didn't understand. Perhaps I had actually caused Burt harm. Perhaps right at that moment, he was downstairs collapsing. I was uneasy until I saw Burt again later that afternoon and realized he was just fine.

The rest of our weekend was fairly uneventful. We attended a number of sessions, but still had time for relaxing in the room, visiting friends, and exploring the city. I was able to put the psychic out of mind for most of the weekend, although my dreams still focused on it. On both Saturday and Sunday I woke up with the strong impression that I should try again in my next session with Dick to contact Joey. I had planned to begin work on past lives, but I can't think of any reason *not* to do auto-writing instead. This time I'll use paper and pencil. I'm ready to learn who my tapper is and what he wants.

THURSDAY, APRIL 1, 1976

Tomorrow's my session with Dick, and I definitely feel ready to do auto-writing. I had an experience this week indicating that it's time.

On Monday, I did my usual yoga and meditation as soon as I got home from work. But this time, I felt a lot of energy in my arm and sensed the presence in the room. So I prayed for protection, and opened myself up to communication. I felt the energy enter my arm and the arm shoot up into the air. I decided to try something different. Instead of letting the arm produce meaningless circles, or perhaps a word or two, I tried asking yes-no questions.

"Are you open to answering yes-no questions?" I queried mentally.

The word "yes" was written out by my arm.

"Are you Joey?"

A "no" was written out. This was indeed puzzling. I tried again. Again a "no."

"Are you a new spirit who hasn't contacted me before?"

A "no" again was written in the air. I was really confused.

"Are you the same spirit who contacted me before as Joey?"

A "yes" this time.

"Were you the spirit who was born into the body of my little brother Joey?"

"Yes."

"Do you want me to call you Joey?"

"Yes."

Again I tried, "Are you Joey?"

"No."

It seemed my spirit was into playing games, or was a stickler for sematics. "Are you a friend?"

"Yes."

"Do you prefer contacting me with paper and pencil?"

"Yes."

"Would Friday, during my session with Dick, be a good time to do this?"

"Yes."

"Do you know what kind of verification for authenticity Dick has in mind?"

"Yes."

"Can you produce that verification on Friday?"

A long pause. Perhaps it wasn't a good question, I reasoned, because I could too easily influence the answer consciously. I was about to retract the question when a "yes" was written out.

"Do I have psychic ability?"

"Yes."

"Will I be able to use that ability to help others?"

"Yes."

"Are you here to serve as a guide to help me?"

"Yes."

"Will you be able to help me find ways to help others?"

"Yes."

"Do you have any other message for me today?"

"Yes. Love." As the word was written out, I felt surrounded by warm, loving vibrations. My arm dropped to the floor, so I continued my meditations. I felt as though I had entered a different reality, where love, peace, and joy were the nature of the universe. It was as though I were being taken places by guides and shown things about the universe, but the experience was too intense to be absorbed consciously. I could only sense the feelings. After a time, I felt I was being told that I had had contact with enough energy for one day, and it was time to come down to an earthly reality. I felt fantastic all evening.

I'm looking forward to tomorrow's auto-writing session. I think this is the first time I haven't dreaded a session with Dick.

FRIDAY, APRIL 2, 1976

I feel more depressed than I ever have after a session with Dick. Even though our sessions never go the way I expect them to, this one was a terrible experience for me.

I asked Dick about my attempts to channel energy for Burt's headache, and my concerns about hurting him.

"All right," Dick responded, "as long as we're going to start with the basics on natural healing—which, by the way, is a more accurate term than psychic healing, because it deals with natural law, God's law—you've got to take a spiritual approach. Now something you've got to remember, is that it's not my will, but Thy will be done. Do you understand that?"

I nodded, but didn't really understand.

"All you're doing is offering up yourself to be a channel. That's all you're doing. Sandy Gibson is not healing anyone. So if Sandy Gibson isn't healing anyone, Sandy Gibson isn't hurting anyone. Now why should you take the blame for hurting if you can't take the credit for healing? This is very important, Sandy. If Burt had dropped dead on the spot, your response should have been 'Thank you, God.' As cold and brutal as that sounds, it's not my will, but Thy will be done. There's greater peace after leaving the physical, and it's God's will to return to that peace. If you got shook and emotional about it, that would be selfishness. Now isn't it strange that Burt should have such a severe headache when he's never had one like that before?"

"What do you mean?"

"Think about it. How else could you have the initial exposure to the potential that lies within? How else would you develop the confidence?"

"Well, it was very spontaneous. With anyone else, I would have gone through a lot more head trips, and probably would have decided not to do it. With Burt, I just did it."

"Again, you're being led, being spoon-fed. Recently, I worked with a burn victim. It was predicted that he would need plastic surgery; he had burns on 60% of his body. But I went up to the hospital every day and combed out the etherial body—or aura. It's creating a charge in your hand, like a magnet, to attract all the defective atoms that are vibrating into the etherial body from the physiological problems. By changing that, you're actually sending back smoother vibrations into the physical. And the body begins to speed up the healing process. He recovered quite quickly without any surgery. There are some scars still on his back, but there are no visible scar tissues. Dick Smith didn't do it. I was merely a channel. You're the same way."

Then I explained that instead of beginning past life work, I wanted to try auto-writing for the rest of the session.

"Sure. Just understand my attitude. Whatever happens, happens. No expectations, OK?"

"OK." I had plenty of expectations, but saw no point in going into them. Either the contacts were authentic, or they weren't, and I was going to find out within the next forty-five minutes.

"Do you want to keep the recorder running? It doesn't matter to me."

"Yes, I would like to."

"Now, we'll walk into it. Sit back and relax."

"Does this chair go back?"

"Sure." For the first time, I pushed back on the chair, making it into a recliner. With my feet up and my head back, I was practically lying down. Dick helped me move the tape recorder out of the way, and then he leaned over and closed the window. "Your bodily functions will slow down, and the breeze might be too chilly for you." At last, we were all set. "What I'd like you to do is hold this pen and rest your hand lightly on the pad of paper. Now go through the motions and see how far you can go comfortably with the paper in this position." I practiced, and found a position in which I could move freely. "Now let's begin by letting our minds go passive." I pictured the white light coming from the disc and going into every part of my body. I could tell that Dick was white-lighting me, too. I was feeling more and more relaxed; more groggy. Dick spoke softly to me, encouraging me to relax further. I felt my eyes begin to move rapidly, and knew that my body must be asleep. I thought about asking Dick if that was the case, but it seemed such an effort to speak, I didn't bother. Again, there was a long pause, but at the time I wasn't aware of time passing. "Now as you relax physically and as you relax mentally, I want you to imagine that your body is in perfect health, totally free from harm or danger of any kind, and that there's an energy, very slowly, very, very slowly, entering your right arm. Just the right arm." By this time, the pen had slipped out of my hand. Dick picked it up and curled my fingers around it.

"Now place the pen on the paper. That's right. This energy is very warm, and the white light remains around your entire body. You feel a warmth around the right arm, very secure. A very secure feeling." The familiar energy was in my arm, and after a few moments it started to move. Circles. My eyes were closed, but I could tell it was making circles. And more circles. "That's right, just let the arm go. You're perfectly safe. White light is totally surrounding the body." I felt secure. And relaxed. But I was getting discouraged. After all my hopes for this session, was I to get only circles? "Do you wish me to ask questions?" I murmured my assent, but wondered what the point would be if I were to get only circles.

"Please identify yourself if necessary." The answer was immediate and I could tell at once what was being written. Squiggles. More meaningless nonsense. Was it true, then, that it was all my imagination? That's all it had ever been and ever would be? I felt foolish wasting my time and Dick's with nonsensical squiggles. But Dick didn't seem distrubed. His voice went on. "What shall we call you?" More circles. "Where are you from?" More of the same. I felt that something was trying very hard, but without success, to get through. "Do you have a message for us today—especially for Sandy? Is there something you would like to relay to us at this time?" I felt Dick's hand moving my clipboard up a few inches so that fresh paper would be directly under my hand. But I couldn't see that it mattered since only meaningless nonsense was coming through. "Is that symbolic of something?" I doubted it, and only more scribbles came through in reply. I felt Dick move over and tear off the first sheet of paper.

Suddenly, something happened. The energy intensified, my arm took off. I felt as though I gave up fighting it. Words were very, very slowly and awkwardly being written. I knew what they were because they flowed into my head before my arm wrote them on the paper. "Sandy...is...blocking...my communication."

"Is there something you wish to know?"

My arm moved slowly and deliberately in response. "I . . . am . . . here . . ." Some more squiggles. "I . . . am . . . here . . . to . . ." Dick reached over and tore off the sheet. I must have been at the bottom of the page. The words continued on the fresh page. " . . . help . . . I . . . am . . . here . . . to . . . help."

"Are you here to help Sandy?" Dick asked.

". . . Yes . . ." was written out.

"What is it that you are trying to help Sandy with?"

"Sandy...needs...help."

"Is there anything specific Sandy should do to receive your help?"

". . . Relaxing . . ." was written out. I didn't realize until later that the word was totally illegible. Dick tore off another page.

"What type of help would be best for her? How should she be helped?"

The question was ignored as I felt my arm writing out its own message. "It . . . is . . . hard . . . to . . . communicate."

"Yes, it is," Dick responded gently. Then he returned to question what purported to be a visiting spirit. "Is it safe for her to practice this a little more often, either with me or alone?"

I sensed strong feelings with that one, and the word written in response came quickly: "Absolutely." Dick chuckled.

"Is she safe doing it alone?"

"Yes" was written out.

"OK. As long as she uses the white light?"

Again "Yes" was written out, but I got many more feelings in response. I got the feeling that the white light was more psychological than anything else, because I was perfectly safe even without it—I was well protected.

"Is auto-writing the best approach for her to use in this time period?"

The words were coming faster and more easily. "Telepathic ... is ... best ... but ... she ... blocks ..."

"Was she very involved in metaphysics, or in this type of work, in a past life, or in many past lives?"

I froze with apprehension. I wouldn't let my arm move. Dick started talking to me. "Whatever you receive, you are able to receive in context, recognizing that each and every life-cycle is a very valuable experience. It is to our advantage to view it very carefully, very accurately and objectively." Still no response from the arm. "Sandy, you'd better tell me what you're thinking about." No answer. I didn't know what to say. "Are you frightened?" I shook my head. "Do you still feel relaxed?" I nodded. "I keep looking at you so darned relaxed, I want to go to sleep!" Dick chuckled, and then returned to his questions. "Is this a life she has chosen not to remember for some reason? Is there something here she refuses to reveal to herself?"

One word was written in response: "... fear ..."

Dick decided to drop the subject at that point.

"Was Sandy used as a channel while working with Burt in New York?"

"... Yes ..." was written out. I was feeling very foolish. I didn't believe that consciously.

"Is this an ability that she has in this life cycle that should be developed?"

No way was I going to let another embarrassing answer come through. "I'd like to stop," I murmured.

"OK, just relax now. You got quite a bit out today. Just relax. Relax your body, relax your mind. You're doing very well. Just keep the white light around you for a little bit. Now I want you to picture your gold disc and coming from it is going to be a very soft pink light. Now we're going to let the shade come out on its own. It'll be the shade most suited to give you energy. We're going to give you energy now because you have been relaxing so deeply for so long today. We want to be sure to make you totally alert and totally functional again. It's going to turn the white into a soft shade of red now, for a little energy shot. It'll filter in. Now, I'm going to count slowly from 1 to 8, and you'll feel your body returning to a perfectly functional state of consciousness, perfectly functional. As I count your subconscious and superconscious mind will put your body back into perfect harmony. You'll sleep well, extremely well tonight. 1—you're perfectly safe now, and you remember everything you're supposed to remember." Dick continued counting. I felt myself rise further to normal consciousness with each number. And my embarrassment became more acute. I had been fantasizing all of those answers, obviously. "Take your time; let your eyes open all by themselves."

I opened them to see Dick reading through the pages with large, scrawled words on them. "Did you expect that much?" he queried. I just shrugged. Actually, I had expected a lot more. Because of my expectations, I had just made up the whole thing. It was too simple, easy, and natural to have been spirit communication. I felt really glum, and wanted to just leave it right there.

Dick handed back my tablet and clipboard. "Now I'd like you to write these words for me: 'Sandy, my, here, help, absolutely, blocks, fear, yes.'" I wrote them and then handed the tablet back to him. I sat looking out the window morosely while he compared the handwritings. So that was his verification: comparing handwritings. I knew that I'd failed. I had produced all that myself. I was a failure, a fraud. I felt very embarrassed.

"Well, nobody took you over." I became even more dejected at Dick's words. He was trying to pick a gentle way of telling me I had made up the whole thing. "What's the matter?"

"Nothing," I said with a shrug.

"It's still you, Sandy. Nobody has possessed you. It's still you. Do you remember what you wrote?"

"Yes." How could I forget, having made up the whole thing?

"Do you remember what you wrote at first?" I nodded. "Do you understand that you were blocking because you're not accustomed to it? You understand, that's normal and natural."

"Umhum." I had blocked anything at all from coming through, and had fabricated the whole thing, obviously.

"That's very important. I'm trying to think of the title of a book I read some years ago. It was about a woman who did auto-writing. She was a housewife, and it was her very first experience with it. It turned out to be her husband who had passed over. She had the same turmoil, torments and questions that you do: Am I really doing this? Am I some kind of freak? Am I flipping out? Am I being possessed? She finally got the attitude that 'Well, God must want me to do something.' And it turned out to be her husband. He wanted to let her know that he was all right and was going to look after her and the kids. It was really a good book."

I could tell Dick was trying to make me feel better with that little story. He was trying to tell me that someone else had once imagined she was doing auto-writing, too, only she had imagined it was her husband. At least she had a good excuse; she was grieving for a loved one. I had no excuse. I was just a fraud. I must have an unconscious desire to be a medium, and would resort to trickery and fraud to convince others I was one. What a despicable thing to do! I wished I could just crawl in a hole and die.

"How're you doing?" Dick asked.

"I'm disappointed."

"Disappointed! With all of that!" Dick seemed surprised. "That's the first time you ever wrote anything, and that's disappointing?"

"But it was just me doing it."

"What did you want to do?"

"Well, with the communication I've done this week, I got a message that I should try the auto-writing today and that the verification you had mentioned would be produced today."

"I'm in no hurry. And obviously there's no immediate urgency, so why rush?"

"But maybe this shows that there really isn't anybody trying to contact me, and it's all my imagination."

"Well, I can give you something to try if you want; that's to forget the whole thing. What do you suppose would happen?" I shrugged. "With free will you could choose on a soul level to forget the whole thing. But if consciously you try to forget it, while spiritually you're still trying to grow in this direction, you'll continue to grow. You can't deny that you're here for a reason. That's real. You *can* deny fulfilling that reason. Being an Aries, I have an empathy for where you're at. I would love to see something materialize in the room, and give me a heavy message. I'd really be convinced. Then, a week later, I'd be asking, 'Now, was that really my imagination?' And it would materialize again and say, 'Here I am again,' and I'd believe. But a week later, being mortal and being Aries, I'd ask myself, 'I wonder if that really happened?'" Dick paused a bit and lit a cigarette. "Now, that was a lot for the first session. And I'll tell you why. The first session usually consists of lines, meaningless lines, or circles, meaningless circles. That's all the first, second, and sometimes third session usually consists of. That's exactly the way you started out. And then, suddenly, we developed a rhythm and you began to write legibly enough that I could read it. It sometimes takes quite a few sessions to get a person to reach that point."

"But what's the point of it if it was just *me*?"

Dick let out a sigh. "Perhaps it's assurance that nobody's going to possess you. It's still Sandy. It's your handwriting. I know what you feel; it comes through. You're not quite ready to let go. Which is fine. There's no hurry. Any more questions?"

I shook my head. What did it matter? I was obviously a

fraud, and I just wanted to go home. I doubted that I'd ever be back, but decided to set my next appointment in case I changed my mind. Burt's parents would be visiting the following Friday, so I set it for Wednesday, but felt certain I'd cancel beforehand. There must be a part of me that wants to be a fraudulent medium, making money by charging people for services I can't perform. Perhaps I'm discovering dark depths of myself that I never knew existed. I wonder if I have the ability to make spirit contact, but blew it this one time by imagining answers. Or if I don't have, and never have had the ability. It doesn't matter. I'm quitting. I only kept going this long in order to get some real proof. Now I have it. I'm a fraud.

SATURDAY, APRIL 3, 1976

It's a relief to be giving up the psychic search. It's become too painful and agonizing. I can go back now to living a normal life, focusing my attentions on Burt, my job, my friends, and a few hobbies. The psychic has been consuming too much of my time lately. My search has been draining and traumatic; I long for the simple boredom of every-day routine.

I came home from my session yesterday in a deep depression. I felt I was an unstable personality who was having hallucinations and needed psychiatric help. I spent the entire evening in bed, not wanting to talk about my feelings with anyone. Burt tried to talk with me, but I wasn't very responsive. When I'm depressed or angry, I get uncommunicative. I know that's not good. And it's very frustrating for Burt. I've been working on learning to express anger, and I'm getting much better at it. But when I get depressed, I just want to be alone.

Burt understood, and left me alone for the evening. I also spent most of today in bed feeling absolutely miserable and not eating. Burt finally enticed me out of bed this evening by offering to take me out for pizza. That offer has never failed to interest me. Despite my lack of appetite, I was able to consume pizza, salad, and beer at a near-by Italian restaurant. I'm feeling better now, but I still don't want to discuss my feelings about being a fraud. I want to forget the whole thing.

SUNDAY, APRIL 4, 1976

I was roused from a sound sleep this morning by the ringing of the telephone.

"Sandy? It's Judy." She sounded upset.

"Hi. What's up?" I rasped, in my just-waking-up voice.

"Have you seen anybody suspicious hanging around the house?"

"No, why? What happened?"

"Someone broke into my garage yesterday."

"You've got to be kidding!" I remembered the evil-looking figure I had seen and Judy's uneasy feelings.

"No, I came home yesterday to find things messed up in the garage. And a gasoline can was left in the middle of the floor, like a warning that the person would return. I don't think it was kids; it seemed more like it was somebody who wanted to scare me."

We discussed the incident briefly, then said goodby. I lay in bed for a long time thinking. It was very disturbing that I had "seen" that figure just a few weeks ago. Was it really coincidence? Or a clairvoyant experience? Will I ever know? Will I be plagued by "coincidences" for the rest of my life?

This afternoon Judy invited me up for tea, so I climbed the staircase to her apartment. As usual, everything was spotless, quite a contrast to our generally cluttered apartment which always seems in need of a cleaning. Judy served peppermint tea as we sat and talked at her kitchen table. I told her about my last session proving I was a fraud and that I was giving up spirit communication.

"That's absurd," Judy asserted, as she squeezed her tea bag into the cup and then tossed it into a small bowl. "It was the first time you ever tried auto-writing. It seems

104

perfectly logical that you wouldn't be ready to let some energy take over your arm. Even if you wrote the words yourself, the messages might have come telepathically from Joey. Or he might have been guiding your arm in some way."

"I never thought of that," I muttered, blowing on my too-hot tea.

"I have faith in what you're doing. I've felt for a long time that whatever's out there, you're in touch with it. I'd hate to see you give it up just as you're finally getting messages through."

That was the most encouraging thing I'd heard in a long time. I had a lot of confidence in Judy's psychic ability. Her belief that the contact had been real made me consider for the first time in forty-eight hours, that perhaps I really wasn't a fraud.

"What exactly did Dick tell you after you did the auto-writing?"

"That it was just me doing it." My tea was finally cool, so I started sipping.

"Well, maybe you misunderstood him. I can't believe he would tell you you're a fraud and then just end the session, without helping you understand why you imagined it. Talk to him about what he meant."

"I don't plan to see Dick again. I'll continue to be a member of the Foundation, but no more private sessions. And no more personal psychic searching."

"I hope you change your mind. Frankly, I think you will. Your drive to understand is too strong for you to quit now."

"Maybe," I said doubtfully, draining my cup.

"Want some more?"

"No, I think I'll go to the Prana open house this afternoon. Want to come along?"

"No, I don't think so. I have a lot of other things to do."

I left, still depressed, and drove the eight minutes to the Foundation. There was a small turn-out and a lot of food. I chatted with Dick and a few other people, trying to hide my depression.

After speaking with everyone I knew, I considered

leaving. Then I noticed a book shelf in the corner that I had never seen before. I went over and started browsing through the collection of books on the occult. I pulled one out to see its title, and saw, with revulsion, that it was on witchcraft. I quickly put it back, disgusted that a spiritually oriented place should have a book on such a horrible subject. I said hasty good-byes and left.

As I drove home, I was suddenly struck by the oddity of my reaction to the witchcraft book. I had always reacted that way to books on the subject and, although feeling a fascination with that area, had never been able to overcome my hesitancy to read a book on it. "Now, really," I thought to myself. "That is rather strange. Why should I react so violently to a book?" It occurred to me that perhaps I really had been a witch in a previous life. Although the idea sounded absurd, it seemed worth exploring. The alternative was to spend the rest of my life avoiding the subject. And also to spend the rest of my life wondering why I had a strong feeling I had been tortured on an alien planet. There were just too many questions I wanted answered to give up now.

I smiled to myself. Didn't I really know it all along? I'm not going to give up my search until I have some satisfactory answers. I'm thinking about the happenings of the weekend that led me to this decision: the phone call from Judy about the break-in in her garage; the book at the Foundation's open house; all the words of Burt and Judy. Some force, or energy, or series of coincidences is making it extremely difficult for me to give up the search, just as a series of events made it impossible for me not to begin it.

Well, Wednesday is only three days away. I'll tell Dick that, although I can't trust myself sufficiently to continue spirit communication, I do want to explore my past lives and continue to try to understand the psychic. I just told Burt my decision to continue.

"Of course," he commented with irritating confidence, "I knew you would. I was just riding out the storm till you came to your senses again."

WEDNESDAY, APRIL 7, 1976

I asked Burt to come with me to today's session. I wanted moral support.

"How're you doing?" Dick started out, making himself comfortable in his chair.

"OK," I responded. "Actually I'm surprised I came back. After the last session, I decided I wasn't ever returning. But I changed my mind in a couple of days."

"Well, it doesn't matter whether you come back here or not. As I've said, we'll love you whether you do or don't. As long as you continue to search on your own, that's the important thing."

"That's what I wanted to stop doing."

"That's heavy," Dick said, lighting up a cigarette. I noticed that Burt also took out his pipe and started to fill it.

"Well, I was very depressed."

"She kept calling herself a fraud," Burt added, as he lit a match. I gave him a dirty look. I didn't want to discuss anything related to spirit communication.

Dick looked at me curiously, and I felt the need to try and explain. "I felt like a fraud because the whole thing was my imagination."

Dick sighed as he took a puff on his cigarette. "I know it's impossible to unscrew my head and loan it to you, but if I could, I'd do it in order to give you an idea of how many people there are in this world who feel the way you do. I really mean that. You're dealing with such intangible knowledge. You can't touch it; you can't show it to anyone. What you're doing is of such a high level, on such a high plane, you'll always question. Look, if you stop questioning, I think you'll have a serious problem."

"But Friday I got definite evidence that it was only my imagination."

Dick looked confused. "What happened Friday?"

"Well, whatever was being written was written in my own hand."

"Oh, I thought you meant something had happened afterwards." He still looked confused. "You said it was your imagination? Where did you get that idea? I merely made the statement that you were not possessed."

Now I was getting confused. "Maybe you'd better explain that."

"OK. You wrote some words automatically, and then you wrote some words consciously. Then I did a comparison, and I said it was still you. It was confirmation for me, and also for you, that there was no possession taking place. You still had conscious control of your faculties. You were a channel. Your characteristics showed up in that writing, meaning that whenever you wanted to, you could have stopped and slowly opened your eyes. So you were still you, and that's very positive. I don't know how you construed that to mean it was all your imagination. It *wasn't* your imagination. Well, I shouldn't say that. But all evidence points to sincerity."

"In other words, you're saying that what happened Friday is not necessarily proof that it was my imagination?"

"Right. Unless you've read a lot of books on auto-writing, unless you've witnessed somebody go through the techniques, and on top of it be a damned good actress, you can't fake it. If you were trying to duplicate things you've read, you did a beautiful job, because it was all quite authentic. These are all the things I take into consideration. Oh, I've worked with people who grab a pencil and start writing and think they're doing auto-writing. But it's imagination. My own gut feeling is that what you experienced was very authentic. Mainly because of the REM. You went through it again. You manifested many physiological characteristics of going into a deep state, a most profound state of rest. And you just don't turn that on and off. You see, it's so natural for you, and you have no idea of how much training it takes people to do it. To get to that depth so quickly—in seconds. You take it for granted."

I paused for a moment, staring out the window, then took off on a different track. "I've been very depressed lately. It seems like I leave depressed after every session."

"Right. And why is that?" Dick looked at me intently. I felt he was looking right through me.

"Well, it's like nothing satisfies me."

"Why?" It wasn't a question to gather information. He already knew the answer and was trying to get me to face it.

"If I feel that I have some real psychic ability, I get depressed. And if I feel that it's all imagination, I also get depressed."

"Why?" The "why's" were becoming relentless.

"Well, for some reason, I have enough curiosity and drive that I want to keep exploring. I'm just not able to walk away from it. But I can't accept it, either. I'm stuck in the middle."

"It's like living in two worlds. One portion of you is struggling very, very hard to be awakened in the spiritual sense. And the other portion of you, which is quite mortal, understandably wants to remain on *terra firma.* And you're not secure dealing in areas so far beyond the physical. Mainly because of other factors, such as past life experiences. So far, we've been working most superficially." Superficially? I wondered to myself. If all the trauma and depression I've been experiencing was the result of superficial therapy, I wondered what deep therapy would do to me. "Sooner or later, you're going to have to face your past. You can do it in this life cycle or in another one. But you're going to have to do it."

"That's why I decided to come back. I can walk away from these sessions, but I can't walk away from everything that's been happening." I told him about the phone call from Judy on Sunday morning. In response, I saw him trying to stifle a grin. "I know what you're thinking," I accused, "I know exactly what you're thinging."

"OK," he chuckled and then let out a hearty laugh. I didn't join in. I knew he was convinced that another incident proved the determination of some guardian angel or protective energy to keep moving me in a spiritual direction.

"All right. I'm ready to start work on my past lives. Where do we begin?"

"Let's spend the rest of today's session on a simple, introductory exercise. Burt can do it, too."

Dick had us both get very relaxed, and then move back into the past of this life to some very pleasant experience. I recalled a trip to the beach several years ago and really enjoyed the chance to "relive" it. Then the session ended and I made an appointment to come back in a week to start probing a past life.

I have a lot to absorb after that session. I had convinced myself that I was a fraud, weathered a severe depression over it, and decided to give up auto-writing, all on the basis of a misunderstanding. In reality, Dick thought what I did was authentic. Perhaps he's lying to me. Perhaps he's convinced that I am a fraud, but feels that telling me will plunge me into a suicidal depression. I think I'd rather believe anything than that my auto-writing is authentic.

THURSDAY, APRIL 15, 1976

The past week has been very busy—Burt's folks came out from Illinois for a visit. I enjoyed seeing them, and we had a lot of fun together, but I wish I had been more sociable. I was very preoccupied thinking about my auto-writing experience, and wondering what past-life therapy will be like.

I feel isolated. Dick, Burt and Judy are the only three people in the world in whom I can confide the very deep emotions I'm experiencing. I'm not sure exactly why I don't discuss my experiences with any of my other friends, but I have a strong sense that it wouldn't be wise. I know of very few people who would even discuss it seriously with me. If I told my co-workers about white light and auto-writing, I'd become the butt of many jokes, and that's one thing I can't take right now. Other people might shy away from me, seeing me as freaky. I remember getting that kind of reaction in the past, the few times I tried to discuss my psychic experiences with others. Another reaction I've received bothers me just as much: people looking to me as "a psychic." I can remember a few times having discussed some of my experiences with someone, and having them then ask me what I saw in the future for them. That's something I can't deal with.

Something else I was preoccupied with this past week is the entire concept of psychic or holistic healing. I didn't know anything about it before I started my counseling at Prana, but now I'm gradually developing an interest in this area. I just purchased a book on the subject called *We Are All Healers* by Sally Hammond. I've been hesitant to read books on the occult, because I don't want to prejudice my own experiences with imagination. But I'm an intellectual, academically-oriented person, and I learn best from books. If I'm interested in a subject, I go to the library and get an arm-load of books on it. If I'm feeling lazy, I find nothing more relaxing than a mystery book and a comfortable chair. So, for me, the easiest and most natural way to learn about the occult is by reading. I used to hesitate to read about the subject, because learning about anything in this field frightened me. But I'm less frightened now, and more ready to learn.

I have a lot of questions about psychic healing. A couple of weeks ago, I felt myself coming down with a sore throat. While meditating, I had a strong urge to use my hands to send energy to that area. My hands felt tingly and full of energy so I put them on my throat. I could feel warmth from them, but when I tried moving them several inches away I felt much more energy. After a moment of this, my hands started shaking violently. That was upsetting to me, and I stopped immediately.

I'm continuing to feel contacts almost daily while I meditate. I usually feel a presence, and then either sense a message flowing through my mind, or feel an energy in my arm writing out a brief message, such as the word "love," or "faith." Monday's meditation was typical. I sat down to meditate, and gave myself the suggestion that I'd slip into a deeply relaxed state for ten minutes, and then would come out of it automatically. I also told myself that if there were messages I should receive I would be receptive to them. Very shortly I was in a deep meditative state and felt a presence. I felt a message coming through: I should relax and let myself go, let myself drift. I would be helped into even deeper states if I relaxed more. And it was important for me to learn how to go into deep states. I meditated for awhile to a mantra, and then felt my eyes open at the end of the ten minutes.

On Tuesday I decided to try auto-writing again on my own. Since I'm not a fraud after all, there's no reason to give it up. In fact, there's an excellent reason to continue: *I want proof.* I want incontrovertible proof that the auto-writing is either authentic or imagination. The only way I can think of to get the proof is to keep trying it. So I asked Burt to work with me, to ask the questions, and move the paper as Dick had done. I did feel apprehensive, but more relaxed than the first time. I lay down on the bed in my study and Burt sat in a chair next to me. I white-lighted myself, and got into as deep a relaxation state as I could; I felt my eyes going through REM again. I felt the energy in my arm and the presence. Mentally, I asked: Who are you? And ...Joey..." was written out. Burt took over asking questions.

"Why are you here?"

"I ... am ... here ... to ... help ... Sandy ... help ... develop ... psychic." The words came out slowly, with large, sprawled letters.

"Should Sandy contact you more often?"

"... Yes ..."

"Where is Sandy?"

"... Here ..."

"Is she asleep?"

I sensed a great amusement, as though the question were too complicated to fully answer, because I was actually more awake than in my normal waking state. The answer reflected this complexity and amusement: "In ... a ... sense ... so ... are ... you ... in ... a ... sense."

Burt picked up the humor in the remark. "Do you have a sense of humor?"

"Yes ... of ... course."

"How often should we contact you?"

"As ... often ... as ... Sandy ... feels ... able."

"Why didn't the handwriting change in the session with Dick?"

"Sandy ... is ... in ... control."

"Is this a strain on Sandy?"

"No ... she ... is ... very ... relaxed ... I ... am ... very ... protective ... of ... her ... well ... being ... but ... enuf ... for ... today ... goodby ... peace ... love."

I felt the energy drain out of my arm, but continued to stay in the relaxed state for a few minutes before slowly bringing myself out of it. That experience could not possibly have been authentic. It was too natural, too easy.

Words like "auto-writing," "trance," and "spirit communication" are heavy words, and I've always assumed that they were accompanied by heavy experiences. I was just lying there feeling totally at peace and having experienced a warm loving presence around me and a warm energy in my arm. It was so natural. No lights flashing, no fireworks, no objects flying across the room, no profound messages from God. It *had* to be imagination.

I think that if I could just jump into a blind belief in my auto-writing I'd feel better. If I could *believe* that I was holding conversations with a spirit named Joey, that I was a medium in the making, that I had lived before and would live again, that there was a God who sent protective white lights, then all would be well—I would be at peace. As those thoughts went through my mind, some recollection from the past was kindled; something I had once read by Neitzsche. I rummaged through some books until I found it:

> *If you wish to strive for peace of soul and pleasure then believe; if you wish to be a devotee of truth, then inquire.*

I do get tired of inquiring sometimes.

FRIDAY, APRIL 16, 1976

As I walked from my car to the Foundation across the street this afternoon I noticed West Rock looming up in the distance. It was a gorgeous sight and a beautiful day. It would be glorious to spend the next hour in the park at the top of that rock enjoying a lovely spring afternoon, I mused. Instead I was about to spend the next hour cooped up in an office trying to relive experiences that would be terribly painful, that would leave me depressed, and that probably had never happened anyway and I was paying $25 for the privilege. I really must be either crazy, or a masochist.

I had a few questions to ask before we began with the past life work. Actually, I rather hoped we'd become so involved with the other questions we'd never get around to past lives. "I want to ask about clairaudience. You said one time that anyone who does auto-writing is clairaudient. But I don't hear voices; I just get words in my head."

"Same thing. It means telepathic. You don't hear voices like you do physically."

"But I don't know how to tell them from my own thoughts. I'm not engaging in a thought process, but the words are there just like my thoughts are there."

"There are some clairaudients who hear as clearly as we're talking. That's a real, true clairaudient. Others hear thoughts mentally. The problem is that it's hard to know your thoughts from thoughts that are coming to you. This will always, always, be a problem as long as you're mortal. In time you may learn to distinguish a fine line there. It's still you, but it's a *higher* you, the oversoul. Even if you never have anyone speak 'through' you or to you doesn't matter, because your soul has a rather extensive history and itself contains a storehouse of knowledge. That's why I keep emphasizing not to worry about where it comes from. As long as it's common sense, you're not hurting anybody. Use it. Even if it's 'just' from you—it's from the higher you. Which is part of cosmic consciousness."

I dug up a few more questions to throw out. But as the session progressed I began to relax more. And in glancing at my watch, I realized that time was passing fast. If I didn't want to spend another week worrying about what might come out, I'd better get it over with. So I gave up on questions and put my list away.

"OK," I said with as much bravery as I could muster. "I'm ready to start on the past life work."

"OK, now we're going to walk into your past lives and play it by ear. We're not going to look for any specific thing, but just try to get a feel of it. We're going to get you used to the idea of traveling, because you'll either go into regression or revivication. If it's regression, you'll go back to the past. If it's revivication, the past will come to you and you'll watch it happening, like in a movie. But we're going to do it very slowly. At all times you'll be able to hear me clearly. And at all times, you'll respond instantly to what I say, as long as it's not against your morals or principles. We'll have a link mentally, even though you may not remember that I'm Dick Smith. OK?"

"OK," I responded weakly. I was wishing I were outside on top of West Rock.

"Now get comfortable." I pushed back the chair and did my best to relax. "Now put yourself in your own relaxed state. Don't think about what's going to happen or what you're going to say. Just adopt a very passive attitude." There was a long silence, during which I relaxed as I did at home, and felt my eyelids fluttering during the now-familiar REM state. "From now on," Dick continued, "I'll be talking to your superconscious mind, or soul level. So whenever I ask a question, it will automatically be directed to the soul level. It may be a little cumbersome to answer me, but you'll find that you'll be able to do so quite comfortably."

By this point, I had reached a state where I had blocked

all noises except for Dick's voice. In hearing the tape later, I was surprised that there even had been other sounds: cars passing by outside, the phone and typewriter in the outer office. I was oblivious to all of it. I was feeling relaxed, peaceful, mildly curious as to what would happen next.

"Now, we'll both pause mentally for a few seconds and we're going to visualize a very familiar symbol placed above your head in gold, and allow the white light to enter and fill your body." There was a long pause, as I drifted further and further away from any conscious awareness of Dick's office. "Now I'm going to count very slowly backward from 10 to 1. By the time I reach the count of 1, your superconscious mind will have a time period that we can investigate today. Take your time, and let it be very natural."

For most of the count, I was in a dark void, not really consciously aware of where I was or what I was doing. I felt very peaceful and relaxed. "One. Now tell me what you see and what you feel."

Suddenly images popped into mind. I was looking at a busy street scene, with people bustling about in old-fashioned clothing. "I see a carriage," I muttered as my eyes focused on one particular aspect of the scene. "There's a horse."

"A carriage and a horse? OK. What else do you see?"

"A cobblestone street."

"What is the year?"

"1898." I surprised myself with the answer. If I had thought about it, I wouldn't have known. But the answer came from nowhere without my realizing what I was going to say.

"What is your name?"

My eyes focused on a young man bustling down the street. That was me; I knew it. "Ashby."

"Ashby? What is your first name?"

"Edward."

"What are you doing, Edward Ashby?"

"I'm hurrying down the street. I have an appointment."

"What is your position?"

117

"I'm a solicitor." The scene began fading from my mind. I tried to hold onto it, to learn more about Edward Ashby, the solicitor. But it was a losing battle. The details of the street became fuzzy, and soon all was darkness again.

"Is this appointment that you're going to important?"

I tried again to tune into the scene so that I could answer the question, but I couldn't. "I don't know. The scene is gone."

"What country were you in?"

I had known that all along; I just wasn't asked. "England."

"And what city?"

"London." I paused for a long time. "It was so sad."

"What was sad?"

"That life."

"What was sad about it?" A long pause, with no answer. "What was so sad about the life as Edward Ashby?" I heard the questions, but they no longer had any meaning. I had long since left the English scene. I didn't know where I was or what I was seeing, but it was terrifying. So terrifying, I didn't want to talk about it. I saw a woman, dressed in colorful, gypsy-type clothes. She was hunched over something, like a crystal ball. Or her body was. She herself was floating somewhere outside her body, absolutely terrified. That woman was me.

"You're perfectly safe now, and free from any harm. I want you to tell me what you're seeing and feeling."

"I . . . I'm out of my body," I let out, in an agonized voice. "I don't want to look down. There's somebody else in my body."

"OK. Do you know what or who is in your body?"

"I . . . I don't know!"

"Do you still feel secure?" What a strange question, I thought. And then I remembered. I was really Sandy Gibson, sitting in the office of Dick Smith, trying to remember some past lives. But this couldn't be a past life, so there was no point in dwelling on it. I wanted to get away from it. But at least I felt more secure remembering who and where I was.

"I guess so. I'm being pulled away from that scene."

"You're in full control, and you can respond instantly to all suggestions that do not violate your morals or principles. Superconscious mind, where are you taking Sandy today?"

I didn't know; there was a dark void. Then I started to get a sense of where I was going and tried to resist it. But to no avail. I found myself facing a hot, rocky, alien planet.

"I don't know where I am. There are a lot of rocks."

"How did you get there?"

"I had to jump out, and I landed here."

"Were you in some sort of aircraft?"

"Umhmm."

"Are you from this planet?"

"No. These people are hostile to my people. I'm scared."

"Are you all alone?"

"Yes."

"What is your name?"

"I don't know. I've been confused since the crash. I'm so thirsty, and so hot. There's somebody here. Dressed in strange clothes. I . . . I'm following him. I don't have any choice!"

"Where is he taking you?"

"To a building."

"Is it a modern building?"

"It's very different. We're walking down this long corridor. I don't understand what's happening!" I was feeling absolutely terrified. "I'm being taken into a room!" A long pause.

"What's happening in that room?"

"I don't know. I don't want to know." I refused to follow the events of that scene into the room. I knew it would be a horrible experience in there, and I didn't want to look at it.

"What do they do to you after they're finished in that room? Do they take you back outside?"

"Yes . . . to die in the sun by the big rocks."

"Superconscious, is it important that Sandy remembers what happened in that room?"

"Yes."

"Is it safe to tell her why it is so important for her to remember?"

"Yes."

"Please tell her exactly how that period of time she was recalling has affected her in her life today?" The answers came out without my understanding where they were coming from.

"It produces fears."

"What is it that she fears?"

"The energies that were used for torture in that room."

"Tell her more specifically, either mentally or verbally, exactly how those fears are still with her today."

"Energies were used to hurt. She is afraid of them now. She is afraid she will be hurt again through the use of energy, and is unable to see that energies can also be used for good."

"Does Sandy understand exactly how this experience has affected her today?"

"Not consciously."

"Is it safe to tell her?"

"I think so."

"All right. I want you to explain to her exactly how this experience affects her in her present life cycle, consciously or unconsciously." There was silence for a few moments, as I slowly began to understand. I felt a weight lifting from my shoulders.

"The energy was being used to hurt me."

"Why were they trying to hurt you?"

"They wanted to hurt my people."

"Why?"

"Because of what we were doing."

"What were you doing?"

"We wanted to unite the planets. This planet didn't want to see unity. They wanted to control. They wanted to destroy us."

"Is this a lifetime Sandy experienced during earth lifetimes, or prior to them?"

"Prior to them."

"OK. I want you to relax now. Let your mind go passive. Let your body sleep. Just relax. Now you're going to return to the physical. You will have microscopic recall of everything you've mentioned here today, as long as it's safe for you to remember it. I'm going to count slowly from 1 to 8. And as I do, your subconscious and superconscious minds will bring you to a state in which you're completely functional. Totally free from stress or strain, worry or fear. You will dream each and every night, if necessary, to add additional information to that which we're retrieving during these sessions. You'll remember all that you're supposed to." Dick counted slowly, and I found myself gradually being aware of where I was and why, of the office, of the noises around me.

"Hi, there! It was pretty heavy."

I nodded. "But I feel better now. I feel I've let go of something that's been dragging me down. I feel freer than I have in weeks."

"You're going to find that each time you hit a home run, a rock comes off your back. It's like being squeezed in a vice, and all of a sudden, somebody slowly unwinds it. I understand why you circumvented some of the nitty-gritty details of both lives, because you did select two that were emotionally taxing." I wasn't sure if Dick had any idea of what was going on in between those two lives, when I talked about being out of my body, but I had no intention of bringing it up. I wanted to forget it. "Like I said, we'll take our time and walk into it. Within a reasonable length of time, you'll go into the room, and you'll be able to dig it all up. That's the biggest step you've taken, though. It's very interesting that you went prior to earth lives. I've had others do that, too."

I left feeling so good, so relaxed, so high, I wondered what I had been so afraid of an hour before. I don't care one iota if I uncovered information that is absolutely accurate, or if I fantasized the whole thing. I somehow released a great deal of pressure. I feel a little more confident, and a little less afraid of the psychic. After so many years of fear, that's a lot to accomplish in an hour.

121

THURSDAY, APRIL 22, 1976

I've had a lot on my mind this past week. I made a definite decision to leave my job when my contract terminates next month. I don't know what I'll do. If I can't find a job involving counseling, I'll do volunteer work. I'd rather work with people and not get paid than be paid for doing research.

Now the insecurities are setting in. My life will be severely disrupted in three weeks, and I have no idea how. I have no idea what a typical day will be like one month from now. It's a shaky feeling.

I called Vanessa, the woman Pete hired at his counseling agency. She's very enthusiastic about my doing volunteer family counseling there, but right now there aren't any families needing treatment.

I've spent my free time this week reading Sally Hammond's book, *We Are All Healers*. The book answered a lot of my questions. Hammond claims that we are all capable of channeling energies for healing, although some people have more ability than others. She said that some people heal by touching the body, while others touch the etherial body several inches away. That's apparently what I was doing when I moved my hands several inches away from my throat.

Her ideas are very intriguing. I never took psychic healing seriously before. I assumed it was the same thing as "faith healing," which, in my mind, was another form of positive thinking.

I've also been very preoccupied this week with past lives. I'm haunted by the vision of that woman out of her body. I remember the terror I felt in viewing that scene under hypnosis in Dick's office and my urge not to deal with it in any way. It couldn't possibly be a past life. Perhaps it's a fantasy of my fears of possession. In any case, it's insignificant, and there's no need to discuss it with Dick. That's how I feel, but it's becoming harder and harder to forget the scene. As I drift to sleep at night, the scene comes into my mind and I suddenly "know" something else about that woman. She was a fraudulent medium, using trickery and deceit to get money from people. She was living in Amsterdam in the 1600's. And she was me.

On the nights when I'm not plagued by visions of this woman, I find myself in touch with more information about the life on the other planet. Just before falling asleep, I'm often jerked awake with another "memory." Or sometimes while meditating, another bit of information pops into my mind. It's quite disconcerting, especially since the information coming in is not very complimentary to me.

I keep seeing visions of a planet more spiritually developed than the earth; a planet populated by very advanced souls. Education was an intricate part of life there; but it was an education oriented to the spiritual. There were many very advanced souls there to serve as teachers for those who were less advanced. Everyone had an attitude of helpfulness, desiring to guide others less advanced. Well, not quite everyone. I, for example, was a definite exception. I was stubborn, bull-headed, and totally recalcitrant. I had no interest in learning or in growing. I preferred to go my own way, scorning the advice of the advanced teachers of my people. Despite many warnings to the contrary, I stubbornly embarked on a mission that landed me on an alien planet. It was as I lay dying in the hot sun of that planet, after a brutal torture experience, that I finally understood what I was doing to myself. When I passed over, I opened myself to advice for the first time. And I was advised to enter a series of incarnations on the earth in order to develop greater maturity. Apparently, I took the advice.

SATURDAY, APRIL 24, 1976

I saw Dick again yesterday. I told him about the new information that had come to me regarding the planet scene, adding "I feel like I might have developed many psychic abilities on my home planet, but I didn't learn the spiritual values that went along with them. Later, when I came to earth, I think I got into the black arts."

"It all makes sense," Dick commented.

"I know," I answered, and then proceeded to tell him about the medium "memories." I noticed him jotting down notes while I talked and looking rather grave. Then I asked tentatively, "Is it possible for that kind of thing to happen?"

"Umhumm," Dick responded noncommittally. "Why does that bother you?"

"Well, at the time I 'saw' the scene last week, it was very upsetting. I could sense everything this woman—me—was feeling. I could sense the me out of my body, and this feeling of great confusion and terror; not understanding what was happening. I didn't have any feelings of being reassured; it was a very frightening experience."

"Do you think this life in the 17th century might have been one in which you were a witch?"

I paused to think about that. I couldn't understand why Dick kept referring to that scene as a past life, when it was probably just a fantasy enactment of my fears. But I decided to go along with the possibility that it could have been. "I don't feel that the medium was also a witch. I think they were two separate lifetimes."

"For what it's worth, the very first impression that I received about you was that you were very much involved in the psychic arts. And you might have used them unwisely."

"How did you get that impression?"

"Instinct. Intuition. Whatever you want to call it. See, there are different types of psychics. Clairvoyants, clairsentients, clairaudients, and intuitive. Theoretically, those that are intuitive are supposed to be more evolved. It's in cosmic harmony, a rapport, so to speak. Again, theoretically, I'm supposed to be intuitive, but I have nothing to prove this. I do get tingles when something less than acceptable is nearby. I do at times sense presences quite strongly. Which life do you want to probe into?"

It seemed a strange question. I didn't want to pick any one. I responded dryly: "Pick my trauma for the day?"

Dick chuckled. "Yeah, pick your trauma for the day. Or if you have enough confidence in the superconscious mind, we can let it make the selection. Of course you still have free will, like about whether or not you enter that building. Sooner or later, you'll have to."

"Why?"

"So you can face it in context. So you can see it for what it really is—an experience that's over and done with."

I thought about that for a minute, glancing out the window. Then I turned back towards Dick. "I'm afraid of the pain."

"You won't feel it. You'll recall having felt it, but you won't actually feel the pain. You might feel emotionally upset and frightened. I'm not going to lie to you—you'll feel a very real emotional reaction, but that's only another means of verification. A strong emotional reaction to a past life is one means of establishing its authenticity."

"Let's let the superconscious mind decide where we go."

Dick helped me push the chair back and move the small table with the tape recorder out of the way.

I couldn't think of anything else to delay things, so tried to relax, and not to think about the possible traumas around the corner. Dick started talking. "OK, just relax and let your mind go passive. Once again, picture your symbol, the disc, in gold. A very clean, warm, secure white light comes out and fills your entire body." There was a long pause, as I felt myself slipping into a relaxed state, shutting out outside sounds as I retreated into myself. Dick continued his induction procedure as I slipped deeper into a trance state.

"Now as information comes to you, you will be able to relay it to me comfortably, easily. Give me your first impressions, thoughts, feelings." There was a long pause. "What do you see?"

"I'm on another planet."

"OK, at all times your conscious mind is able to perceive the facts. Earth time, it is 1976. The experiences are those of the past. You have lived through them. You are once again whole, and you are living in the body of Sandy Gibson. What are you seeing?"

"I just landed on this hot, rocky, alien planet. I'm alone and confused." My voice was barely audible. It took a great deal of effort to speak. I was very absorbed in the vivid scene being played out before me, and which I seemed to move in and out of. Sometimes, I seemed to be in the scene itself; other times I was watching it.

"OK, keep watching."

"There's this man walking towards me. He's dressed strangely . . . I think maybe he's a friend." A pause. "Wait, he's not. He's an enemy! I didn't pick up his vibrations right!"

"There's a reason for that, Sandy," Dick offered gently, "keep watching."

"I have to follow him; I don't have any choice."

"Yes."

"I'm afraid."

"Is he leading you into a building?"

"Yes."

"All right, don't analyze what you're experiencing at this time. View it objectively."

"We're walking towards this building."

"Yes."

"I'm very frightened. I don't know what will happen."

"Yes."

"We're going in. There's a long corridor."

"Yes."

"We're walking down the corridor." Again I stopped,

as I did after virtually every sentence. I seemed to need constant encouragement to keep watching and talking.

"OK, keep watching."

"We're going into a room."

"OK."

"There's a table in it. I'm put on this table. There's a light overhead. It's shining on me. I feel very strange— very far away."

"That's OK. Just keep watching."

"I'm very woozy. They've made me feel strange. My hands!"

"What are they doing to your hands? Remember now, you're only recalling in memory."

That's right. It was all in the past. I kept forgetting that; the scene was so real. The feeling in my hands was so real.

"Oh, the pain!" My hands were burning with incredible pain.

"Are they using some type of electrical equipment or sophisticated machinery on you?"

I tried hard to look, but some of the details in the scene were blurred. It was something like that.

"What is it they're trying to do?"

"They're trying to break me."

"Why are they trying to break you?"

"To learn secrets from my planet."

"Do they know of your planet?"

"Umhmm."

"All right, now continue to watch carefully. What else are they doing?"

"They're hurting more parts of my body."

"You're perfectly safe; just keep watching."

"There's a lot of pain!"

"There was *at the time*, yes."

"They keep probing."

"What are they getting from you?"

"Nothing; I don't know what they want."

"What kind of questions are they asking you?"

"They don't have to ask questions; they can get information straight from my brain."

"OK."

"I just don't know what they want to learn. I'm not a very important person on my planet."

"OK, keep watching."

"They're angry now because I don't know anything. They just want to hurt me and make me suffer."

"You're perfectly safe now; all of this happened in the past and is over. Keep watching."

"My legs! There's pain in my legs! And now my arms!" My body was alive with pain.

"Yes, what's happening now?"

"I feel on the verge of dying! I can't stand the pain. But I'm going to fight to stay alive!"

"Yes, keep going."

"I'm breathing deeply, trying to relax. Trying to bear this pain." The pain became duller and I relaxed more. "It isn't so bad now."

"OK."

"The heat! Now there's heat! It's unbearable! I feel like my body's burning up!"

"Remember, now, this already happened and it's all over. You're almost through now, and you're doing fine." Dick's gentle voice and constant reassurances were all that kept me going.

"My body's all wrecked up! It was a good body!" There was agony in my voice. "I was young and healthy. Now I'm like an old man!"

"Yes."

"They're taking me off the table now, taking me outside."

"Yes; they've left you by a rock."

"It's so hot here. I don't want to die. But I feel myself slipping away."

"Has the soul left the body?"

"Not yet. But I'm starting to feel peace."

"The pain is gone?"

"Umhmm."

"And there is peace?"

"Umhmm."

"Has the soul left the body yet?"

"Umhmm."

128

"And there is peace?"

"Yes."

"Now, superconscious mind, bring her back to the present. Your body will remain in a very deep, rest-filled sleep, totally freeing itself from any stresses, strains, fears, or anxieties. You're coming back to the present, with your mind passive. Your superconscious is still in rapport with us. Superconscious, what is the significance of this life with Sandy today?"

"She already understands that this experience makes her afraid of the psychic. She doesn't believe that energy can be used to heal instead of to hurt."

"OK. Is there anything else that Sandy should know at this time?"

"She needs to relax more; to understand how these past life forces are still affecting her today. They are the root of her fear and tension."

"Have her past life memories up to now been accurate?"

"Yes; quite accurate. She has chosen to remember them."

"Does she understand why?"

"Yes, but she does not accept it. This is an important lifetime, and in order to complete her mission she must understand the forces from the past."

"Are these sessions beneficial to her from now on?"

"They're essential."

"OK. Is there anything specific I should know concerning Sandy in order to help her?"

"There is a lot of fear; a lot of resistance. But also a strong drive. Move slowly."

"Has the approach been practical for her so far?"

"Yes; it's been excellent."

Dick then had me relax, and fed me some positive suggestions in a soft voice, while counting me out of the trance state. He finally reached the count of 8. "Good afternoon!"

"Hi," I responded in a soft voice.

"That wasn't so bad, was it?" Dick asked, leaning back in his chair and lighting up a cigarette.

"Well, not now that it's over," I answered, rubbing my eyes, trying to fully wake up.

"Well, you're still here. You're body's still intact. Right?"

"Umhmm."

"Try to appreciate that I'm not really that cold. I know what you're going through. As mortals, we fear the unknown. As you keep living through it, you realize that you do come through it and come back all right. There are a few goodies still around there, but I have a feeling they started you off at the top of the ladder."

"Do you think it really happened?"

"Well, let's put it this way. If it didn't, you're a damned good actress. Logically, why would you bother to make up something like that?"

"I don't know. I can't think of any reason."

"Of course, to myself, I have to ask questions, like: Is she on an ego trip? Is there lack of affection in her life? Is there something missing in her life to cause a total void? I don't see anything to indicate this. You seem to be fairly content with your marriage, you appear to have a busy life and to be accomplishing something tangible. So when you start piecing together all of the factors, then, logically, you may really be onto something. I don't think you'd just get better if there weren't some validity to what you're coming up with. Now you've been coming here since February 1st. It's now April 23rd—almost three months. What have those three months been like for you, compared to the previous months?"

"There's been an improvement. The main thing is that I have fewer fears. I'm more open to experiences and looking at my experiences. I don't fight them like I used to. I don't necessarily believe all the explanations you give, but I'm more open to looking at them."

"If you're feeling a little bit more inner peace, a little more confidence or self-assurance, a feeling of the rocks falling off your back, that's all I care about, Sandy. The end results. Any questions?"

"No." I still didn't feel totally awake. I made an appointment for the following Friday, and then made my way out into the warm April breeze. I wondered if I was awake enough to drive safely, but since it was the only way I'd get home, I decided to chance it. I drove slowly, trying hard to concentrate on the traffic.

That evening I decided to stay up alone after Burt had gone to bed. I lit a candle and sat alone in the living room. As I sat there quietly, staring at the candle, I received a great many impressions about several past lives. I saw myself resenting the advice from my home planet that I incarnate on the earth for awhile, feeling rejected by my own people. I came to earth unhappy, lonely, rejected. I also came to earth with a large arsenal of psychic skills that I had absorbed from my own culture, but without the maturity to know how to use them wisely. I was eager to make friends on my new planet, but wasn't sure how to go about doing it. So I reached for the one skill I had that might impress and influence others; psychic powers. I was quite surprised by the results, for the people of the earth were largely helpless in the face of my skill. On my own planet, I couldn't have gotten by with anything; most everyone else had greater skill than I did. Here, most people had less. I began to use my powers out of loneliness, but then got drunk on power. I became very involved with the black arts. That lifetime, I felt, came around the 1400's, and was probably in Europe. Within a century or two, I chose to punish myself by becoming possessed while working as a fraudulent medium in Amsterdam.

I stared moodily at the candle for a long time. Those were depressing thoughts, following a draining afternoon. But I had to admit that I was starting to feel better. I was starting to feel that I understood myself for the first time. I blew out the candle and went to bed.

I woke up this morning feeling absolutely fantastic. It was a beautiful day, so I decided to walk through the park after breakfast. I got there early so the park was quiet. I strolled down the path that wound through woods along a brook, listening to the birds and ducks. I felt at peace.

I feel I know myself like I never have before. It's as though I had amnesia for my entire life up until age 25.

But the amnesia is starting to lift. So many things about myself make sense if I accept that I really had been tortured on an alien planet, banished to earth by my people, become involved in the black arts, and then punished myself through possession. Of course, all of this could be nonsense. But the explanations provide a framework on which to fit the pieces of my life and myself that had puzzled me before.

I also realized that the terror is disappearing. I dreaded the thought of looking at past lives and resisted it for a long time. But what I feared was knowledge. And that knowledge is far less frightening than the not knowing was.

This inner peace is a great change from the turmoil and intensity I've been feeling. Now I know what I'm looking for, and I can slow down, move at an easier pace. I'm ready to decrease the frequency of my sessions. I won't need them every week any longer. Perhaps twice a month now.

FRIDAY, APRIL 30, 1976

I tried auto-writing twice this week. On Monday evening, Burt and I began with the usual white-lighting procedure. Then "...Hi..." was written out.

Burt asked, "Who are you?"

"...Joey..." was the response.

"Why are you here?"

"...To help Sandy..."

"Can you help us help Pinky get better?" (Pinky was a plant of ours that we were concerned about.)

"...Yes, pray..."

"What do you mean by pray?"

"...Unite with higher energies..."

"How can we unite with higher energies?"

"...Faith. It is difficult to communicate. Sandy is still tense..."

"How do we know you're not Sandy's unconscious?"

"...That will be difficult to prove. What do you suggest?..."

"Tell us something Sandy doesn't know."

"...Sandy knows everything she needs to know on deep levels. So do you. Life is continuous. There is no death. Do you believe that?..."

"I thought I was asking the questions!"

"...Don't I get a turn to ask questions?..."

"Sure."

"...How can I help you believe?..."

"You're doing a pretty good job right now."

"...Good. Glad to hear it. I wish Sandy felt the same. She believes I am a figment of her imagination. She's hard to convince. Can you read this?..."

"Yes. Your handwriting is much improved. It's at least C+."

"...Thank you..."

"OK, here's a question for you, Joey. If you are a higher power, how come I have to keep moving the paper?"

"...I must communicate through a mortal; and a very resistant one at that. It's not easy..."

"Do you have any message for Sandy that will help her in finding her path at this time?"

"...Faith and prayer. Sandy knows her path. It is a process of making contact with the internal..."

"What part does Dick Smith play for Sandy?"

"...He is a guide and is very crucial at this point in Sandy's spiritual development. So are you. Enough for today. Good-by. Have faith!..."

I felt discouraged after this attempt. I always feel apprehensive before trying auto-writing, and depressed afterwards. I want so much to obtain some evidence that would convince me whether or not it's authentic. I decided to try again on Tuesday evening.

This time "...Greetings!..." was written out before Burt's first question.

"Greetings, Joey!" Burt responded. "Any messages for us?"

"...I'm glad to be back..."

"Anything else?"

"...I'm glad to see that Sandy is growing..."

"Anything else?"

"...Communication is still very difficult because of Sandy's fears. They will pass in time, but slowly..."

"Why don't you provide a dramatic demonstration of your existence?"

"...I will in time, but not yet..."

"Can you give us any idea when?"

"...When Sandy is ready and more relaxed..."

I was very aware of all answers as they came through; I received them mentally before they were written out. That answer impressed me as a definite cop-out.

"Is the information Sandy has been receiving about her past lives accurate?"

"...Yes. Very accurate, for many reasons. She needs

her past life information for present growth..."

"Why does Sandy always get anxious before trying auto-writing and get depressed afterwards?"

"... Fear. Very deep fear based on past life experiences. She would prefer to forget them and ignore the psychic. Very understandably. She needs support. That is why I'm here..."

"Does the information Sandy has been receiving about her past lives come from herself or from you?"

"... Both. Mostly from herself. I help out from time to time..."

"When will I finish my dissertation?" Burt's dissertation had become a real struggle, and he often wondered if he'd ever get it done.

"... When you decide that you want to finish it. You must face very deep resistance in yourself. Right now you fear to finish it. You cling to the structure it provides your life. And you fear to face your own spiritual growth which awaits you at its termination. Such growth is scary and often resisted. Ask Sandy..."

"When will I finish it?"

"... There is free will, you know! Life is a continuous process of growth—on any plane. That is the main message I wish to leave with you this evening. Also to congratulate Sandy on her facing some past life traumas. Keep up your support of each other. You have chosen each other for important reasons and have important work to do together. I leave you with love and bid you both a fond good evening..."

As usual, I felt mildly depressed afterwards, thinking, "I've just wasted my time with a lot of bullshit!" But I had to admit that we received some inspiring messages. I felt good about the congratulations and assertions that I was making progress. And the message about Burt's resistance to his dissertation made sense.

I went into today's session with Dick not only with my recorder and list of questions, but also with a folder of auto-writing. I decided I needed a respite from past lives and I wondered if the evidence Dick was looking for had come through yet.

I arrived at the Foundation a few minutes early, so I chatted with the other staff members, whom I was getting to know, and got myself a cup of tea. Then I nestled into the big green chair in Dick's office, almost looking forward to the session since I wouldn't have to go back to another past life. Typically, every Friday morning I have to fight an impulse to call the Foundation with some excuse to cancel my appointment. But I felt that this one would be, for a change, untraumatic.

I handed Dick a folder with my auto-writing in it.

"You know," he said, glancing at the writing, "even though you may feel the presence of a guide, all contact should be directed to a God level. In other words, we shouldn't talk to Joey as Joey; we should talk to God. This is very important." I looked confused. "Maybe we should expand on this; OK?" I nodded, as Dick lit up a cigarette and leaned back in his chair. "You may feel confident that, say, Dr. Josepth Glutzheimer from Sweden is a spirit working through you. But you don't *pray* to Dr. Glutzheimer. You pray to God. If God sees in his infinite wisdom that it is Dr. Glutzheimer who's supposed to help you, he'll let Dr. Glutzheimer make the contact. And it's no offense to Glutzheimer. Higher energies know that there are lower energies around who'll try and throw a monkey wrench in the gear train. So always address your thoughts mentally to God. Or Christ, or Christ-consciousness. Not Joey."

"I do that anyway, because I always pray to God for protection before I start."

"That's good. Also ask that whatever you receive will be for the highest good of mankind and yourself."

Dick read the pages of auto-writing.

"Do you have any impressions you're willing to share with me?" I asked, as he finished.

Dick paused. "Well, I have a lot of thoughts about this. But I have to ask myself, 'Are these thoughts to be shared with you? Are they to be shared at this time?' I'm mortal, too. My ideas could be my imagination. And by sharing them I could lead you."

"I feel it would help me to have some objective impressions on this."

"But, Sandy, I really don't want to lead you. I'll say this: nothing is out of line. Based on what you've asked, all of the answers are consistent with a spiritual philosophy."

"Do you still have a gut feeling that this stuff is authentic? Do you see any evidence?"

"Yeah, it's still gut feeling."

"What about the handwriting?"

"It's changed enough to reveal that it's not all you, but there's enough of you there to indicate that you're still in conscious control. And that's very important. Unless you're developing into a trance medium, and I don't think that's your calling. Telepathic, maybe. Probably. But not trance medium. Let's go back to what I've said before. Let's go to extremes, and assume that it's your imagination. As long as you continue to come out with things that are of help to others, so what?"

"Well, then I'm not being very honest with myself. If it's my imagination, but is claiming to be a spirit guide, then I'm being dishonest with myself."

"So what? It's still you. It doesn't matter if we call it your imagination or your soul, it's still you. If you come out with information that helps you and others, what difference does it make?" I felt glum; I wanted evidence. Dick picked up on my thoughts. "I know where you're coming from in wanting tangible evidence, but I understand completely the answer you got on that. You're not ready."

"Are you saying that so far there's no tangible evidence of authenticity?"

"Well, so far, everything you're doing is tangibly correct. You have, without realizing it, followed the format that real auto-writers follow."

"Couldn't people follow this format without being legitimate auto-writers?"

"I haven't seen it. I've had people bring in papers that they think is auto-writing, but there's nothing there. You can see it; you can sense it."

"But it sounds like there's no way to verify the real auto-writing."

"Yeah, there is. When you start asking questions and getting answers that you don't know anything about."

Dick wrote out some questions for me to ask, and folded the paper over. I slipped it into my purse and made an appointment for two weeks later. I walked into the warm April breeze feeling very disappointed. I had hoped Dick would have more answers.

FRIDAY MAY 7, 1976

I've continued my work on auto-writing during the past week. On Monday, I went into the usual trance state and Burt asked the usual introductory questions. Then he asked: "Have you known Sandy in a previous lifetime?"

"... Yes. On another planet..."

"Can you give us any information on this?"

"...I can try, however Sandy does not care to remember, so may block. I was her guide or teacher—named Kirk. It was long ago. She was a stubborn pupil. But is more receptive now. We are still struggling with the same lessons. It takes time. I have great patience..." I could feel the patience as the message came through. I felt surrounded by complete love, understanding, and acceptance. I felt no criticism in being called stubborn; it came through with acceptance and warmth.

"Can you give us more details of how you plan to be of help to Sandy?"

"...I will be around for a long time to serve as a guide and teacher, both personally and professionally..." I started to get feelings that I was to use this communication as a tool in a future counseling career. But the message was confusing to Burt.

"I didn't know you had a profession, except as a spirit."

"...I mean Sandy's..."

"Who is Andrew Carter?"

I suddenly felt dizzy and confused. Where was that question coming from? Of course, it must be one of Dick's questions that he'd given me last session. I suddenly became tense. A question like this one would be definite proof of whether or not this experience were authentic or

139

imagination. With this one answer, I would know for sure either way. I felt terribly threatened. I didn't want the answer to come through. What if it were wrong? I would have to give up this nonsense. But I knew from experience that everytime I tried to give it up, I went into a deep depression. I didn't want to risk that again. I had to block the answer. I realized that I was receiving messages from the presence.

"Relax. I can answer that question. Give me a chance to do it." I refused. It was too risky. If it were wrong, I would be plunged into a deep depression again. I wasn't ready for such a definitive test. My decision was accepted, and the following answer was written out: "... Sandy is blocking. She is not ready for that question..."

Burt inserted one of his own. "What is the relationship between drugs and spiritual growth?"

"... Drugs are a menace and a barrier to spiritual growth. They inhibit the body's vibrations and the soul's ability to unite with higher energies. While under a drug the body is less able to make contact with higher energies—as in prayer or meditation. However, some drugs can release certain inner channels to simulate some spiritual experiences. For some people they can be an impetus to spiritual growth, but are no substitute for the real thing. Real growth is preferable..."

"Do your messages get through clearly or are they distorted?"

"... Both. The basic message gets through..."

"Do you have any message to leave with us this evening?"

"... Yes. Sandy needs to practice relaxation. It would help in providing a clearer channel. You must learn to focus your attention on the goals at hand. There is a universal peace. It is found in the souls of all people. Cultivate this peace in your own soul and it can be a step to world peace. Good night..."

I slowly brought myself out of the trance, feeling increasingly depressed as I did so. I had failed the test. If all this were really happening, the answer would have come through. No answer was the same as a wrong answer. It was obvious that the whole thing was my imagination. I felt very withdrawn the rest of the evening. Burt picked up on my vibes, and left me alone.

I went to work the next day without feeling any better. I thought a lot about what was happening. First, my feelings. I could not deny that I *felt* that there was a presence in the room every time I did auto-writing. I felt that presence as strongly as I could feel Burt's, but in a different way. I was using different senses to feel that presence. And I felt a definite personality coming from that presence. I felt emotions coming from it. I couldn't deny those feelings. I didn't want to give up trying to understand that experience. I owed it to myself to continue to explore those sensations that were so real to me. But it was obvious that I couldn't provide any kind of evidence that would be meaningful to others. In that respect, I was letting Burt and Dick down. How could I expect either of them to continue to be supportive when the only evidence I could provide was my own feelings?

That evening, Burt and I had a long talk, and I told him about my feelings. His attitude was surprising.

"But I *want* to continue working on this with you."

"Why, Burt? I can't provide any evidence."

"I can wait. We've been told the evidence will come in time. And I believe that."

"You really think there's going to be evidence someday?"

"Yes, I do."

I watched him light up his pipe, while I sat silently for a few minutes. "*Why* do you think so?"

"I've never really doubted it. I think you're in contact with something. I don't know what, exactly, but I'd like to keep at it and find out."

"Do you mean that you believe that Joey really exists? Or Kirk, I guess we could call him."

"Yes, I think I do."

"That's a strange attitude for a scientist."

"Not really," Burt said smiling. "I believe in you. I don't think you'd imagine this. You're stable and intelligent and there's just no reason why you'd imagine it.

And when I'm communicating with Joey in the auto-writing, I really feel that I'm talking with a personality. Not you."

Later that evening, while meditating, I again felt the presence and felt a message coming through. I was told to remember exactly what had happened during the auto-writing—that I was the one who had refused to let the answer come through. Joey was willing to give it. I had to admit that was true. I felt much better, and went to bed that night with my depression lifted.

That evening I went to see Vanessa, the woman who received the job I had applied for. She called me earlier this week to tell me that there was a family needing counseling from the agency. She asked if I'd like to work as a co-therapist with her. We were to meet the family the next day, so we got together to discuss our respective therapeutic styles. Vanessa told me that it was a large family, with six children, and the parents had been fighting a lot. Many of the present problems probably stemmed from an affair the husband had had five years ago that the wife still resented.

When I got home that evening, Burt was out, but I had an urge to do some auto-writing on my own. I put myself into a trance state and asked questions mentally. I felt in close telepathic rapport with the presence. I got answers more complex than the words that were written out; at times, no words at all were written out because our telepathic communication was much faster and richer.

At first, I got only squiggles. I asked mentally: "Is someone here?"

"... Yes ..."

"Who?"

"... Kirk ..." I sensed that this was to be the preferred name now. We no longer needed to use the name from this lifetime.

"Are you the same entity known as Joey?"

"... Yes ..."

I felt an urge to ask about the family Vanessa and I would be seeing the next day. "Do you have any information on the family we see tomorrow that will help in counseling them?"

"... Move slowly and gently. The mother drinks. The father is often depressed. They will try to hide this information from you. Stay objective. Don't let your energy be drained. You can be of help to them..."

"Do you have any other message for me tonight?"

"... Love and faith—incorporate them daily into your life until they cease to be words and become living realities..." With that, the presence vanished, and my arm fell to the bed.

I was eager to find out if there was any validity to the information on the family. Vanessa knew nothing about my interests and involvement in the occult, and I didn't intend to tell her. But I would stay alert to any mention of issues around drinking and depression.

The next day, after seeing the family, it was quite evident that the father was depressed. There was no evidence, however, that the mother drank. I couldn't help but feel down as I drove home. I thought to myself, "The information seems to be wrong. I should give up this nonsense. By listening to it, I could do harm. I might be looking for problems in areas where there aren't any and could become less effective as a result." I kept reminding myself that I would have to be patient.

Burt left yesterday for a four-day conference, so I'm alone for the weekend. I decided this evening to try some auto-writing by myself. I wrote out a list of questions which I then asked telepathically in the trance state. Again, I felt the close telepathic rapport, and received many impressions and feelings that couldn't be put into words. I asked for further information about the life Kirk and I had had together on the other planet and other past lives of mine. The answers certainly didn't give the specifics I had been hoping for.

"... As you are ready, this information will come. Please move slowly. In the past you lacked sufficient patience for spiritual growth. You still have the same tendency. If you force issues and recollections the harm resulting will understandably push you away from your chosen spiritual path. Slow growth is preferrable to none. Haste is very mortal. Once you fully understand and appreciate the nonexistence of time you will come to value the fullness of the present moment without rushing into the next..."

I then asked if there was any further message. "... Yes. Trust your own feelings. They are a valuable guide in this life. They will serve you well and keep you on the right path..."

Afterwards, I sat quietly for a few minutes thinking about the experience. I enjoyed it, and felt extremely comfortable throughout. I felt surrounded with warmth and love. Two months ago I was afraid to be alone at night because I would sense a presence and hear tappings. Now I've moved beyond fear into enjoyment. I'm making progress.

THURSDAY, MAY 13, 1976

This week has been difficult. My boss talked me into staying for another six weeks to finish our research project and give him time to find a replacement. I agreed, on condition that I could take some time off to continue the family therapy work with Vanessa.

I have mixed feelings about staying on longer. On one hand, I feel relieved that I won't have to face the insecurities of unemployment in just two weeks. But on the other hand, I hate the thought of continuing for another six weeks with a job that I don't enjoy.

I'm glad that I'm able to do some family counseling. I'm continuing my volunteer work one evening a week, and work with Vanessa two afternoons a week. We work well together, and I hope I can continue my volunteer work there when I quit my job in six weeks. I've been interested in obtaining more formal training in family therapy, and Vanessa is also considering training in this field. We're looking together at various schools in the area to see if we can find one for this fall.

Vanessa and I saw our clients again on Tuesday afternoon, and I found a good opportunity to bring up the subject of alcohol. I learned that the mother seldom drinks because it poses problems for her when she does. I didn't pursue the subject with them, but realized that I had obtained definite evidence of inaccurate information from Kirk. I decided to do some auto-writing that evening, and ask for clarification.

I gave Burt a list of questions to ask, and then put myself into a deep relaxation state. After a few scribbles, my arm began writing.

"...Good evening..."

"Is someone there?" Burt asked.

"...Yes, indeed..."

"Please identify yourself."

"...Kirk..."

"Why are you here?"

"...To be of assistance to Sandy..."

"Is communication easy or difficult tonight?"

"...It gets a bit easier each time but it is a slow process and Sandy has a long way to go..."

At this point, Burt was silent for a long time. I had a strong sense of what was happening. He was trying to communicate telepathically with Kirk. I began feeling very uptight. I was being tested again, and I resented it. I wasn't ready for that. After awhile, Burt asked, "Can you read what's in our minds?"

"...At times. I have better rapport with Sandy..."

"Why do you have better rapport with Sandy?"

"...Past life links for one thing..."

Then Burt read the main question I wanted answered. "Could you clarify the extent to which your messages are received accurately and the extent to which there's distortion? In particular, Sandy is wondering about the family in which you stated that the mother drank, but she claims she does so seldom."

"...Yes. There is some distortion at times. To be expected at this stage. But the basic message is received. This is a slow and difficult process and Sandy has much to learn to develop her receptivity. Regarding the family in question: be alert to reference to her use of alcohol. It points to a deep underlying problem which will manifest itself later as therapy continues. Sandy needs great patience in this process. It takes time..."

"Do you have any past life information for Sandy that would be of use to her at this time?"

"...There would be no point in attempting to convey such information at this point. Sandy would block it. She can better obtain such information in her dreams where she is less inhibited or in sessions with Dick where she is more relaxed—not so concerned about this process..."

"Do you have any past life information for me?" Burt asked.

146

"...Yes, but this is not the time. You are not ready to hear it and Sandy is not ready to serve as a channel for it. In time..."

"Do you have any further messages for us this evening?"

"...Yes. Patience. I understand the difficulties and frustrations. I sympathize. Sandy should let her feelings guide her and trust in the reality of her own experiences. Denial results in depression. Peace to you both..."

As I brought myself to a normal waking state, I again felt depression come over me. I had failed another test: Burt's telepathic experiment. It had to be imagination, but yet I couldn't give it up. I decided that what I really needed was a good psychiatrist to help me understand my need to create a fantasy spirit guide to send me spiritual messages.

It's time to return to past life work. Probably the possession experience in Amsterdam this time. One part of me wants to delay that experience for at least twenty years. Another part of me wants to deal with it right away and get it over with. I already know which side will win.

FRIDAY, MAY 14, 1976

I started today's session by telling Dick that I wanted to go back to the Amsterdam lifetime.

"OK," he responded, "let's talk about this trance medium incident. We're definitely going to use a revivication technique. If we get into regression, your soul level or superconscious mind could possibly allow you to experience what you once experienced as a trance medium."

"Could you please explain trance medium again?" I had never heard that term before meeting Dick, and was having a hard time understanding it.

"OK. A trance medium is an individual who is capable of altering their state of consciousness so their ego, or conscious mind, has very little to do with the words coming through their mouth. Now it's possible that some things happened in the 17th century that blew your mind. It was frightening because it was new and unexpected. And maybe some negative results came out of it. So we're going to use revivication rather than regression. You'll be recalling; viewing."

"But didn't I experience revivication with the planet scene? It was very painful."

"Yeah, but there was a lot of regression involved, too. One part of you had to be there to prove to you, to *you*, that this was very emotional and traumatic. Now, with a trance medium lifetime, where we don't know much about the forces working through you, it's safer to use revivication. It'll be just like watching a movie. And you may react to it emotionally, like you would to an emotionally-charged picture. But the profound fear won't be there. You'll feel, but it may be 10% of what you actually felt. Any questions?"

I wished I could think of some to delay things, but I couldn't. I lay back, trying my best to relax.

"All right, now, we'll start with the white light." Dick went through our usual introductory procedure. I slipped into a deeper and deeper state, feeling my eyes going through REM, and losing rapport with my surroundings. "Now, I'm going to count slowly from 1 to 10. As I do so, you will see a grey cloud in the distance becoming closer and closer. By the time I reach 10, you will be able to clearly distinguish a scene in this cloud. It will be a scene that is important for you to remember today. And you will observe it carefully, telling me everything you see." I felt myself becoming more and more tense, as Dick counted, although I couldn't see anything in the grey mist before my eyes. "Five. Six." I was tensing my muscles and starting to breathe heavily. I knew I was coming close to a very heavy trauma, although I still couldn't see anything before my eyes. "Seven. Eight. Nine. Picture's fuzzy, but starting to take shape now. Ten." I still couldn't see anything, but the emotions were there. "You're perfectly safe now, viewing a past life objectively, in context." I was gripped with a powerful emotion. My breathing had become short and heavy as I attempted to keep my surging emotions under control. "Let it out, Sandy. Let it out." I began sobbing. "Keep going. Let it all out." The sobbing went on and on. Several minutes later, Dick said softly, "Now relax, Sandy. Relax now. Just relax. Relax." My muscles relaxed and the sobbing gradually subsided. "Now you are able to look at it logically, as though it were a dream, and explain what it was you've seen." That was rather confusing, since I still hadn't seen anything. But as I kept looking, images were taking shape before my eyes from that grey mist.

"I see a woman. Who was me. And she's dressed in very strange clothes." After every statement, Dick gave me an encouraging "hmhmmm" which made it easier to continue. "And she's in a small room. She's looking at something. Maybe a crystal ball. Trying to contact a spirit. She doesn't seem like a very nice person. She has to have this experience."

"Yes."

"Because of all the things she did before. But she doesn't know that consciously."

"OK. It's a karmic lesson, then, is that correct?"

"Hmhmm." As I looked at the woman, sitting before me in my mind, I understood a great deal about her. More than she did about herself at that time. But I also knew that I had *been* her. "She doesn't know consciously what's going to happen. She's saying strange things. Then all of a sudden something happens."

"Hmhmm. What's happening?"

"Well, it's like she's sitting up startled. She seems kind of stiff." I stopped, not wanting to go on.

"Did her body become possessed?"

The comment caused me to see what I was blocking in the scene. The woman was out of her body; something else was in it. "Hmhmm."

"What was it that possessed her?"

"I don't know."

"OK. Look at it objectively, now, just like watching a motion picture. As long as the superconscious mind wants you to watch, you will watch." The scene remained before my mind, but I didn't want to talk about it. "What's happening now?"

"She's very frightened. She doesn't understand what's happening."

"Yes. That's understandable."

"She wants to scream. But she can't." I stopped again, overcome with emotion. I wanted to cry.

"That's good. You're doing great. Keep watching."

"She's out of her body!" I started sobbing again.

"Let it out; all of it." The sobs kept coming. "Just relax now. Just relax," Dick said gently after several minutes. "Let your mind go passive. Very, very passive. Relax. Now listen carefully. Your superconscious mind will help you remember microscopically all details of today's session that you need to know to help you place your soul's history in context. You are now here in 1976, in a new body, eager to learn the right lessons, eager to fulfill the obligations you've accepted on the earth plane to accomplish, with an intuitive feeling that you are easily and comfortably releasing those pressures from the past. I'm going to count slowly from 1 to 8. As I do, the subconscious and superconscious mind will work together to bring you to perfect balance and harmony." Dick counted slowly, and I felt myself slowly gaining awareness of my surroundings and returning to normal consciousness. "Take your time, and let your eyes open by themselves. Good morning!" I just smiled weakly. "It's strange the feelings I got while you were going through that. I felt a great empathy—a compassionate love. Something inside kept saying you just had to get that out. It's like pulling out the weeds before they can grow back." We both chuckled. "When you first mentioned this to me, I had a feeling it was going to be a zinger life. It may be one of the things that was blocking you from the telepathic communications. I think you knew it, too. You surprised me, because I didn't think you'd get into it today."

"I don't think I saw the whole thing."

"No, but you saw enough to realize its importance, and that it has to be totally weeded out. Not thrown away. You've got to remember it so you won't do it again. As it comes into the conscious, it makes it easier to make choices in this life with discretion."

"Do you think I'll have to go back to it again?"

"Yes, I feel quite strongly that you will, but I could be wrong. I think you got the heaviest part today, and it will be a bit easier next time. Tell me now, everything you remember from that."

"Well, first I've got to get a drink of water." I left the room for a short break, and then returned to discuss the incident I'd just experienced. I nestled into the chair, and Dick leaned back in his. "I started feeling the emotions before I saw anything."

"I know. You wanted to stop."

"You knew that, huh?"

"Yeah. Forgive me, I'm really not a sadist. It's not a comfortable thing to do with patients. Nobody enjoys this part of therapy. But you can't pussyfoot around too long, if the soul wants it. And obviously your soul did, or you wouldn't have opened your mouth today."

151

"I knew I'd be going back to that today."

"I didn't know you were going to do it today, but it's good that you did. How much of it do you recall?"

I remembered it all, and summarized the details.

"That part where you described wanting to scream and not being able to is an indication of an actual possession that might have taken place." I looked up startled. "I know what you're feeling. But it's got to come out. That's usually what happens. It's like losing conscious control of the faculties. When you're dealing with the higher energies, and it's something you chose to work on in that lifetime and all that, there's nothing to fear. Possession seems to be a very real thing. It's nothing that we encourage. I'd never encourage anyone to become a trance medium. Or even get involved with it. That's why we discourage Ouija boards, we discourage pendulum-type things, mainly because you are opening your centers to trance mediumship." We continued discussing the scenes I had seen for awhile. "Now it's important that you keep today's session in mind. Whatever you do, don't block it out. If it makes you afraid, be afraid. You've got to get it out till it's just like a movie, at the same time knowing that it was you, that you did these things, that it was part of training. You should not try to suppress today's session, like with, 'I don't want to talk about it.'" We both laughed, remembering all the times I'd said that.

"Have I ever said that?" I asked in mock surprise, and we both laughed again.

"Well," Dick responded, "maybe it's crept out once or twice. You've got all the documentation!" he added, pointing to the tape recorder. "You know, maybe someday you could put this whole thing in a book. Maybe someone might be able to benefit from it." I thought that was a crazy idea, but had to admit that the idea had occurred to me once or twice. Perhaps that's one reason I've been so diligent about keeping this journal.

"What are you feeling now?"

"A little shaken up still, drained. But I feel a great release of pressure." We chatted a while longer, and then I set an appointment for two weeks later.

PART II

SATURDAY, MAY 15, 1976

Burt and I both slept late this morning and then spent a
leisurely morning in bed making love. Then Burt kissed
me good-by and went out to run some errands. I had a
brunch, and then crawled back into bed to rest. I felt
physically drained from the love-making. And I still felt
emotionally drained from the previous day's session. I lay
in bed, contemplating all the events of the previous three
months, from the time I first started counseling at the
Prana Foundation. I thought about all that had been
happening to me during those months. And suddenly, out
of the blue, a thought struck me. It was possible that all of
those things really *were* happening. It was possibly that I
really *did* have a spirit guide. It was possible that I really
was able to establish telepathic rapport with this guide. It
was possible that I really had been tortured on an alien
planet. It was possible that I had been involved in the
black arts. And it was possible that I had been possessed
while working as a medium in Amsterdam centuries ago.
It was possible that life was far more complex, far more
mysterious than I had ever before imagined. I had had all
of these thoughts before, but they had been only of the
most intellectual, abstract nature. Suddenly, I realized
there was a difference. For the first time in my life, I
accepted the possible reality of these occurrences without
a thick, impenetrable shield. For the first time, I was
saying from my very deepest self that such events might be
real.

The dam broke. I sobbed and sobbed for what seemed
like hours. I knew that I had given up a defense and would
never again hide behind it.

I feel very vulnerable. I'm not used to living without my shield of defense. Perhaps we really and truly never die, but live as many different people in different ages, working through karmic debts in each life cycle. Perhaps there really are higher energies all around, seeking to serve and guide earthly mortals to higher reaches of consciousness. Perhaps some people really are able to communicate with such energies. The possibilities seem so vast and limitless, that I feel dizzy contemplating them.

I know that I've turned a corner, and will never again be quite the same.

I'm not accepting the reality of my experiences; I need much more objective evidence before I can do that. But for the first time in my life, I'm truly, honestly, and spontaneously open to their *possibility*.

My goal has changed. I arrived at Prana in February in search of help to stop my psychic experiences from happening. Instead, they increased, and I've been investing a great deal of energy in blocking, denying, and resisting them. Now, I'm ready to learn about them.

SUNDAY, MAY 16, 1976

I went to bed last night feeling great peace. I drifted easily into a deep sleep and slept soundly for several hours. Then I awoke with the impression that I would have some experiences with trance mediumship. I found that thought frightening. If I'd been possessed before, I could be possessed again. I drifted into a troubled sleep.

Today, I decided to do some auto-writing and ask for clarification of those impressions. Burt had to be out for most of the day, so I decided this evening to do auto-writing by myself. I sat down with paper and pencil and went through the usual introductory procedures. I had trouble making contact, however, and could not capture the sense of warmth and well-being I usually feel. I felt cold vibes around. I concluded that they were my imagination, however, and proceeded. Things began as usual.

"Who's there?" I asked telepathically.

"... Kirk ..." was written out, with what appeared to be the usual handwriting.

"Could you please tell me what experiences I need to undergo to prepare myself for mediumship?"

"... You already know the answer to that ..."

"Could you please clarify it for me anyway?" I persisted mentally.

"... Follow the plan ..."

"What plan?" I asked with trepidation. The answer was written out slowly, and I only received one word at a time telepathically.

"... Allow ... yourself ... to ... be ..." I couldn't believe that the next word was really the word I was receiving telepathically, so I let the first four letters be

155

written out. "...poss..." I jerked my hand away instantly, breaking whatever contact I had had. Trembling, I stuffed the papers into a drawer and ran out of the room.

I fixed myself a cup of hot tea, and sat at the kitchen table trying to get hold of myself. There was no doubt that "possessed" was being written. "Allow yourself to be possessed" was the message. What a horrible message! It was true that I didn't feel the usual warm vibrations. On the other hand, I felt that I had surrendered more control of my arm than I ever had before. There was more energy in my arm than ever before, and I felt less involved in the process than ever before.

Could Kirk have given me a message like that? I have trouble believing it. Could I have been in touch with some hostile entity claiming to be Kirk? Was I really in danger of being possessed? I'm through with auto-writing. It's too upsetting and too dangerous! I want out!

WEDNESDAY, MAY 19, 1976

I saw Dick today for an emergency appointment and told him about Sunday's traumatic experience. He was puzzled.

"I don't get negative vibes," he said, looking over the papers of auto-writing. "I do question why the word 'possession' would be used. Maybe it's suggesting using regression on the Amsterdam possession experience. That would be real, tangible evidence to you that it actually occurred. It would also be a mind-blowing experience. I'd be rather reluctant to put you through that now. Look, Paul Solomon is going to be here tomorrow and he'll be giving the foundation a reading Thursday night. I'd like to throw in a question about you. But I have to have your permission."

I paused. That sounded threatening. What dreadful things might come out in a reading like that? But the truth is very important to me. I want to know. "OK."

"His batting average is very high. He's very talented. We'll get some straight answers from him. I will, of course, audio-tape it. No guarantees, of course. In the meantime, keep up the white light."

"OK, but I'm giving up auto-writing."

"I wouldn't do that. It's too easy to grab onto an excuse to turn your back on it."

"I know, but I'm scared. I'm giving it up."

On that note, the session was ended. I left feeling better, but still disturbed. I hoped Dick would have more answers, but he, too, seems puzzled. And the idea of a reading is unsettling. Maybe I'm on the verge of being possessed. Or maybe the whole thing is my imagination. Perhaps I'm a fraud after all.

SATURDAY, MAY 22, 1976

Burt agreed to go to the lecture with me Thursday evening. He hadn't planned to attend, but readily changed his mind when he saw how nervous I was about it.

Burt, as usual, took longer to get ready than I did. I sat in the living room, thinking about the lecture and my possible reading. "OK," Burt finally called out, "I'm ready to go!"

I glanced up as he entered the room. "It's already done," I murmured.

"What's done?"

"My reading. It's already done."

"I thought he was going to do a reading *after* the lecture," Burt mused.

"That was my impression, too. But I feel that it's already done."

With that, we were off to the lecture. We drove to the Ramada Inn, and walked into a conference room already crowded with people. I caught a glimpse of Dick across the room and we waved at each other. Then Burt and I sat on the side where we could set up our tape recorder, and the lecture began. Solomon spoke about healing, and I suspect it was a very good lecture, I was too preoccupied to hear much of it. After about an hour, there was an intermission. Burt and I continued sitting and holding hands, waiting quietly for the second half.

Suddenly I was aware that Dick was standing over us. "You got your reading, Sandy," he said, sitting down in the row in front of us.

"You're kidding!" I exclaimed

"No, he gave it this afternoon. Very unexpected. We were all just sitting around in my office chatting. He was

158

sitting in that big green chair there and started drifting off to sleep. We started joking about his going into a trance state, and as it turned out, he really was. Then we were told, 'You can ask questions now.' So I asked about you. It came out in a booming voice, very different from his usual voice. It's all on tape. And it's a good reading."

"But, Dick, what did it say? I'm dying to know. Is it real or imagination, what I've been experiencing?"

"Well," Dick paused, choosing his words carefully, "Some of it's real and some of it's imagination. He suggested you stick to prayer right now for awhile. The main thing is, you've got some chemical imbalances affecting your emotional state. Niacin and some others."

"Well, how soon can I hear it?"

"When you come in for your next session."

"But that's nearly two weeks away! Isn't there any chance I can hear it sooner?"

"I can't promise. I'll do my very best, however. How're you doing?"

"OK."

"Any more questions?" I shook my head. I just wanted to hear that tape. "OK. I've got to go and talk to some other people. Are you sure you're OK?"

"I'm sure." I didn't hear anything further in the lecture that evening. I kept staring at him, wondering if he was really as good a medium as I had heard. He seemed to be a warm, together, spiritual person. And his account of how he discovered his ability and how he had helped others was fascinating.

The next day I called the Foundation to see if I could stop by and hear the tape on my own, but Dick was out. I kept wondering how I would feel about the reading. What if its message went against my own feelings about my path and my experiences? The more I thought about it, the more it seemed to me that I would have to put more faith in my own perceptions than in a reading—even one by Paul Solomon. That conclusion enabled me to relax more about the reading. Whatever it said, I didn't have to believe it.

Today Judy and I had tickets to a family therapy

conference. We were up and out bright and early—and almost on time. As we drove, I told Judy about my reading and my feelings about it. I was able to put it out of my mind as we listened to a lecture, and I resigned myself to having to wait nearly two weeks to hear the reading.

"You know," Judy said, as we sat outside later nibbling on the wretched box lunches provided at the conference, "I'm not getting anything out of this program. Interested in splitting?"

"Actually," I responded, biting into a piece of cake, "I was thinking the same thing. But I can't believe it's going to stay this bad. Let's listen to about half an hour after lunch. Then we can go if it doesn't get better."

Judy agreed, and reluctantly, we both walked in from the gorgeous May afternoon to sit on hard chairs listening to irrelevant comments on family therapy. After about forty minutes, we exchanged meaningful glances, and slipped quietly out the side door. It was good to be out in the warm breeze. "Well," Judy asked, "how shall we pass this afternoon that we now have free?"

"I don't care," I shrugged, "as long as it'll help me keep my mind off that reading."

"You know what I feel like doing? Spending the afternoon drinking wine coolers!"

I agreed that that sounded delightful, and we drove straight to the liquor store for a bottle of wine. Judy mixed the wine with bitter lemon and ice and we both sat in her kitchen getting progressively more tipsy. We had a great time giggling and laughing over life in general and some of the absurdities in the family therapy field.

"You know what I think?" Judy asked after a couple of hours. "I think I hear your phone ringing downstairs."

"Couldn't be. I don't hear anything."

"No, it's your phone. I'm sure it's your phone."

I staggered downstairs, wondering who would be calling me in the middle of Saturday afternoon.

Judy was right. The phone was ringing. I picked it up. "Hello?" I said, trying to sound sober.

"Hi! It's Dick. I'm down here at the Prana office trying to catch up on some paper work, and thought you might

160

like to come by and hear your tape. Can you come right away?"

"Sure," I said, "be right there." I hung up before I remembered that Burt was away for the weekend at a conference and had our car.

I ran upstairs and told Judy my plight.

"I'll be glad to take you. Get your tape recorder and let's go."

I breathed deeply of the warm, fresh air, and found I was sobering up fast. "You know," I commented to Judy on the way, "it really was lucky that we decided to leave early. If we had stayed for the whole program, we'd still be there and I wouldn't have been able to hear my tape today."

"I know. Another one of those coincidences. Call me when you want a ride back."

"Actually," I responded, "I think I'd rather walk. I'm sure I'll just want to be alone for awhile. Then how about joining me for supper? I've got some fish thawing."

"OK. Look, I'm going home to sleep, because I only got a few hours last night. But anytime you want to talk, just wake me up."

"I won't unless I need you, but I may need you. I don't know how I'll react to this." We hugged good-by, and I made my way into the Foundation. I found Dick in the outer office on the phone. He motioned me to go on into his office, so I set up my recorder and made myself comfortable. Dick came in a couple of minutes later. "This session will be unofficial; off the record. I called you because I know how eager you must be to hear the tape."

"I called yesterday to see if I could pick up the tape and hear it on my own, but you were out."

"Solomon told me specifically that you were not to hear this tape by yourself; that I was to be here and interpret it to you. So the answer to that would have been 'no.' I'll start the tape now, and we'll stop it every few lines so I can explain it to you. This is a fairly short reading. Short and to the point."

I wondered apprehensively what the point would be as Dick put the tape on the recorder. I was amazed at how

161

fast I had sobered up after an afternoon of drinking. As the tape began, I heard the soft and soothing voice of the man who helped the medium into trance. "You are now relaxed and turned within yourself, giving the consciousness to the Higher, the Divine that may speak through you. You will answer questions as I present them, giving that information that the Divine would have us know, being limited only by the Word, the Divine Father. In doing so, I command that you be surrounded by the holy presence of Jesus, the Christ, for protection, as we pray." The words struck me as very deep, mysterious, as a preparation for a very spiritual experience. The voice continued on with the Lord's prayer, and then said, "You will now find yourself resting in an enjoyable state in the arms of the Divine Father, and giving yourself to His mystic experience. Upon completion of the channeling, you will return to the body, and awaken feeling refreshed and filled with energy." Then the question for the reading was presented. "You have before you the soul record and the inquiring mind of Sandra Gibson, born April 10, 1947. You will comment on purpose and personality past and present, relationship with the universal forces, those problems that trouble this one concerning her fear of possession and you will answer questions as I present them. What is the basis for the fear this one experiences about possession?" There was a pause and I squirmed uncomfortably in the chair. Then the man's trance voice, much deeper than his usual voice, began to speak.

"Yes, we have the records. Quite a number of influences here at work, partly from soul memory and partly from present experience or relation to universal forces and attitudes toward the self. In earlier times this one has had experiences with use of communication with forces beyond the self and has misused . . ." Dick punched down the "pause" button on the recorder.

"He's talking here about a past life. Just like we've already discussed here. You misused psychic forces in the past. Now this is coming from the Akashic record. It's right from the horse's mouth. I didn't tell him anything about you in advance, by the way." The recording resumed.

"In this time there is very little ability . . ." I pressed the "pause" button this time.

"Does this mean, Dick, that I have very little ability to use psychic forces now in this lifetime?" I started to feel relieved.

"Wait," Dick cautioned. "Hear the entire sentence." He released the pause, and rewound the tape to the start of the sentence. "In this time, there is very little ability to believe that such can be used properly."

"You see," Dick said, stopping the tape again, "you don't believe that you can use these forces for good. You're still stuck in the past. Hear the rest of this section."

"There is a feeling of a need to be punished from the past. A feeling that such cannot be used for proper good and elevating purposes until after there has been some suffering as a result of using such for the control of others in the past. For this reason will subject the self to a period of possession for the feeling of cleansing the self or righting that which has been upset in the past in the use of psychic or occult forces."

"In other words, Sandy," Dick continued, "you have a need to punish yourself because of what you did in the past. You need to understand karma. It's not punishment. And there's no need for you to punish yourself. You've learned your lesson, and it's time now to use your abilities for good. You don't need to suffer first before you can do that. Let's go on."

"At the same time, in the present, such should not be developed, should not be used by this soul until the attitude toward the self has been changed. There are feelings here of guilt, of unworthiness. A new personality structure need be built concerning the self and the self worth, the ability to express, the right to express, the value of self, and self love. These things must be instilled in this one lest there is the feeling here that through channeling the consciousness of another, I can be a channel for that which is acceptable, while I am not myself acceptable. Thus, negating the personality of self, promoting an outside or external force which gives way to the dangers of possession. Watch out for this. For if this one should open and become a channel under these

163

conditions, will crucify self in the sense of no longer expressing that which felt unworthy when there is found that which is worthy, or a stronger personality. This then will dominate the life of the present personality as such." I paused the tape.

"I don't understand what he's saying."

"OK," Dick answered. "He's saying that you *could* open yourself up to possession because of a need to be punished from the past. It's the guilt that's still there."

"Well, is he saying that this guilt, this feeling of unworthiness comes from what I did in the past?" Dick nodded. "But supposedly I was already punished by the possession experience in Amsterdam. Why wasn't that enough?"

"You have a lot of guilt," Dick explained. "And it's still there. And will be until you fully understand that you don't have to punish yourself for what you did. Accept it as your past, and go on from there." We continued with the tape.

"Work first on establishing a sense of self worth, a sense of self love, a sense of right to express, a sense of being acceptable as she is in present personality."

"How can I do that?" I asked.

"By being helpful to others. You've hurt people in the past, and you're having trouble believing that you can help them now." We resumed listening.

"Then, develop further the abilities to be receptive to influences both within the self and outside the self. Train and orient the mind to understand that the higher influences of psychic forces need not come only from without self, but can come as well from within. Then ask that such as automatic writing or even trance communication come from within the self, that the seeking be directed there." Dick shut off the recorder again.

"Look, he's saying that the ability's there. You do have the ability to be a channel—even a trance medium. But you don't believe that you can use the ability for good. You need greater self-confidence before developing yourself further along these lines."

"For as long as the body, the mind, the consciousness,

expect that these things can only come from without, this will be the orientation or the seeking. So that when this one will bring through a message or channel psychically, it will come only from without the self. Change the orientation pattern of thought, the expectancy, and will be able then to tap the highest that is within the self and higher consciousness of self rather than external entities. Far safer when approached in this manner."

"I don't understand," I said. "What's he saying about channeling with the self?"

"You can get all the information you need from inside yourself. You don't need to contact external entities for that purpose. It's all within you." I still didn't understand, and suspected I wouldn't for a very long time.

"Now this last section," Dick said, "is truly amazing. The whole thing is. But here's where he really gets specific."

"Should comment here that there are imbalances in the physical body contributing to the lack of control over these as well. And should be careful about the dietary balance, especially in the endocrine system, the pancreas in particular, and presences of minerals that are needed for the thought process, the control of emotions, the control of energy, and the control of self. And should add to the diet a supplement of chromium, magnesium, manganese, and zinc. And to supplement the diet with niacinamide or pantothemic acid and vitamin B6 and vitamin A. These will assist in the thought process, the elevation of mood, the stabilizing of energy, and if the diet is controlled so that we avoid starches, carbohydrates, and sugars, especially refined substances, will not find such fluctuations of energy from ecstasy to depression. And during the periods of depression some shakiness in receptivity to influences about the self and external.

Building the health then both mental-emotional, and physical, will stabilize the conditions about this one that allow that the development be of a higher nature and in balance about the self." Then I could hear some talking in the background as Dick posed another question: "Quantities recommended in the food comments?"

The trance voice continued. "In niacin: 50 mg. twice a day. In the minerals or the metals, should be trace supplement. Recommend very small amounts—not therapeutic or megadoses at all. In B6 and vitamin A should be therapeutic quantities rather than prophylatic. Not megadoses. That is sufficient for this reading."

"So that's your reading," Dick said, turning off the recorder. "And the message should be clear. You've got to develop more self-confidence. By the way, right after the reading, while energy was still flowing through him, I gave him a list of all your past lives we've discussed. He said it was amazingly accurate. That's rare, you know, to have that much recall of past lives. How're you feeling?"

"Relieved. I didn't know what kind of material would be in that reading. But it all makes sense. It sounds like me. And it gives plausible reasons for things. That diet is going to involve some changes, though. My diet's pretty good, but it does include a lot of carbohydrates. Breakfast today was a donut and coffee at a conference. And lunch was a sandwich and cake."

"Well, that diet is part of your problem right now. I'd suggest you get started on those changes and the vitamins. Consult a doctor or nutritionist first, if you want. In fact, we can recommend a doctor here who's sympathetic to what we're doing."

"Well, maybe. I'll let you know."

"Any more questions?" Dick asked.

"No. I just want to go home and try to absorb all this. I'll keep my regular appointment next week."

I can stop the auto-writing for now; I've been advised to do so. That's a relief. I can concentrate on meditation for awhile, and then, when I feel more confident, go back to the auto-writing. When I go back to it, I won't be worried about possession. And because that fear will be gone, so will a major block. When I resume auto-writing it will be with a different attitude, and perhaps with much more dramatic results.

FRIDAY, JUNE 25, 1976

There have been a lot of changes in my life in the past
month. The reading has been a turning point. Physically,
I can't remember ever feeling better. I discussed the
reading with a nutritionist who told me more about
low-carbohydrate diets and suggested I read a book on
low-blood sugar. Then I saw a doctor whom Dick
recommended. He prescribed a similar diet. With a lot of
protein, few carbohydrates, frequent small meals during
the day and lots of vitamins, I feel full of more energy than
I ever thought possible.

I've also undergone a lot of changes professionally. I
quit my job earlier this month, and began spending a
couple of days a week doing family counseling with
Vanessa. I also quit the volunteer work I was doing one
evening a week as co-therapist—my work with Vanessa is
far more rewarding. Recently, Vanessa learned that Pete
is resigning, effective as of September 1st. Vanessa will
automatically be promoted to his position, and her
counseling job will be open. The Board of Directors wants
me to take the job. I was their second choice before, I've
been doing volunteer work for the agency, and they don't
want to go through the application procedure again. I'm
very excited. I remember my conflicting feelings in April
when I felt strongly that I would receive the job, but that I
wasn't ready for it. Both feelings proved to be true.

The job would entail counseling, administrative work,
and educational work in schools. Vanessa wants to divide
the functions of director and counselor, so that we each
perform both jobs, and receive the same salary. Dick calls
my new job a promotion, and pointed out that it came
into my life just at a time when I'm ready for it.

During the rest of the summer, I'll spend a couple days

a week at the agency and several days a week working on my dissertation. My advisor sent it back recently, asking for some extensive revisions. It'll take months to complete them.

Burt's been feeling very discouraged about his job. He's tired of working with statistics, and wants to work with people. He's seriously thinking about switching from research psychology to clinical psychology. He comes home from work almost every night in a bad mood. We've had many discussions on the subject lately, with Burt asking my advice and impressions. There's not much I've been able to tell him, except to follow his own feelings.

I've followed the advice of the reading, and have temporarily abandoned auto-writing. Instead, I meditate diligently every day.

However, I had a very startling experience last week. My Mom was visiting from the midwest. The first afternoon she was here, I meditated as usual. After I got into a deep state, I felt Kirk's presence. I told him to go away because I wasn't supposed to have anything to do with him.

"Now, remember," he transmitted to me telepathically, "exactly what Dick told you. He said to continue meditating and to listen to that voice of silence inside. That's all you're doing now—meditating. These thoughts you're receiving are part of your own voice of silence. I have a message here from your grandmother which is for your mother. It's an important message, and very important that your mother receive it."

"Well, I'm very uncomfortable with these telepathic messages. Unless I see it written in black and white I don't know if it's just my own thoughts." At that point, a slate suddenly appeared in my mind, and word by word a message was written on it. I felt Grandma's presence as these words were written: "Tell your mother that your Grandmother is well and happy. Thank her for her prayers."

I sat silently for a few minutes. I couldn't possibly give that message to my Mom. She didn't believe in praying for the dead.

I had already told Mom about my work with Dick and my reading. She was interested although cautioned me to be certain that what I did came from God. As we did the dishes together, I asked, "Mom, do you still think about Grandma even though she's been dead a year now?"

"Yes," Mom responded, "I think about her a lot. In fact, I pray for her often. I know I never used to believe in that, but I read something somewhere about how prayers can help confused souls on the other side. And it just felt right. So I've been praying a lot for her."

I felt rather shaken up inside as I proceeded to tell her about the message I had receive earlier that day. Mom was pleased. "It's a good feeling to think that I may have helped Grandma," she said.

I lay awake for a long time that night thinking about the incident. It was the first time I had received some information that I didn't know consciously but yet that had been verified to my satisfaction. Was it really possible after all that my messages were more than imagination?

I've had three sessions with Dick since the reading. I've taken in lists of questions trying to fully understand the reading. My main confusion has been the difference between information that comes from within and that which comes from without. I was advised to concentrate on channeling from within rather than trying to contact external entities. But I've found that very confusing. Wasn't Kirk an external entity? I asked Dick about it.

"You've heard the expression, 'as above, so below,'" Dick responded. "In the more profound philosophies of life, reference is made to man being a microcosm of a macrocosm. We're all one—all a part of a whole. Externally, you can make contact with Kirk, but the same knowledge, the same vibrations, the same frequency, the same essence of life is contained within you."

'You've said that when I do auto-writing, I'm in telepathic communication. If the information is coming from inside, then with whom am I in telepathic communication?'

"As we turn our thoughts inward, we transmit those thoughts to a higher state of consciousness. And the higher state of consciousness responds and transmits the answer back."

"So I'm in telepathic communication with *myself*?"

"With your *higher* self. Your oversoul."

"My soul?"

"Your *oversoul*. It's cosmic consciousness."

"Is that different from the soul?"

"Technically, no. It's all one. Mortally yes. Let me see. How can I explain the oversoul to you? Think of it like a corporation. A very large corporation. There's one person who's Chairman of the Board. He has a number of board members who work with him. They're responsible for executive decisions on a very high level. Then beneath the Chairman of the Board we have a president and a number of vice-presidents. Then we have superintendents or general managers. And beneath them we have a foreman. Now think in terms of us on the earth plane as being workers. And God is Chairman of the Board. Now the worker sends a message to God, and it may have to go through a chain of command, before it gets to God. Now with our analogy, you can pick up a phone and call the Chairman with a question. And the answer may be sent down to you through the chain of command—telepathically."

"But that sounds like it's coming from outside me."

"I know, but it's not. Everything's inside of you. That truck outside the window is inside of you. The universe is contained within each of us. I know this is frustrating to understand. You have to grasp it intuitively."

"Well, are you saying that even though the auto-writing supposedly came from Kirk, it could have come from inside of me? That Kirk's words and messages were already inside me?"

"That's correct."

"Where does the information come from for trance mediums? Inside?"

"It depends. Sometimes the source is inside. Some trance mediums are actually 'possessed' and it comes from outside them."

"Well, I'm still confused on how you authenticate auto-writing."

170

"First of all we look to see if it's offensive. If anything offensive comes through, or anything you're uncomfortable with, we discard it and assume it's coming from outside. Then we look to see if it's information that's logical, spiritual, makes intuitive sense to you, and fits into a pattern of your life that is helpful to you. If it's offensive or evasive, we forget about it."

I still didn't understand after that explanation, so came back two weeks later (this afternoon) with the same question. At first, I got the same answers. Then Dick tried a different approach.

"Instead of thinking of it in terms of a personalized vessel of information, think of it as cosmic truth. Universal truth. Names are no longer necessary." Dick paused for several minutes. "Wow, what's coming to you! Holy mackerel! Look, instead of assuming that information is coming from Kirk, in your mind, eliminate the name. Think in terms of cosmic knowledge. There really is no need of a guide; you are the guide. As evolution continues, the reality of the oneness will become more consciously recognized."

"Suppose I do more auto-writing, and I get a name?"

"Fine, assume it's coming from God. Ignore the name."

"That makes sense. It all made sense from the beginning except for the name."

"Just eliminate the name! It was that simple!" We both laughed. "That came through me like gangbusters and I started to float. It wasn't for me—that was a message for you!"

I understand it better now. I'll forget about Kirk's name and assume that the information comes from "Cosmic Consciousness" rather than from a specific entity. But I still don't fully understand it.

We've also been talking about karma this month. I don't understand why I still feel guilty about my work in the black arts if I'd already paid the karmic debt through possession in Amsterdam.

Dick explained: "It's like the attitude that those who live by the sword die by the sword. On a soul level, as we try to grow, we're much more harsh on ourselves than a judge would be. If you stole my old, beaten briefcase and I caught you, you might feel so guilty that you'd want to buy me a new one. I'd just want my old one back. You may have felt that the only way to balance the books was to let yourself become possessed. But it doesn't have to work that way. Instead of punishing yourself, you can pay off karma by helping others. If you killed me in a past life, that doesn't mean I have to kill you now to pay off the karma. It means you may have to save my life now or be of help to me in some other way. In theory, the reason I'm here now working with people is that I was a warlock in Atlantis. That's what you're getting into, too. You're going to be helping people in this life to pay off that past karma."

"What can I do to overcome these feelings of inadequacy and guilt?"

"You're doing it. The most important thing you're doing is facing it bit by bit and beginning to understand it. You're also learning about karma, that you can pay off your debts by helping others who may be going through similar problems to what you've been through. Also, keep working with the white light. By the way, I heard a new approach with that to recommend to you and others. We all have while light within ourselves. Call on that light within rather than letting it flow from a gold symbol outside. See it coming from your solar plexus or from your heart and going into all parts of the body and surrounding you."

Dick concluded today's session with a reminder to remain discreet about what I'm doing.

"The medium recommended in his talk that anyone who's in touch with a source of information work with it themselves for at least six months before being open in public about what they're doing. You're doing this yourself automatically—and I highly recommend it. Realistically, it will be at least six months before you feel confident about the material that's coming through you. Let's put it this way, you're 1000% better than when you started, but you're only 80% positive. And you know what I'm talking about."

Yes, I know what he's talking about. I'm still hesitant

about going back to auto-writing. For now, I'm very happy to do without it. It really doesn't seem to matter much, however, whether I'm doing it or not. I still receive messages telepathically during meditation. Ever since that message for Mom from Grandma, I've been getting some message every few days. Usually, it's something reassuring, like a reminder that I am part of a larger whole or that I'm surrounded by much love and protection. I'm becoming more comfortable with these messages, so I think that I'll be ready to return to auto-writing fairly soon.

SATURDAY, JULY 24, 1976

I'm finally beginning to understand how information can be received from inside. It occurred to me one day while meditating. I visualized a giant computer that contained all that ever was or will be; it could be called God or the oversoul. Everything everybody does or thinks is fed into the computer and stored in its memory. Each soul is a little computer terminal. If we know how to utilize the computer properly, then we can obtain from it anything we want to know. Just like terminals, we can plug into the Central Computer at any time. I drew a diagram to illustrate my concept. (See diagram on page 175)

I can communicate with Kirk directly (telepathically), or I can communicate with his essence in the Central Computer.

Dick was impressed with my diagram. "Yes," he said, "that's exactly what I've been trying to explain. That's a very good way of illustrating the concept. In fact, if you really want to make this accurate, you've got to realize that in time all those terminals will be absorbed into the Central Computer as it gets larger and larger. They'll still retain their individual identities, but they'll be part of the Central Computer. And new terminals will hook into this larger computer. In time, they'll be absorbed, too."

"This theory makes a lot more sense to me," I responded. "It's obviously easier for you and me to communicate directly, but we could contact the essence of the other within the Computer. In fact, each of us has that ability. If we could all use the Computer well, we wouldn't need teachers or reference books on the physical plane. Most people don't realize that they're connected to this Central Computer, and those who do usually don't know how to utilize it properly."

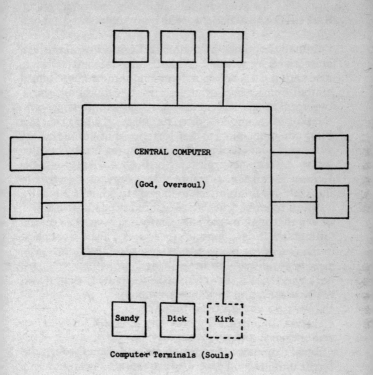

Computer Terminals (Souls)

Dick smiled. "I think you're about ready to graduate." That made sense. As I learn to obtain more answers from within myself, I'll have less need of Dick.

I saw Dick again later this month to do another regression session. I'd been receiving more impressions about that life in Amsterdam, and I had a strong feeling that I needed to experience it again to understand it more fully.

Before we began the hypnosis, I told Dick about the latest impressions I had received. I had seen myself as a little Dutch girl who was very much loved by her parents. But I disgraced them in adolescence by running away and joining a group of very disreputable people who were involved in the occult—perhaps gypsies. I later made my living by pretending to tell fortunes and contact dead relatives. I could fool people into thinking I really had the ability to contact spirits. So I tried. And became possessed. But I wasn't sure what happened after that, and I felt it was important to know. I told Dick I might be resistant to looking at the scene, but I needed to do it. We agreed that Dick would push gently if necessary. We went through the usual hypnotic procedures. I again went back to the day of the possession experience. Dick questioned me. "What do you do for a living?"

"I tell fortunes. And contact dead spirits. I just pretend. I fool people, and they pay me money."

"Why do you do these things?"

"To make a living. I'm not very honest. I just want to make money, and this is an easy way."

Dick proceeded to question me, as I went through the events of that day. I described attempting to conjure up a spirit, and then related in an agonized voice that I was outside my body and couldn't get back in. I was unable to move my body that was in Dick's office and became concerned. I lost contact with the scene.

"I can't move! I'm frightened!"

"You're perfectly safe and no harm will come to you." Dick's voice was very gentle. "However, it's very important that you return to the scene in Amsterdam. It's important that we know what happened to your body there."

176

"I don't want to see it!"

"I'm going to talk now to your superconscious mind, Sandy. Is it important that Sandy watch this scene to learn what happened to the body in that life?" I felt my head nodding an affirmative response. "OK, Sandy, now I'm going to mentally guide you back. You're perfectly safe." Dick's gentle but firm insistence gave me the courage to return to the scene, as I witnessed a tormenting series of events. The low-level entity in my body taunted me and laughed at me. Then it ransacked the room destroying my most valuable possessions. I started to cry.

"I'm very poor; I don't own many things. But everything I do own and that is valuable to me is being destroyed!"

"You're able to look at this scene objectively. You realize that these are only material possessions, and they really don't matter. Now I want you to keep watching. What happens next?"

"There are friends approaching my house. They've come to visit me! They don't know about this thing that's taken over my body!"

"All right. Keep watching. What happens to your friends?"

"They see my house destroyed. They see that I'm possessed. They run away frightened. They go for help!"

I next described how a local religious leader came to perform a kind of exorcism which was unsuccessful. I described how the local law-enforcement official came and decided that I must be locked up pending an investigation of my condition. But a large crowd was gathering outside, and they were convinced I was possessed. And they refused to wait for any investigation. I was forcibly taken away by the crowd and tied to a stake while a fire was lit.

"This thing is laughing at me!" I wailed, terrified. "It says it won't be here for long!" Suddenly, I found myself back in my body just as the fire began to burn it. I cried.

Dick gently brought me back to the present, reminding me that the scene was in the past and that I could now view it objectively. We discussed it after Dick brought me out of the hypnotic state.

"You know," Dick commented, "nobody but yourself was hurt. You don't need to feel guilt for having hurt someone in that life."

"I don't think I do. But I think I feel guilty for a lifetime before that when I was involved in the black arts. This Amsterdam life was fulfilling a karmic condition."

I had been deeply hypnotized during that session, and hung around the Prana Foundation for a couple of hours before I felt able to drive. I felt drained, but thought that I had worked through a very important emotional block. I was relieved.

This regression was the final experience I needed to prepare myself to return to channeling information. I don't know if I'll return to auto-writing, however, or try some other technique. I don't know when I'll start or under what circumstances. But I think I'll be ready soon.

SATURDAY, AUGUST 28, 1976

Burt and I just got back from a week in Illinois. Burt's grandfather died, so we went there for the funeral and to visit our parents. I enjoyed seeing our parents and other relatives again, but I'm really glad to be home. So much has been happening this past month, that I'm eager to return to my psychic explorations.

I've recently started channeling information again. It started several weeks ago, when I was concerned about a family that Vanessa and I were counseling. She and I disagreed about the best therapeutic approach to use. She wanted to refer them to another agency, but I had a strong feeling that referral would be inappropriate for them. I was confused about the interpersonal dynamics in this family, and about how Vanessa and I could resolve our conflict. The confusion was making me depressed. As I sat home alone one evening, I felt an overwhelming urge to do some auto-writing. I hesitated, becasue I hadn't done any since the reading three months ago. I wondered if I was ready to resume the contact. But my urge to do it was so overwhelming that I set aside my apprehensions. Burt was at the office working late, so I proceeded alone. I received a long and reassuring message. I was told to trust in my own intuitions and follow my instincts as a counselor. I was also told not to be concerned with the different approaches of Vanessa and myself. Everyone, I was told, has a different perception of reality. That doesn't make some right and some wrong; it makes all of us unique. I was also told that, in a practical sense, it didn't matter what approach we utilized because this family would not accept any referral and would drop out of counseling in a very short time. I felt marvelous after

179

this contact. The love and peace surrounding me totally dispelled my depression and left me feeling relaxed and confident. I decided to go along with Vanessa's approach. But the family did not accept the referral and they stopped seeing us a couple of weeks later.

I still wasn't certain that I was ready to begin regular contact again even after that experience. But the contacts came to me. I continued to receive messages while meditating. For example, Vanessa and I applied to a family psychotherapy training program and I was concerned about whether our applications would be accepted. I knew that the competition was stiff. One day while meditating, I saw these words written in my mind: "You have been accepted into the family training program. You will receive your letter next week." I was uncomfortable after that message: What if it were wrong? But a week later I received my letter of acceptance.

I was beginning to feel more confident about my messages. But they were becoming harder to remember because they were getting longer and more complex. When I mentioned this to Dick, he suggested that I turn on a tape recorder and speak the messages as I received them.

I discussed it with Burt. We decided to resume regular contacts on a weekly basis. So, a couple of weeks ago, we began. I went into a trance state and Burt turned on the recorder and then asked questions. I saw words written mentally, which I read. Later, as the trance deepened, the answers came telepathically.

"Are you ready to answer questions?" Burt asked.

"Yes."

"What is the source of this information?"

"This information is being channeled through Sandy's subconscious mind and originates from high energy levels. The information is available to all who are able to make contact with it. The information at this time is not being expressed through the personality of another entity. This is necessary at this time in order not to confuse Sandy. In time, this information will be received through a spirit guide. At this time, protective entities are present,

180

but they are serving to help Sandy make contact inside herself. This is an important aspect of the training procedure for Sandy."

"How often should this contact be made?"

"As often as Sandy feels able. It is crucial that Sandy be comfortable when contact is made. It is also important not to waste time and to take advantage of every available opportunity."

"Do you have any suggestions on how to meditate?"

"At this time, we would say this to you. Meditation is most effective when you allow it to happen. If you *try* to meditate, you will defeat your purpose. If you judge yourself and say, 'Now I'm meditating well' or 'Now I'm not meditating so well' then you also defeat your purpose. Meditation is a state of complete passivity, when you allow yourself to become receptive to your own inner voice. You must *allow* it to happen; you cannot *try* to make it happen."

"Is there any further message for us?"

"Yes. Tonight we shall briefly consider the importance of faith. Faith is not a blind acceptance of that which you cannot know. Rather, faith derives from your own inner self. It cannot be emphasized enough that your psuedo-scientific culture has cut people off from the flow that is within. Your task now as a people, as a culture is to reacquaint yourselves with that inner flow. Each of you as individuals must make that contact. As you discover yourself you will discover your uniqueness as an individual. And you will also feel the universal flow that unites you with all of humanity. As you make contact with that inside of you, you will understand that faith is knowing that these inner energies are always there and they will guide you when you need guidance. You can turn to them at any time. The more rapport you maintain with this energy within, the more your life itself will flow. Faith is understanding this flow in you, through you, directing your life if you will allow it. That is the meaning of faith. You must understand at this time how very important it is for you as individuals and for your culture to make this contact. Are there any other questions tonight?"

"No."

"Thank you for your attention. Good night."

After we finished, I felt great peace and relaxation. The experience had been very pleasant, and I didn't feel any fear. Several days later we tried it again, and we received more material on faith.

"Tonight we will continue our discussion on faith. Faith is a description of something internal. It cannot be sought outside of yourself. It cannot be understood by another person. It cannot be grasped by an intellectual process. It can only be encountered by each inside of the person. You will find inside of yourself a deep reservoir of knowledge, understanding, intuition that you cannot grasp intellectually. You cannot fully comprehend it intellectually. You cannot put it in a test tube. You cannot see it under a microscope. It is something your scientists have yet to understand. Yet its discovery, its use, its flow through your life and lives of countless other individuals on your planet is the only way at this time the planet can save itself. You must start with yourself and your own inner searchings. You must start by caring for your body. It cannot be emphasized enough how important proper diet, proper exercise, and proper frame of mind are to this process. In your culture, at this time, it is extremely difficult to obtain an adequate diet. That is why you must take great care to make every attempt to avoid chemicals, to avoid processed foods. Strive to purchase and prepare foods as pure and natural as possible. That is the message for tonight. Do not try to analyze, to understand my words. Rather, let them filter into your consciousness. Good night."

Shortly after that session, I had a very vivid dream. In it, I was visiting a psychic for a reading. She had two messages for me. One was that I was well-protected in my explorations and had nothing to fear. The other was that I was to begin writing a book. When I woke up the next morning, I had an overwhelming urge to organize and expand my journal so that it would be understandable to others. Most of my journal has been on tape rather than written. And I haven't transcribed any of my sessions with

Dick. But I felt a compulsion to begin organizing all of this material into book form. I hesitated for several days, but the feelings were so strong I couldn't ignore them any longer. Now I'm spending every spare moment transcribing tapes and going over old notes. It's very time-consuming, but when I work I lose all consciousness of time. I think I've been writing for fifteen minutes, but an hour has passed. It'll take many months to organize this material. And I have no idea how such a book will end, or what its title should be. Or even if it'll ever be published. But as long as my need to write it is so strong, I'll continue working.

Burt asked about the book in the next trance session. As usual, the answer was vague.

"Do you have any comments on the book Sandy is writing?"

"Yes. Sandy should continue to work on this book. The project is important, but the reasons cannot be fully understood at this time. But it is important, and your help and support of Sandy is crucial to her, at this time. You can help through your encouragement, your interest, and by striving to keep yourself in a state of harmony and peace."

Our last trance session was held just before we left for Illinois. Burt received a phone call from his Mom saying that his grandfather was very ill and might not live much longer. That evening we did a session, and Burt asked about his grandfather. We were told that he could continue to live for as much as three to four months if he chose. But he was being advised by spirit guides around him to leave the body earlier. He was, however, clinging to the body because he was afraid of death. But if he followed the advice being given him, he could leave at any time. We were then given some information about death.

"As you contemplate the death of one you love, it is a good time to think upon the meaning of death. To die is to be born again. It is merely a change of form. Just as changing your clothing does not change your essence, neither does the change in physical form known as death alter your essence. Upon death the soul is liberated from the physical and faces new joys, new challenges, new opportunities. It need not be a time of mourning. It is more appropriate to make it a time of rejoicing. Be grateful that this man is finally about to leave the body after a long and productive life. He will be glad afterwards that he did so."

Three days later, Burt's grandfather died, and we went to Illinois for the funeral.

Yesterday, I went to see Dick for what may be a final session. At least, it will be the last session for awhile. I want to see if I can manage on my own without his answers and support. I showed him the trance material and he thought it was very spiritual. He encouraged me to continue working along that line as long as I felt confident.

Dick also told me he's working with another woman, named Jan, whose doubts and uncertainties are similar to mine. She hears voices and has been writing down their messages. Dick read me some of them—they were very beautiful and spiritual. I asked him to ask her if she'd like to get together sometime. I'd love to talk with someone whose struggles are similar to mine.

In just a few days I begin my new job. I'm looking forward to it. I've been putting in a lot of volunteer time this summer, and it will be good to work full-time and to earn a paycheck again. Burt has decided to start looking for an internship in clinical psychology but feels discouraged about his chances. I've been talking to him a lot about faith and how our paths work out the way they're supposed to if we open ourselves to our inner voices. But I have doubts, too, that he'll find what he wants. Internships are difficult to find anyway, and most of them were assigned in the winter or spring.

SUNDAY, SEPTEMBER 26, 1976

Burt has a new job! He answered an ad for an internship and was told that the position had been filled, but they recommended another institution that had an opening. He called for an appointment. He went on a Friday for the interview, and they offered him the job on the spot, if he could start that Monday. Burt accepted, and quit his research job over the weekend.

He loves his new work. He's an intern at a progressive, private psychiatric institution. He's receiving training at seminars and classes, and does individual, group and family therapy with patients. Burt's become happier and more self-assured in the past few weeks.

So we both started new jobs this month. They've entailed a lot of changes in our lives. For one thing, our income has dropped considerably. It's been more difficult than we realized to adjust to this drop—especially since it happened so fast. And we're both adjusting to new jobs, and feel insecure about them. Burt feels insecure about counseling, which he's never done before. I also feel insecure about counseling, wishing I'd had more training. And I feel scared of all the responsibility involved in being co-director of an agency. We've been tense and short-tempered with each other.

Despite our busy schedules, we've been finding time to continue our trance sessions, holding one every few days. The answers to our questions are general and spiritual, rather than providing advice. For example, Burt asked early this month where his career should be going (this was before he made the decision to look for an internship).

"It is important for you to make your own decisions

based on your own inner feelings. You have important work to do on this plane. It is important for you to understand that your life has been preparation. There is no wasted time. Every experience is assimilated by the soul for its growth. You need to understand this. You need to accept yourself. You need greater confidence in your own inner voice. Do not think in terms of having wasted the past or wasting the present. Continue to search for the most fulfilling work for yourself but still seek meaning in the present and study the past for what it shows."

"I don't understand how there can be free will and at the same time no wasted time. If I'm not free to waste time, am I really free?"

"You are free to spend your time however you choose. Whatever you do can be made into a productive lesson for the soul and utilized for its growth. On a soul level, you have already chosen a path that is designed to develop particular qualities in yourself. It is a path designed to teach specific lessons to the soul. However, you have the free will to reject that path and to choose any other. To choose a different path is not to waste a life. Rather it is to absorb different lessons, to develop different potentialities. The path your soul has chosen is designed to develop the lessons most needed at this time. But it is possible to learn different lessons, ones perhaps not as needed, perhaps fewer potentialities would be developed. But the soul can utilize any experience for its growth."

"Now I'm more confused than ever." After a pause, Burt continued. "I think this is the first time I've said something and not gotten a response."

"You haven't asked a question."

"Is this a non-directive approach? The question is, Why am I so confused?"

"You are confused because you are seeking outside of yourself for answers. You are confused because you are using your intellect to analyze concepts that you can best understand intuitively. The answers will not make sense to you until they come through you, from you."

"Does this mean I have psychic abilities that haven't

been developed?" I sensed great amusement at this question.

"Of course. Everyone does."

"OK. Anything further that you'd like to tell us?"

"I think it is advisable to return to our discussion on faith. We must continue to return to this area because it is so important, and so easily misunderstood. A true understanding of faith will answer many of the questions you are asking, and answer many questions unasked in your soul. To have faith is to understand that life exists beyond the self. It is to understand that the universe is a swirling mass of energy forces, interacting with each other. It is to understand that life flows smoothest when you align yourself with the energy forces around you, above you, and within you. When you try to isolate yourself from this energy flow you feel confused, doubtful, alienated, alone. When you allow yourself to flow with the energy you feel unified and intuitively your questions are answered."

Several days later, we received this: "It is important to understand and accept the meaning of patience. All life is a cyclical process of growth. Steps must be taken one at a time. Yesterday's steps must be taken before today's. And today's steps must be taken before tomorrow's. Growth can be likened to the grades in a school. Second grade material would have no meaning to a child who had not mastered the first grade. It would be inappropriate to give college level material to students in grade school. By the same token, you are in the school of life. You must understand that today's lessons must be accepted and learned for today. Tomorrow's lessons will be the outgrowth of today's lessons. It accomplishes nothing to make haste on the path of life. One must tread slowly and surely, mastering each lesson as it comes. It is important for your growth to understand these words and integrate them into your lives."

I asked Burt to ask a question in the next session about drugs in our culture. This is the answer we received: "In your culture, at this time, there is a worship of drugs. You must understand that the human body is a miniature society in itself. With proper care, it can maintain itself in perfect balance and harmony. The introduction of drugs into the body disrupts the natural harmony and flow within. This is true for any drug administered for any purpose. Most drugs will not kill or permanently damage the body. All drugs cause temporary disruption of the body's processes. Some drugs can facilitate religious awareness. However, such awareness can more safely be obtained without the drug. In your culture at this time it seems necessary upon occasion to allow doctors of medicine to prescribe drugs for healing purposes. This is necessary because it is the only means your culture has at this time to effect healing. However, the use of drugs inflicts violence upon the body, a reflection of the violence that permeates your society. In time, if your culture matures and develops, your people will learn how to heal the body by respecting its natural rhythms and processes. In time you will know that it is not necessary ever to use drugs in the body for healing purposes. That knowledge will be a long time in coming to your medical profession, however."

Then Burt closed with his usual final question: "Do you have any further messages for us today?"

"Today as your portion of the earth is preparing for the fall season, I wish to draw your attention to the miracles of nature that exist all around you. It is too easy for your people to rush to work in the morning, to rush home at night, and then bury themselves in front of a television or a newspaper and never notice the world around. You ask for miracles to prove the existence of God when miracles exist in your very midst. The miracle itself of the trees that seem to die in fall yet bloom again in the spring should orient your minds to the reality of reincarnation. Would God allow the trees to live again and again, and not provide the same miracle for human souls? As your season is changing, notice each day the beauty of the trees as they assume their glorious fall colorings. Enjoy the pure, crisp air as the heat and humidity of summer fades behind you. Enjoy the sights, the smells, the sounds, of your fall season. You are in one of the most beautiful sections of your country during this time of year. Take time to enjoy it. Take time on a daily basis to notice the miracles of nature around you. Breathe deeply of the fresh air outside and give thanks that such a beautiful world is yours to live in. Good night."

I felt uncomfortable with that analogy. I don't consider the cycle of trees to be evidence of reincarnation. I don't even consider it a good analogy. I wondered again if perhaps I was imagining the messages or really was in touch with higher energies. I wondered if I would ever have an answer to that question.

I decided that I needed to understand more about the process. So during last week's session, I gave Burt a question to ask: "Can you give us any further information about the source of this information and Kirk's role in it?"

The answer didn't provide very much clarification: "This is understandably confusing to you. It must be greatly simplified to be explained, and cannot be fully grasped with your conceptual framework. Sandy is receiving information telepathically through the subconscious mind. Sandy is able to maintain a rapport with superconscious reality. Kirk's role is first as protector to ensure that no harm shall come to Sandy while in an entranced state. Second, to serve as trainer or teacher to help Sandy learn step by step how to become a channel. Third, Kirk's role in transmitting information telepathically is important for its accurate reception."

I occasionally ask about clients I'm seeing, and that evening, Burt decided to ask about one of his patients. I felt a moment of panic as he read me a name. I wasn't accustomed to channeling information on somebody I'd never met before. What if the information was wrong? Perhaps Burt would rely on the information in counseling and would make the patient worse. I received a very strong impression to relax and stop fighting. I did my best to quiet my conscious doubts to allow this information to come through.

"Look here into a relationship with the father or father-figure in this person's life. There is emotional imbalance from a troubled relationship."

I couldn't wait to get out of the trance and find out if there was any accuracy to the information. But Burt proceeded with another question: "Who is Jesus?"

"Again, you ask a question that appears simple, but the answer is highly complex. Think of Jesus in terms of a set of ideas, a philosophy of love and caring and good will. The true story of Jesus contains many distortions as recorded by your historians. But if you seek to understand the philosophy and seek to acquaint yourself with the energy force and the force that can be characterized as the spirit or essence of Christ, then you will know much more than the historians about Jesus and you will understand what is really important."

Then he asked his closing question: "Do you have any further information for us tonight?"

"There is so much to be imparted, it is difficult to choose what is most important to say to you tonight."

At this point, I felt surrounded by emotions. It was similar to the feelings of an older, kindly uncle who had so much advice to pass on, that he didn't know where to begin. After a pause, the information continued.

"I think it is important for you both to realize that you are entering periods of your profession in which you are very busy. You are both doing productive and important work that you have chosen to do. However, it is important for you both to remember to take time every day for each other and for yourselves, take time to notice and appreciate your world, to smell a flower or feel the wind. Take a deep breath of fresh air. It is important for you each to have time alone to explore yourselves and to make contact through meditation with the highest energies that are within and around. It is important to find time to relax and feel peaceful and to discover and recognize the peace that is within in the midst of your busy lives. That is all for tonight."

When I came out of the trance, I asked Burt about the information on his patient. He said that the information was true since this woman's father had died when she was young and she married an older, father-figure. However, he also said the information was so general that it could apply to anyone. I decided that Burt was right and felt depressed. We did find the final message meaningful, however. We've been working so hard that we have little time left for relaxation.

I've been feeling discouraged lately about these trance sessions. The information is always so general that I don't consider it evidential. I'm still waiting for very definite proof that I'm not imagining all of this. I want some profound information to come through that I couldn't possibly know consciously. Until I get that kind of evidence, I can't help but wonder if I'm wasting my time.

I met Jan recently. She's been working with Dick for several months, ever since she started receiving messages from a voice. I invited her over for lunch, and we read each other's messages. Hers are very spiritual and profound. I'm convinced that her source is of a very high spiritual level. I felt charged with warm energy just by reading her messages. That meeting with her left me feeling more strongly than ever that my messages are virtually meaningless and are probably imagination. I think it's about time to see Dick again.

THURSDAY, OCTOBER 7, 1976

Something rather strange has been happening. Several
weeks ago a mother and daughter came into our agency
for counseling, and I was assigned as their counselor.
During the initial session, I saw a big patch of red near the
daughter's head. It disappeared for awhile, then came
back. Later in the session, she told me that she had a great
deal of anger for her mother. I know that red in auras can
indicate anger, so I wondered if the color I saw was related
to her mood.

During their next session, I again saw patches of color
near the daughter, but the colors changed. During most of
the session the color was a murky blue, but when she
spoke to her mother, it changed to red. In the following
session, I began seeing colors near the mother, too. And
during the past week, I've been seeing colors near other
clients. I doubt, though, that I'm seeing auras, because I
see only a patch of color. Auras surround the entire
person.

There's also something else I need to discuss with Dick.
I'm discouraged. I haven't done any trance sessions for
over a week. I'm tired of devoting so much of my time to
something that may be pointless. It takes a couple of
hours a week to hold the sessions, then another two to
three hours to transcribe the tapes. I also spend several
hours a week working on my manuscript. I must be crazy
to be devoting so much time to this nonsense.

I've been stopping by the Foundation every couple of
weeks to drop off copies of my trance sessions, but I
haven't had a session with Dick in two months. I called
him last week to request an appointment.

"You must be telepathic," he said when he came to the

phone. "I was just thinking of calling you. There's something I want to talk to you about."

"I called to make an appointment. I have some things to talk over."

"We're having a meeting next Friday afternoon here for some people interested in the Foundation's work. Why don't you attend? You can help explain what we're all about. You could come by at 11:30, and we'll talk, then go for lunch, and come back for the meeting. How does that sound?"

I agreed, but felt apprehensive, wondering what Dick wanted to talk to me about. I think on some level I already know what he wants to talk about; it's something I don't want to face.

SUNDAY, OCTOBER 10, 1976

I saw Dick on Friday, and left the Foundation wanting to
give up this psychic work. I arrived very late for my
appointment, the first time I've ever been late. Resistance,
perhaps, to hearing what Dick wanted to talk to me
about? I showed him copies of my latest trance sessions.

"No holes," he commented. "I don't see anything here
that deviates from a spiritual course."

"But there's nothing *evidential* there."

"What do you mean? There's lots of material here
that's evidential. You're just expecting too much. If you
receive a bit of information that's accurate, you feel good
about your work for a few days. Then you begin to doubt
and want something else tangible. If you get it, you want
still more the following week. Ever heard of faith?"

"Yes, I'm hearing more than enough about it from the
trance material. I want concrete proof. The material I've
been getting on clients is too general."

"You've got to have patience. Look, you were told that
a woman had a problem with a father-figure, and it turns
out that her husband is a father-figure. There are many
people that that information would apply to, but it
wouldn't apply to everyone. Do you think it's coincidence
that it just happens to apply to the person you're doing the
reading on?"

"I don't know. I just want more detailed information."

"Part of the problem is the conditions under which
you're working. Under ideal conditions, you'd have the
name, and perhaps the birthdate, or whatever is needed,
on someone you've never met. And you would have the
confidence that the reading will be evaluated by an
impartial person. Perhaps none of it is shared, but if

applicable, is utilized to improve a counseling relationship. Ideally, you're not the only one doing a reading, but your reading is compared with others done by other channels. These would be experimental conditions, allowing, in time, a real assessment of the accuracy of the information."

"I don't understand what you're talking about."

"I think you know exactly what I'm talking about."

Suddenly I felt very apprehensive, and feared that I did understand. "I hope you're not suggesting that I start doing readings?"

"That's exactly what I'm suggesting. I think you've known for a long time that you were approaching this point. It's an ideal experimental approach to determine the degree of your accuracy. Look, Sandy, there's recently been quite an increase in interest in the Foundation's work due to an article about us in the paper. We're trying to co-ordinate the services we have here to offer people. One important service is diagnostic work. I'd like you and Jan to both try doing readings. You'll each have the same names. All I want you to do is relax and let whatever's there come through. Don't analyze or block anything. Then give it to me. I'll go over it carefully. If anything appears accurate, we can make use of it discreetly."

"But I'm not ready for that. I may never be. Something inaccurate could come through and hurt somebody."

"That's why I do an evaluation of the material first. It's a safety device, so that you don't need to worry about that. Your worry about hurting people is one thing that blocks more specific material from coming through. The choice is yours, and I don't want to push you into it. But give it some thought."

I promised to think about it, and felt preoccupied through lunch and the afternoon meeting. I remembered that I never did get around to asking about colors, so made an appointment for next week. Last night I talked things over with Burt. I told him my fears of the information being wrong and hurting someone.

"Well, the information has been extremely helpful to me. I can't begin to explain how much it's helped me or what a difference it makes in my life."

"Really, Burt? I didn't know you felt that way."

"Of course; I assumed you knew that. Look, it helped me find the courage to look for a clinical internship. It's helping me adjust to my new job and helping me meditate better. It seems only logical that it could be of help to others, too."

I still didn't feel ready to begin readings for other people even as an experiment. We decided to ask my source about it during my mext trance session. As I began going into the trance, I felt very receptive, experiencing REM almost instantly. I was quite apprehensive, however, about the questions I knew Burt was going to ask.

"Who or what are we in contact with?" he began.

"You are in contact with high level information that is being channeled through Sandy..." I started feeling apprehensive, and considered ending the session. Then, telepathically, the sentence was finished in my mind with gentle humor: "... despite the fact that she is offering great resistance and refuses to believe that she is in contact with such information." I was advised mentally to deal with the apprehension by paying attention to the vibrations around me. As usual, they were loving and comforting. Verbally, the answer was completed: "Kirk is present to serve as a guide and protector."

"Do you have any comments on the possibility of Sandy doing readings for the Prana Foundation? Is she ready to do such readings and is this the appropriate place and approach for her to be doing them?"

"Yes, Sandy is ready to do such readings..." At that point, I realized what I had just said and felt upset about it. I was convinced that the opposite answer was true and couldn't understand why I had said that. I felt like a helpless bystander as words came out of my mouth that I didn't believe and wouldn't consciously choose to say. The sentence continued: "... although she herself does not believe this. It is important to understand that Sandy is undertaking a training program. She is not a perfect channel but has the potential to do much better. An excellent training device is to do readings on strangers.

196

This reduces conscious interference which is more likely with people she knows. The information received must be evaluated carefully because Sandy still has much to learn about being a channel. However, enough helpful and accurate information should come through to be of use to other people and at the same time serve as a training device for Sandy."

"Can this source of information be used to give readings on physical health states?"

"It must be understood that Sandy has already chosen a path for using this source of information. She has chosen at this time to use this information primarily for counseling purposes. Because this is the type of training she is undergoing at this time the bulk of the information received will relate to emotional forces and past life forces that work in the individual. That is not to say that no information on physical health will be received. But it is not Sandy's primary goal as a channel. She could of course change her decision on the matter. At this time, that is what she has decided."

"What information on an individual should be provided in order to receive a reading?"

"The name is desirable but not essential if another means of identification such as a file number can be provided. Birth date and sex can be helpful but are not essential."

Then Burt threw in a question about a patient of his. I felt panicked. I was afraid of making a mistake with the information. I received a very strong telepathic message to relax and stop my thinking processes. As soon as I did so, words started coming through. I felt very uncomfortable as the words came out. I had never heard of this woman, and for all I knew, she didn't even exist.

"This is an individual who is beset with confusion and worries. This person must be helped to straighten out her thinking and thought processes. Intensive counseling along these lines is essential. Slowness and patience from the therapist are important. There is a good prospect for improvement."

"Any other information for us tonight?"

"Yes. Some words on this subject must be addressed to Sandy. It is essential for her to understand the meaning of patience. The process of developing into a channel is a slow one and we can only take one step at a time. It is essential for her to have faith in the process itself and not to expect miracles. She is still being trained and must expect there to be times of conscious interference and inaccurate reception. That is only natural at this stage. On the other hand, she must develop confidence in her ability to serve as a channel and to use this ability for the benefit of others. Remember that very traumatic past life forces are at work leading to great resistance to use this ability, and leading to an inability to believe it can be used to help others. Keep an open mind, develop patience, and confidence will be increased as we proceed in the training process. That is all for tonight."

I was eager to come out of the trance and find out if anything I said about the woman was true. I was amazed when Burt told me it was completely accurate. The woman had brain damage and was definitely suffering from a confused thought process. Burt agreed that intensive therapy would probably result in some improvement. Receiving that accurate bit of information was encouraging. But I also felt discouraged that the material hadn't been more accurate. Why couldn't it just have said, "This woman has brain damage?" I'm afraid I don't have the patience and faith that Dick and my source keep talking to me about.

SUNDAY, OCTOBER 17, 1976

Yesterday I spent the day at a workshop on holistic healing led by Dick and Joe. Joe is a new counselor at Prana. He's in his early twenties and with his beard and glasses, looks a little like Burt. After an introductory lecture we each picked a partner and practiced feeling the energy from him/her. We would slowly run our palms over an area about one-half inch from the person's body, being very aware of the energy. We were instructed to note areas where the energy level felt different, such as cold, hot or tingly. We were told that this is often a flag to indicate imbalances in the body. Periodically, we shook our hands in the air to dispel any negative charges we might be picking up. We spent most of the day practicing in this manner, and then Dick led us all through a deep relaxation exercise.

The experience increased my desire to learn more about healing. I hadn't realized before how many people there are in the country who are interested in holistic healing. Dick told me about a nurse at New York University who teaches other nurses how to heal with their hands in a course called "The Therapeutic Touch." And I heard recently that Lawrence LeShan (author of *The Medium, The Mystic, and The Physicist*) has experimented with training people to do psychic healings. He concentrated at first on finding people who had had no previous psychic experiences. He devised a training course that taught them how to channel energy, and there were many success stories from their efforts. He's convinced that the ability to heal is within us all, and anyone can be taught the skills. I've been doing a lot of reading the past few months. I find reading very relaxing, and enjoy going to bed early with a book. I usually carry one around with me, so if I'm stuck waiting for a bus or sitting in a doctor's office, I can read. I'm also a fast reader, so I manage to consume about one book a week.

I've been re-reading some of the work of Jane Roberts. I read over her accounts of her early days with mediumship in *The Coming of Seth* and *The Seth Material*. She suffered many insecurities at first before she came to accept this personality who spoke through her in trance. I also re-read the first book that Seth dictated through her: *Seth Speaks*. He presents a very sophisticated and profound philosophy. I still don't understand it all after two readings of the book.

Dick recommended that I join the Theosophical Society. It's an international society that was founded in the 1800's by Helena Petrouna Blavatsky. Their basic philosophy is one of universal brotherhood and the universality of all religions. They don't advocate any particular religion, but they investigate the basis of all religions and philosophies. Their library is one of the most extensive in existence on religions and the occult, and members can borrow books by mail if they pay the postage. I'm considering joining.

I'm also reading books on family therapy, and I'm learning much more from my own reading than I am from the institute that Vanessa and I attend every Tuesday evening. It's quite a disappointment. I've already read far more books in the family therapy field on my own than we'll read and discuss as a class. I think I've probably read more than the instructor. The course is basic, boring, and irrelevant to the counseling I actually do at the agency. It's become quite a waste of time. Vanessa and I leave straight from work on Tuesday evenings and don't get home until after 10:00 p.m. About 10:30 every Tuesday night, I seriously consider quitting the course.

FRIDAY, OCTOBER 22, 1976

I saw Dick again last week. He began by discussing my manuscript. I had dropped off a copy of the first hundred pages of draft material at the foundation the week before.

"I read the material; so did my wife and a couple of other people connected with the foundation. Everyone found something in the material to relate to. It's really a universal story you're telling, because everyone has struggles to contend with. It doesn't matter, of course, whether or not it's ever published. As long as it helps one other person in some way it will have served its purpose."

"Do you have any criticisms or suggestions?"

"The only criticism I heard from the others was that it's not finished, and they would have liked to have read more. I don't have anything to change or add. It's your story. It's your perception of your experiences and our sessions. For me to change anything would negate the kind of philosophy I've been talking about."

I showed Dick a copy of my latest trance session.

"Well," he commented, "I agree with everything that's said here. You're not a perfect channel, but you're ready to try doing readings."

"But I don't think I have the confidence to do readings. I'm afraid of hurting someone. I'm afraid the material coming through is all my imagination." I had said those words a hundred times before. And I got the same answer Dick's given before.

"Faith and patience, Sandy. It'll take time to get the kind of material you're looking for. And you're expecting a lot. It's like you want a miracle a week. I think if Kirk materialized right here in front of you and described in detail what's going on down the street, you'd believe in your work for about one week. Then you'd be asking for another miracle next week to renew your faith. As long as you're mortal you're going to question and have doubts. They'll never completely go away. But you've got to have faith that there's a reason for all of these messages. I can wait for more specifics to come through. I'm in no hurry. And you shouldn't be either." Dick paused to light a cigarette. "Look, *I'm* supposed to be the impartial researcher looking for holes in your messages, and *you're* supposed to believe in what you're doing." We both chuckled. "Let me look for the holes. If I find any, I promise I'll let you know. Continue dropping copies of trance sessions off at the foundation. If I read something that makes me uneasy, I'll get you on the phone right away. So stop worrying and relax. Your worry just causes you to block more material and slow down your growth."

"Well, if I do decide to do these readings, what exactly will our procedure be?"

"I'll use our Prana Foundation worksheets. At the top of each sheet will be a name, a birthdate, if we've got it, and any specific questions to be asked. Perhaps you and Burt could work out a general question like Solomon uses: 'Please give any information that will help this soul's growth.' Something like that. Then when I get your readings and Jan's readings I'll compare them. Not competitively, though. I'm not trying to prove that one of you can channel better than the other. It may well work out that each of you will be proficient in a different area. Perhaps one will specialize in past lives and one in physical health. And I'd also like you to proceed blind."

"What do you mean?" I was puzzled.

"No feedback for awhile. When you begin, you're very likely to make mistakes because you're nervous. If I tell you you're making mistakes, it'll make you more nervous and you'll make more mistakes. But if you know you won't be getting any feedback, in time you'll relax, and you'll start getting really accurate material. And then we'll have something to evaluate. Ideally, we need hundreds of readings to make an evaluation. But do at least 25 before getting any feedback."

"Well, I'm sure I'll want to know immediately after each reading if it's accurate or not, but I think it would help me to relax if I knew in advance that I wouldn't get any feedback. I still need to think about this some more. I'm not ready yet."

We then proceeded to discuss the colors I've been seeing.

"You know," Dick commented, "you're very possibly beginning to see auric colors."

"But I'm not seeing a whole aura."

"You have to begin someplace. In time, you may see much more. As with everything else, you've got to have patience to let things develop one step at a time. This is an extremely valuable tool to have in your work with clients."

"Do you have any suggestions that will help me develop this? Should I study what various auric colors mean?"

"I wouldn't just yet. It's so hard to describe an auric color. What I call red might appear as pink to you. And there are many more shades of auric colors than there are of physical colors. The best thing to do is immediately write down what you see and your interpretation of what it means. Do you take notes when you're counseling?"

"Not usually, except for the first session when we fill out our forms."

"It'd help to get in the habit of taking notes. Then you can jot down colors as you see them. You may need to slightly alter your state of consciousness while with clients in order to see the colors better. In time, you'll learn to slip in and out of the state without anyone being aware of it. Of course, as with anything else, you don't want to invade people's privacy," Dick reminded me as the session ended. "Don't try to read someone's aura without their permission. Unless they've come to you for professional help. If a client comes to you for help, you have a right to utilize whatever tools are at your command—such as your intuition, trance readings, or auric readings. But in other contexts, respect privacy."

A couple days later, Burt and I did a trance session, so

he asked about my seeing colors.

"Is Sandy starting to see auras? If so, how can she learn to do this better?"

"This is a process that Sandy is slowly opening herself to. It must be done very slowly, and taken one step at a time. She is beginning to see colors near and around people which indicate the individual's character and state of mind. It will take much time before she is proficient at seeing and interpreting these colors. The training process will proceed as other training processes have proceeded. The important thing is to be open to the lessons when and how they present themselves and not try to impede or to hasten the process beyond its natural course."

Then Burt asked if there was any further message.

"Yes. Tonight we wish to again address Sandy on the importance of faith and of patience in this process of self-development. It is important for her not to expect too much too soon. It is important for her to accept within herself her own resistances, her own blocks, her own past life experiences that slow down her development now. These are all part of her and must be accepted, like any other part. It must be understood that all of these things can be overcome. They will take time. The process cannot be rushed. Look upon the progress that has been made and be grateful for that. Do not dwell on the progress that has yet to be made and be discouraged by that. These same words have much meaning at this time for Burt, in his personal struggle. Good night."

Last week, I stopped by the Foundation to drop off copies of my recent trance sessions. Dick and several other staff members were sitting around chatting, so I joined them for awhile. When I left, I had a nagging sense of foreboding. I tried to get in touch with it; it seemed to relate to something that might happen to someone who was in the room. I went home and tried to nap, but that feeling kept nagging at me. I had a strong urge to do some auto-writing. So I picked up a pencil, white-lighted myself, and waited for the flow of information to start. My arm began to move. "Is there a message for me?" I asked mentally.

"A . . . message . . . for . . . Dick," was written slowly in sprawling letters.

"What's the message?"

". . . Danger . . ."

"What is this danger?"

". . . Fire . . ."

"Where?"

". . . Home . . ."

Then the information stopped. I was puzzled. Was this a warning I should pass on? Or just nonsense? I sighed, and decided I had an obligation to pass it on. But I didn't sense an immediate danger, and I had to rush off to an evening meeting. The next morning, I was out visiting schools, but by afternoon I had a chance to call the Foundation. I felt very foolish. Dick was out, so I left a message with Pat the receptionist.

"Tell Dick I did some auto-writing last night, and got a message to warn him of a possible fire in his home."

"Did you have any other impressions about it?" she asked me.

"Well, nothing specific. So he'd better be careful of anything. Like smoking in bed. Also, I had a feeling he should make sure his kids don't play with matches. But all the message said was possible fire in his home."

The next day I called to make sure Dick had received the message and I apologized for not having given it to him personally.

"Oh, no problem. You never have to worry if you have a message to pass on to me. I take everything in context, and Pat is completely reliable. You can leave any message with her. By the way, I think the thing you were picking up already happened. Last night, I saw my son walking around hiding something in his coat. I insisted on seeing what it was. It turned out to be a propane torch that he planned to play with, not understanding how dangerous those things are. Of course, I took it away from him and explained why."

I thought about that afterwards. Perhaps I really had picked up on that incident in advance. Perhaps it was more than coincidence. But why in heaven's name couldn't I get things *specifically*? Why couldn't the auto-writing have said: "Tell Dick to watch his son because he may try to play with a propane torch tomorrow night." Why couldn't messages come through like that? It's very discouraging to just get bits and pieces and have to figure out what they mean.

SUNDAY, OCTOBER 31, 1976

In between giving out raisins to the ghosts and goblins who keep ringing our doorbell, I'll try and bring this journal up to date.

I decided to ask my source about the accuracy of the information I've been receiving, so last week Burt put the question on the agenda for our session. This was the answer:

"The information received is in general quite accurate. A great deal of information is blocked and not allowed to come through. What does come through tends to be general. The more minute the details that we attempt to transmit, the greater the chance for error. Most material up to now has been general and is quite accurate. A word misunderstood or a phrase slightly twisted makes little difference with such information."

Then Burt asked if there was any further information, and we got quite a lecture:

"It is very important to fully understand the significance of one step at a time. In your positions you are unable to look at the universe as a whole and understand the nature of reality. If you could, you would see it like a ladder. In your positions now on your planet and at your stage of evolution, you are on a particular rung of the ladder. As you develop as individuals and as a culture, additional steps on the ladder are taken. But this is a ladder on which no steps can be skipped. Every step must be taken. Every soul starts from the bottom and climbs to the top. If you fully understand this, you will realize the total futility of judging other people. There are many souls below you on this ladder. You were once where they are now. They cannot be judged because everybody must pass through the same steps, in order to advance. They can be encouraged to climb higher.

"There is no point in envy. There are souls on higher rungs of the ladder than yourselves, but in time you, too, will be on those higher rungs. But you must move at your own pace. You cannot take another step until you are fully prepared to do so. It is not like school where you can fake examinations, teachers can be misled, where luck plays an important role. On this ladder, you cannot advance until you are fully and truly ready and prepared to do so. You must learn the lessons that are meant to be learned on your present rung. You must understand that as souls you have arranged the circumstances of your lives to be appropriate to the rung of your ladder on which you are presently. The circumstances are designed to teach you the lessons you need to learn. They are designed to prepare you to take the next step on the ladder. You must fully accept your circumstances and take advantage of the opportunities that are presented to you in order to work through all that must be done at your present stage. If you do so with patience, with willingness, with openness, in time you will find that you have moved up the ladder to another step and the circumstances of your life are accordingly adjusted. This kind of process continues not only for a particular life cycle on the earth, but for many life cycles in many stages of development on many planes of reality until, ultimately, all souls are gloriously united at the top of the ladder. Good night."

Burt and I both continue to feel insecure about our new jobs, and we've been receiving encouragement on that. Burt asked in a recent session:

"Do you have any helpful words of wisdom for me regarding my job?"

"It is important for you to understand the vital nature of your work. You have been put in a particular situation where you have the opportunity of interacting with particular people and learning particular lessons. Every day you should begin with the attitude that you are going to try to be of help to as many people as possible. At the end of the day consider all the people you have helped.

208

You are doing valuable work that is of help to others. You should focus on your concern for others and your helping of them, then you will think less about your own insecurities, and you will find them disappearing over time."

"Any further information?"

"You both need to develop greater confidence in yourselves and in your abilities to help others. Focus each day on the good you are doing and you will find your own insecurities become less and less important. Good night."

Earlier this evening, we had another trance session and received a lecture on sin:

"Today we will consider the subject of sin. You have been raised in a culture that teaches the existence of sin, and of evil. The result of such teaching is great guilt and insecurity in the people of your culture. There is much searching for authority figures to learn what is right and what is sinful. There is no understanding of the fact that in the universe itself good and evil are meaningless concepts. The universe itself just *is*. The souls that inhabit the planets are what they are. This is not to imply goodness or evil, but rather to explain the importance of accepting that which is. It is important to understand that everything serves a purpose. To condemn a person or an idea as evil is to imply that no purpose is served in its existence. It is important to strive to understand the purpose in each thing that exists and to seek to learn the lessons that are available from it. All souls are struggling for perfection as each understands that term. Every soul serves a purpose no matter how evil their actions may appear. To label a person as sinful or evil is not to understand the purpose being served by their action, the lessons that are being learned by that soul, and by other souls. It is important for each soul to concentrate on its own development and growth and seek perfection through living in accordance with the flow it finds within. Do not waste time judging other people or attempting to determine what in them is good or evil. Rather, strive to understand that both concepts are confined to your plane of reality. On higher planes the universe is seen as a totality and accepted for what it is. Good night."

I still don't feel confident enough to do readings for Dick's experiment. I'd like fewer lectures and more proof from my source.

SUNDAY, NOVEMBER 28, 1976

I've been feeling in conflict about how to learn the counseling skills I need in my work. The approaches I'm learning in the family training institute run counter to my own intuitions. I've been wondering if I should try harder to learn the institute's approaches or if I should listen to my own intuitions. I asked for advice from my source, and this is the answer I received:

"Yes, there is much that could be relayed on that subject. Sandy is going to hear and read many conflicting theories. She must understand the dual approach that must be taken here. On the one hand, she is practicing therapy in her culture in the present time. It is important to be aware of the theories that are being practiced in that place and time. They help orient her to the state of development of counseling theories and the general background of the clients she serves. However, on the other hand, she also has access to far more advanced theories learned centuries ago on her home planet and that she has been studying over the past years in the sleep state. Therefore, it will also be important for her to draw on this knowledge which is now buried below conscious levels. Part of her task is to bring this more sophisticated theory into consciousness and to practice it in her work. Part of the conflict now is her lack of trust in her own intuitions."

Something strange has been happening in our trance sessions lately. My voice changes. Occasionally, for short periods, it becomes husky and strong, instead of the usual soft hypnotic voice I have in trance. Perhaps it's due to the fact that I'm recovering from a slight cold.

The type of information coming through hasn't

changed, though. We're still getting lectures. This is one of the more recent:

"Tonight we will consider the power of thought processes. It is not fully understood on your plane that your physical reality is the end result of thought processes. Your thoughts create your reality. By the same token, your thoughts can be utilized to give yourself a harmonious and productive life rather than a negative and unfulfilling one. It is important to dwell on the positive and the beautiful and the productive and the fulfilling aspects of your life. To dwell on these things will set up vibrational frequencies which will attract more of these things to you. To dwell on the negative, the ugly, the unfulfilling will accomplish the opposite. When you put yourself in a position where those thoughts will create a negative reality for you, you are not yet able to appreciate on your plane that thoughts create reality. However, you can begin to appreciate some aspects of this by attempting in your own lives to dwell on the positive and you will then be able to see that you're creating for yourself a positive reality in your own life. Good night."

In our latest session, Burt again asked about the source of the information. I'm confused by the fact that sometimes the information uses "I" and other times "we." When Burt asked the question, I sensed a gentle amusement, and was told telepathically: "Well, I'll explain it again but you still won't understand it." The answer that came out of my mouth was:

"We will attempt to provide further clarification. However, it must be kept in mind that this process cannot be fully understood with your conceptual framework. When 'we' is used, it can be understood as a number of friendly and protective spirits working together on this project. Although the information must be understood as coming from within Sandy, Kirk is always present to facilitate the reception of information telepathically."

I was disappointed that the answer didn't provide much more clarification. Telepathically, I received: "We tried to warn you that you still wouldn't understand it."

We also got another lecture in that session:

"Tonight we will discuss the importance of self-concept. It is extremely important to maintain a positive attitude towards the self. For your attitude towards your self projects an image that you adapt yourself to. Those around you come to see this image as the real you. If you have a basic love for yourself, and accept all of yourself, then you will project those images to other people. The thoughts that you have about yourself create the kind of person you are and that other people see you as. Keep a positive mental outlook at all times and you will be amazed at the difference in your self and your life."

I continue to feel discouraged about this information. I often ask about my clients, and receive true, but general, information. Much of it I already knew consciously so it isn't proof of anything. Sometimes Burt asks me about his patients. Recently he asked about a man who, according to the source, felt very lonely and isolated. He needed to feel wanted by other people. Burt agreed afterwards that the man was lonely, but, he pointed out, in our alienated society, we're all lonely, so that statement could apply to anyone. He also asked me recently about a woman, and was told: "This is a woman who is very troubled over certain past behaviors. She can be helped to come to terms with her guilt and come to accept herself. This will take much time." Afterwards, Burt said that there are past behaviors that this woman feels guilty about. But, again, most people feel guilty about something in their past.

I agreed with Burt that my statements were too general to prove anything. Discouraged, I went back to see Dick last Friday. We spent most of the time discussing my doubts.

"I think we're looking at this material very differently," he commented after reading my latest trance material. "For example, this statement about the woman who feels guilty. I think that's a very specific statement. Or, at least it's very directive in terms of where counseling could begin. And, look, something else you've got to remember. You're asking for information on people who did not request a reading. This information is more designed for you or for Burt, as counselors. I think you'd probably get

213

more specific material on people who had requested a reading."

"My main concern right now is: where is the information coming from? I'm definitely not producing it consciously; I'm not making it up. Now if it's really authentic, really from high levels, then it would be coming from my super-conscious. Right?"

"Right."

"Now if it's not coming from that level, then it's coming from sub-conscious or unconscious levels. So what the question boils down to is: does the information come from super-conscious levels or sub-conscious levels. Right?"

"Right. Now, your sub-conscious mind has been programmed from birth. It's absorbed every book you've ever read, every philosophy you've ever heard, every thought you've ever had. And in a relaxed state you can recall much more of this material and organize it more logically. Now, if I were playing devil's advocate here, I could argue that actually what you're doing is utilizing your vast academic background to answer the questions. It's possible. But what I see is that the information is offering you very sound advice. So what if you're organizing and feeding back to yourself your own academic training? That's great. There's certainly nothing wrong with it."

"If the information is coming from that level, then it'll never get very specific. I won't be able to do readings on people I don't know. Right?"

"That's correct."

"Is there any way to find out for sure which level I'm drawing on?"

"No, there's no way to know for sure. We've got certain details, that I consider more specific than you do. Like the man who's lonely. I think that's a very specific piece of information."

"Well, *I* don't consider it very specific."

"Perhaps you're not supposed to get more details. Remember karma. Suppose I told you everything that was going to happen to you in the next week, and it was all traumatic. Then as you lived through it, it wouldn't even affect you because you knew it was coming and knew it would be over soon. So you might lose a very valuable opportunity to grow from that experience. It's just not a good idea for us to know our future in great details."

"I understand that. But nothing has come through yet to convince me that I'm in touch with the super-conscious."

"I'm 80% convinced. I see this material as a lot more specific than you do. It's specific enough for you as a counselor to get a handle on a client's situation. And again, you might get even more specifics if you did readings on volunteers. I anticipated that we'd get into this during today's session, so I already have a volunteer for you. Joe Hebert. You know him, he's one of our Prana staff members. He's volunteered to be a subject for a reading. Now you know his head's together on this stuff. He's not going to freak out from anything that's said. He can evaluate it objectively. From your perspective, you should tell yourself that it doesn't matter if the material is right or wrong. See it as a name to practice on."

"I feel uneasy about doing one on somebody I already know. I'd rather start with a stranger."

"I could give you a name you don't know. A client that I'm seeing. She has not specifically requested a reading, however."

"Well, give me her name, and also write down her birthdate. Maybe I'll do them."

Dick wrote down the information, and gave it to me in an envelope so that I wouldn't see it until Burt read it to me while I was in trance. I'm not sure if I'm going to do these readings or not.

THURSDAY, DECEMBER 23, 1976

I started Dick's experiment this month. I began with the name he gave of a client. I was very apprehensive about doing it, but tried to remain relaxed and let the information come through. Burt asked: "Can you provide any information on the general health or karmic conditions of _____ that would be helpful to her at this time." This is the answer we received:

"Yes. This is a woman who needs much help. At this time she is experiencing many insecurities and needs much reassurance. It is especially important for her to understand that she is able to overcome the insecurities and fears that beset her at the present time. She is experiencing some frightening things that are created by her own mind. Through many reassurances and practicing a more positive outlook this period in her life can be passed through and she can move into a more tranquil period. At the present time she is resisting spiritual growth within herself. If she can learn to accept the power of prayer and if she can learn to maintain rapport with the universal flow that is within she will discover much peace. It is also important that she eat regular meals on a regular basis, taking care to insure proper nutrition and eating slowly in a relaxed manner."

I also sensed a number of impressions as the words were coming through. I saw a circle of dark, murky blue. And I had the impression that she might be experiencing hallucinations or delusions and that she needed to understand that they were not real.

I dropped the reading off at the foundation several days later. Then the following week, I stopped by to give Dick more completed portions of the manuscript.

"Well, Sandy," he said, "your first reading was very interesting. I know I said no evaluations till later, but I want to give you a little feedback that you may find encouraging. That woman definitely has delusions. That's what I'm working with her on."

Dick said that very matter-of-factly, and without surprise. But I found it a mind-blowing statement. Something accurate had really come through on a person I had never heard of. Coincidence, maybe? Or was I really channeling information from some high-level source?

I felt encouraged after Dick's comment, but, of course, the encouragement only lasted a few days. Then I became discouraged again by the usual non-specific material. I also became confused. I read someone's theory that we could develop consciousness to the point of communicating with beings from other planets. I remembered Kirk had lived on another planet. So I had Burt ask: "Is Kirk presently living in body on another planet?" The answer was astounding:

"Yes. In the sense in which you understand this question, it could be said that Kirk is presently living a lifetime elsewhere."

I had always assumed that Kirk was a spirit. How else can one be a spirit guide? I had asked the question out of idle curiosity, never imagining that I'd get a positive answer. Burt asked about it again in our next session:

"Can you explain how Kirk can serve as a guide for Sandy at the same time he is living in body elsewhere?"

"This can be explained, but unfortunately not in terms that will be understandable to you. Kirk is presently living on another planet but is able to serve as a protector spirit for these contacts. It is necessary to understand the nature of space and time in order to fully appreciate how this can happen."

I do get tired of being told I won't understand, even though I'm sure that that's true. I'm also finding it hard to accept receiving nebulous, spiritual answers for very specific questions. We've been feeling overwhelmed with all our bills. We don't seem able to make ends meet on our new, smaller salaries. So Burt asked for advice from our source:

"I'm quite concerned about our financial situation. Can you give us any information or advice?"

"It is important that you maintain contact with the flow that is within. When you do so, you will find that such problems tend to disappear. It is important not to allow yourselves to worry or to engage in negative thinking on the issue. Rather open yourselves up to inner forces within and this contact will give you the faith you need to face such problems with tranquility and to place them in proper context."

Burt feels discouraged sometimes, too, by such answers.

"Why can't the source just give us the winning lottery number for this week?" Burt asked recently over dinner. "That would be a concrete way of helping us with our financial problems!"

I laughed. "If we asked for the winning number, we'd probably get a lecture on the importance of listening to our inner voices, to help us put money in its proper perspective. I also think that if we did get the winning lottery number it would be the last information we ever got. I feel strongly that I'm not to ever use any psychic force for making money. I suppose because I did that in Amsterdam. I'm not even going to keep any money if my book is published. Any royalties will go to the Prana Foundation and perhaps some other charities."

I also get a bit tired of all the lectures. A recent topic has been our concern over financial matters:

"Yes. Tonight we will discuss the importance of living the life as a preparation for death. When a soul becomes immersed in earthly or materialistic concerns, that soul is denying the recognition of the true nature of life. Your life in the earthly cycle is a preparation for further development elsewhere. Your time on the earth should be utilized to prepare the soul for this further development. It is important to seek out the lessons that are to be learned and to experience as many growth-fulfilling activities as possible. Do not allow yourselves to become entrapped in concern for earthly matters. Over-involvement in such concerns will lengthen the amount of time that must be spent in the earthly cycle before advancing elsewhere. Rather keep in mind that the purpose of life is for growth and development of the soul. Keep yourselves open to such development and attuned to the flow within, that makes such development possible."

We also continue to receive lectures on faith. I am trying to pay more attention to the lectures. I must admit that they make sense. And when we try to apply the philosophy in our lives, we both feel much better. I'm still waiting, however, for more proof.

Yesterday Burt received a thick envelope from the Prana Foundation in the mail. It contains a half-dozen worksheets with names and birthdates for readings. I finally feel ready to do them.

We're leaving tomorrow for a week in Illinois, to spend the holidays with our families. As soon as we return, I'll start doing the readings in the packet Dick sent. I want very much to know if the information is coming from the super-conscious, and I'm ready to co-operate in Dick's experiment to find out.

SUNDAY, JANUARY 23, 1977

We devoted most of our trance sessions this month to the names Dick sent. The readings are getting longer, but they're still general. Sometimes the material relates to past life forces or to the path the soul has chosen for this life. It's going to be very difficult to evaluate material like that.

I enjoy doing the readings. It gives me a sense of satisfaction, even when I don't receive feedback. I'm developing a little more confidence that I won't hurt people.

My voice is continuing to change. Occasionally, for a phrase or a few sentences, my voice becomes husky and strong. This happens most often during the readings, rather than while answering personal questions for us or giving a lecture.

We haven't had as many lectures this month. One we received was very encouraging, since we're both still suffering from the insecurities on our jobs:

"Yes. This evening we would like to leave you with a few words of encouragement in your busy lives. It is important to understand that you are both entering new career patterns that entail much growth. This growth produces stress and insecurity. These will pass with proper application of spiritual principles. Utilize these lessons for growth. Strive to maintain your inner harmony and balance. Periods of greater stability and slower growth are ahead. Do not wallow in feelings of insecurity. You are in your present positions in order to obtain the necessary security and confidence for future work. Use these opportunities. Do not reject them. They give you the opportunity to learn the lessons you need. This is all for tonight."

This was a reassuring message, since I still feel insecure on my job, and we've been extremely busy the past few months. I have a full schedule almost every day in the office. In between appointments with clients, I have to find time to do the administrative work, which I'm always behind on. And we're always getting announcements of "Important Meetings" that either Vanessa or I have to find the time to attend, and I've recently started seeing a family at the agency on Saturday mornings. Often, I'm just plain weary. On top of work, there's our family therapy class every Tuesday night. And Burt and I devote a lot of time to holding trance sessions which I later type from the tape. Of course, I'm still writing in this journal when I can find a few spare moments, which isn't often. And I got some very discouraging news this week: my advisor sent my dissertation back (again) requesting that two chapters be completely rewritten. I wonder if my work will ever satisfy him. I wonder if the degree is worth the effort. I'd like to quit, but hate to do so after five years of doctoral work.

Burt has been very busy, too. He's working one evening a week doing family therapy. And his days are also extremely full and taxing. He seldom gets home before 6:30 or 7:00 p.m. evenings. And he's also completing work on his dissertation, which has to be squeezed into evenings and weekends.

We're tired in the evenings. After intense involvement with other people all day, we both need time alone to recharge our batteries. We both meditate, and I do some yoga. Then we spend time quietly reading or writing in the study. Occasionally we watch something on television. It's often 9:00 or 10:00 before we're ready to sit down together and discuss what our days have been like. And that doesn't give us much time before we go to bed. Our weekends are too often a busy round of laundry, shopping, house-cleaning and paying bills. We've been spending most of our weekend evenings at home, listening to music or chatting with each other or Judy. Burt recently brought home some books on massage, and we've been trying some of the techniques on each other.

We need to find more time just to relax together. We can't afford to go away for a weekend. So we decided this week that sometime soon we'll take a weekend as a vacation at home. No chores or errands. We'll pick up a guide book on New Haven and see some of the things in the area we've never found the time for. We can pretend to be tourists in our own town. I sure hope the source is right, that less hectic periods are ahead. I'm ready to start counting the days.

Despite the busy schedule, I still find time to read. A book I'm just finishing is *The Open Door* by Theon Wright. It's the account of his father's experience with automatic writing, and also the experiences of Theon and his brother who developed the ability in adulthood. They received beautiful messages from their source, which I found quite an inspiration.

Of course I thought, "I wish I could receive beautiful messages like that instead of all these lectures which are probably just from my sub-conscious feeding back to me all these books I'm reading." Ah, well. Dick says the doubts will never go away. I guess I'll have to learn to live with them.

SATURDAY, FEBRUARY 19, 1977

I saw Dick early this month and told him I was interested in learning to go into deeper trances. So he explained a new technique we could use involving colors.

"One of the most effective vibrations that the human body is capable of responding to is the vibration of light. White light is the highest vibration, consisting of all light. Black is the absence of all light. What we do is break down the vibrations of white into seven colors: red, orange, yellow, green, blue, indigo, violet. By breaking down the spectrum of white, you allow the body to raise the life-force or kundalini from the base of the spine up through the seven chakras. You'll become intimately involved with each color and actually be able to feel its vibrations. You may feel pretty floaty at times. If you panic, I'll slow you down and relax you. If you can let yourself go, you'll feel more secure than by holding on. This method has been used by psychics, seers, clairvoyants for centuries. You may feel a lot of wild sensations. It's like taking a trip, but without drugs."

"And I can use this technique at home to do readings?"

"Yes, that's why I'm teaching it to you. I'll put it on tape so you can play it back. I'd advise you to be discreet about sharing it with others. It does work. People should know what they're doing before they try it. And someone could flake out a little bit if they used this approach without proper preparation. Not that it's going to hurt them, but they could panic and it could turn them off. In time, after you become comfortable with this technique, you can add the vibrations of sound. One of the most effective mantras is the simple word "om." If pronounced correctly, and this is very important—it must be done correctly—you can chant it seven times after going through the color spectrum. It's a mantra that could literally take you out of your body for many constructive purposes."

Before we started, though, I wanted to cover some other questions. By the time we finished, there wasn't time to do the trance exercise, so I made an appointment for two weeks later. While he was writing out my next appointment slip, I asked if he could give me any comments on my latest readings. The recorder was off, but my recollection of his answer is:

"Over half are very good. They're very applicable to the person in question. The rest stink. I think you're trying too hard. You've got to relax and let the information come through very naturally. You may be trying to get specifics to please me or yourself. You can't try. You've got to let it happen."

I left feeling very discouraged. If almost half my readings were really bad, there didn't seem any point in continuing. I once again decided to give up doing readings.

By the next day, I was depressed. It was an uncommon feeling. In the past months, I've felt discouraged or unhappy at times. But it had been ages since I'd been depressed. I didn't like the feeling. But I couldn't pull myself out of it.

After a few days, I decided to call Dick and see if I could come in sooner than the scheduled appointment. I got an appointment for the next week.

"I want to explain why I requested an earlier appointment," I said when I arrived. "I'm depressed. When you said last week that almost half my readings stink, I got discouraged and stopped doing readings. And then I got depressed. I seem to get depressed whenever I stop doing them."

"I said *what* last week?" Dick responded surprised.

"That almost half my readings stink."

Dick looked puzzled. "Do you have that on tape?" I shook my head. "It certainly doesn't sound like something I'd say. And it's not what I believe. You may have misunderstood me. Let me explain. A little over half of the material you've come up with I can verify as being accurate and applicable to the person in question. The rest, I can't judge. I'm putting it away until my sessions with the clients have developed further; maybe later the material will make more sense. It may be 100% accurate. In any case, it's too soon to evaluate the work either you or Jan's doing. We need hundreds of readings to make an assessment."

"I'd like everything to be completely accurate and verifiable "

"I know that. But, look, Sandy, you've got to realize that nobody is judging you. You've got to believe that. In no way am I judging you. It doesn't matter to me if you hit ten out of ten or zero out of ten. It doesn't make you less worthwhile as a person. If other people are judging you, that's their bag. If you're judging yourself, that's your bag. You don't have to do it."

"I'm still afraid of somebody being hurt by one of my readings."

"That's why we're using this procedure. I examine all readings. I may discreetly share some of the information with the person in question if I feel it would be helpful to them. If I think they're not ready for it, I hold back on it for awhile, or explain it to them in terms that they can accept. Look at it the other way; people may be helped by your readings. Shall we take it to extremes again? Suppose you do a thousand readings, and only one of them is helpful to someone. Wasn't it worth it? It would certainly be worth my time to go through those thousand readings."

"Yes, I guess so. The strange thing is that I get depressed when I don't do readings."

"Look Sandy, if you came in and said that every time you did a reading, you got extremely depressed, I'd suggest that that may not be your path and perhaps you should try something else. So when you say that you get depressed when you don't do readings, I can only suggest that you do readings!"

We both laughed. I was feeling fine again, and was ready to try the color exercise.

Dick went through each color: red, orange, yellow,

green, blue, indigo, and violet. He told me that the color was flowing into every cell of my body and surrounding my body. Then he said the color was changing to the next one on the spectrum. We ended with white, after which he had me pray for protection, and then asked me some general questions. I've never felt so high in my life. I really felt in another dimension—very detached from the questioning process. Afterwards Dick commented on my voice change, saying it sounded masculine.

I also showed him some of the dreams in my notebook, and he noted that my handwriting had undergone quite a change. "It's a bi-vert's writing. That's someone who's neither introverted nor extroverted. A very objective, almost scientific mind. It's excellent in your work. It means you won't get emotionally involved with clients."

"I'm afraid, though, that I do. One of my biggest problems right now, both as a counselor and as a channel, is that I'm afraid of hurting someone. It makes me insecure in dealing with clients."

Dick told me that I needed to get over that fear and develop greater faith. That's easier said than done.

We finished our session about noon, and Jan came by for her afternoon session with Dick. His schedule was light that day, so we all went down the street for lunch together.

"Would you like to borrow my tape recording?" I quipped to Dick. "You'll probably be going over with Jan this afternoon the same things we talked about!"

"Actually," Dick responded, "I've been wondering if you two would like to have some joint sessions. It would cut down on your expense and my time. I do repeat a lot of material for you both. You have the same questions, the same doubts, the same insecurities."

"How often have we each asked: 'How do I know this isn't just my imagination?'" Jan asked Dick in jest.

"Oh, you both asked it once," he responded. We all laughed, since the statement was so obviously untrue.

We decided to hold a joint session the following week. Dick said he'd like to teach us a new technique at that time.

The following week, Dick told both of us to relax, and

he would give us a name of a person. We were to try to picture that person's body, examining it carefully for anything that seemed indicative of disease or illness. He casually threw out Joe's name as one to practice on. After a few minutes, he asked what we had experienced.

"I didn't really get into it at all," I commented. "Shortly after we started, I got a sharp pain in my neck, which was very distracting."

"That's strange," Jan said, "I saw something in his neck that wasn't quite right—like a sprained muscle."

"You both picked up on the same thing," Dick commented. "Joe *does* have a pain in his neck right now. I've been sending him energy, but it hasn't cleared up yet. You both picked up on that in your own ways. That is another very effective technique for doing readings, and one which the two of you could practice together between sessions."

Dick gave us a list of names to use for readings utilizing this new technique. He suggested that the two of us get together and take turns reading the names to each other, jotting down any impressions that came to us. He admonished us not to compare answers until we were all through.

After the session, Jan and I went out for tea. "I feel very discouraged by what happened in the session, Jan," I said. "I have neck pains sometimes anyway from an old whip-lash injury. I'm convinced that the pain I felt was just coincidence. But you were really able to see the pain. I feel inadequate every time I talk to you. Your messages are so beautiful, and I'm convinced you're in touch with a high-level source. But what I'm doing is imagination. That's what I feel much of the time. I don't see any point in my doing readings at all, when you can do them much better."

"I can't believe you're saying that! It's exactly how I feel. I felt very inadequate in there with Dick, because you had actually felt the pain, and I hadn't. I feel the same way about your messages and your readings. I'm convinced that *you're* in touch with a high-level source, and that what *I* do is imagination."

228

We both laughed, and agreed to start turning to each other for support between sessions. We can give Dick a break from all the confidence-boosting he does by doing some of it for each other.

A couple of strange things have been happening lately while I meditate. One is that I recently received a personal mantra. I generally use "om" or no mantra at all. But during a recent meditation, a two-syllable word that has no meaning to me popped into mind. I tried to ignore it, but it kept coming back. I sensed very strongly that it was a mantra devised for my own state of development, and one that would help me grow further. I've been using it, and find that I'm getting into much deeper states than ever before.

MONDAY, MARCH 28, 1977

Jan and I got together recently to try doing health readings. They're much easier than the usual trance readings, because we didn't go into trance, or at least we were in extremely light trances. We just relaxed, pictured a body and tried to tune into the vibrations and visualize anything abnormal. We scheduled a joint session with Dick to discuss our results, but Jan couldn't make it at the last minute. So Dick and I met. He read through our impressions, and pointed out a number of observations that were accurate. There were also a large number he was unable to judge, and a few that were wrong.

"You're still both hitting over 50%. That's above chance level."

I suppose I should be pleased with that, but I'd like more impressive results.

After our session, Dick invited me to join him for lunch.

"I'll come along for a cup of tea," I responded, "but I've got a headache and don't feel like eating. I've had a touch of flu the past couple of days."

"Would you like me to send you some energy?" Dick asked.

"Sure," I responded, curious as to what that would involve.

He had me sit in a straight-backed chair with my eyes closed. I'm not sure what happened after that. I think he charged the aura around my head with energy. I felt a little better afterwards, but there wasn't much change. Throughout the afternoon I felt weak, run-down, and achish. Until early evening. Then I felt a great surge of energy gradually moving through my body. The weakness vanished, as did the headache and body aches. I'll bet Dick's energy charge finally took effect.

Burt and I are holding trance sessions regularly, and some odd things are happening with them. My main problem is that I'm too consciously involved with the material. I listen closely to everything that's coming through, and evaluate it critically. I know I have to avoid that, yet I'm probably too insecure or too unskilled to leave my body during trance. I read something once about ego projection, which involves projecting the consciousness without the astral body leaving the physical. I don't know much about it, but I've had a strong urge to try it during the trance sessions. So during one session early this month I tried to imagine I was in the kitchen. I could see our kitchen easily, and could almost convince myself that my consciousness was actually there. I remembered that Dick had once said you can tell if an image is imagination by trying to change it. So I tried to make the dirty dishes in our sink disappear, and they were gone instantly. "A pretty neat trick!" I decided. That proved that my experience was imagination, but I was having a good time and didn't care. I was barely aware of Burt's questions and the answers that were coming out of my mouth. I decided to try pretending I was in our front yard. I did so, and noticed that the streets were wet. I knew that we hadn't had any rain, so again, I was imagining the experience. But I was still having fun, so projected to a near-by park. I walked along the duck pond, thinking how nice it was to stroll through the park alone at night without worrying about muggers.

After the session, I remembered what had transpired, but my recollections were hazier than usual. I read over Burt's notes. We've recently started a new system of recording the trance material. In addition to tape recording it, Burt takes everything down in long-hand. Usually, my voice is slow enough for him to get everything, but if anything is missing, I go over it on the tape. It saves me a lot of time.

I noticed that Burt had asked about the effects of pot, and received this answer:

"This drug suppresses the reactions of the central nervous system in ways not yet understood. It has a profound impact on the functioning of the brain and its reception of sense data. This is not yet fully understood. It is no more harmful than many other commonly-used substances in your culture. That does not excuse its harmful effects. A truly healthy culture is a drugless culture. True spiritual growth is best attained without these artificial aids. It is preferable to meditate."

Then he asked about pipe smoking.

"Yes. Here we have yet another drug commonly used in your culture. The smoke exerts a noxious influence on red blood cells and the body's oxygen supply. This smoke is breathed in from the air even if not inhaled directly. Understand that this habit will impede the body's development in yoga postures and proper breathing."

"OK," Burt then asked, "how about sex?"

"What is the question?" came out of my mouth.

"Any comments on it?"

"The sexual release of energy is an important aspect of the body's maintenance of harmony and its sense of rapport with higher spiritual energies. It must be understood that all energy flows from the same spiritual source. Sexual energy is no exception. The enjoyment of sex is appreciated on a most profound level when its spiritual aspect is understood. It is best to share such an experience with a partner who also understands its spiritual aspects."

We then did a reading and ended the session.

Several days later we held another session. It had been a hectic day for both of us. We had been doing housework, which neither of us enjoys, and contemplating a possible move, since our house has been sold and the new landlord is considering a large rent increase. I was tired, and Burt was in a bad mood as the session started. I hadn't realized just how bad his mood was until I got into the trance state. Then I became very perceptive of his vibrations. I was very uncomfortable about proceeding with such down vibrations in the room, but attempted to do so anyway. Burt asked about moving.

"It is important to rely on the light that is within. Do not belabor this decision. The path will be clear when the time is right."

I could tell that Burt was very disappointed in the answer, and it increased his bad mood. He started fumbling at the desk where he was writing, and some books fell off. I couldn't stay in trance any longer, so slowly brought myself out.

Burt was grouchy, and complained about getting such a general answer when we needed help. I became very defensive, and said I was doing the best I could and if he didn't like the answers, he could stop asking questions. Later, both our moods improved.

A couple weeks later, we decided to spend a Sunday afternoon looking at apartments to see what was available. We looked at one just down the street, and we loved it. Although not as spacious or with the old-fashioned charm of our present place, it's very pleasant. It's right across the street from the park, has a lovely porch, and even has room in the back for a garden. And it's cheaper than our present apartment. After mulling it over for a couple of days, we realized that we both wanted to take that place, so signed the lease. We move the first of next month. "You know," Burt commented recently, "that answer we received about the move really was more profound than I realized at the time. The path *was* clear at the right time, and we didn't have to belabor the decision after all. Things just happened."

Things have been rather hectic lately preparing for the move, and we haven't been doing many trance sessions. Recently, while meditating, I felt Kirk's presence and realized he had a message for me. I was surprised. I haven't been contacted during meditation for months, not since we began regular trance sessions. I allowed energy to enter my arm and immediately sensed a cheery "Hi!"

"Who or what am I in contact with?" I asked mentally.

"Kirk," came back mentally, with my arm also moving to write out the name in the air.

"Why are you contacting me this way?"

"It's the only way I can contact you right now. You

haven't been using the trance format," I received mentally.

"Do you have a message for me?"

"Yes. Continue the readings."

"Using the trance format?"

"Yes."

"Do I get rusty when I'm away from it?"

"Most definitely."

Then the energy went away. I guess that message was pretty clear.

We did a session the next day, and Burt gave me a name for a reading. I had run out of names from Dick, so Jan had given me the name and birthdate of a friend who was interested in a reading.

"This is a soul whose development must be undertaken in various areas at this time. There is some reluctance here to develop in these directions. The soul knows its history and its path. But there is difficulty in the conscious attention to several areas. Observe the food and the eating patterns. Beware of heavy and rich foods that can have a self-destructive effect on the body. Limit the alcoholic beverages. It is important here to modify the diet along simpler and more nutritious lines. It is important also to examine the sleep patterns. Regular sleep on a routine basis is extremely important, especially for this body.

"There are self-destructive tendencies here. They must be guarded against. It is also important to look to the spiritual development. An inward search is desirable here. Turn the thoughts inside. Search for understanding of the self. Strive to understand the place of self in the universal pattern. Meditation can be of help here. Observe also the relationships with others. Strive to develop greater empathy and concern for other souls. Develop further the need for companionship of others. Strive to make this companionship one that is compatible for others concerned. Strive to develop deep caring and search to understand others. The search to understand others will help in the striving for self-understanding. This will aid in the greater appreciation of universal forces and patterns."

I was concerned about that reading. I knew absolutely

nothing about Jan's friend, and was afraid that it could be very upsetting for someone to receive a reading saying he was self-destructive. So I gave Jan a call and read it to her.

"It's extremely accurate, Sandy," she responded. "I don't know about the alcohol, I wouldn't say he has any alcohol problem. But the rest is definitely very descriptive of my friend."

"But do you think you ought to give him the reading? It could be upsetting."

"Well, he requested it. And we have to have faith that it came through for a reason. Yes, send me a copy and I'll give it to him."

I was extremely surprised that something came through I hadn't known consciously.

I felt very high in that session, and enjoyed my "stroll in the park." Burt reported that my voice change was more pronounced than ever before, being very gutteral and fast-paced.

Pat, Prana's receptionist, recently told me that Joe's brother, John, was starting a prayer group. She hoped to attend, and Joe would be going. I was intrigued. I've been getting very interested in healing, and decided to go to the first meeting. It was held last week.

It wasn't until I started driving to Milford for the meeting that I realized how nervous I was. All my old fears came back to me. Could I help channel healing energy? Or would I hurt people by trying?

I had a very minor auto accident on the way, and arrived feeling tense, a little scared, and with a neck ache. Joe was there, and I met his brother John. Their sister Sue was also there, and another woman named Cindy, with her husband. They were all in their late 20's or early 30's. Sue, John, and Joe had been involved in another prayer group last year held weekly at Dick's house, so had some experience. Joe explained the procedure.

"Absolutely anyone can come to our group any Wednesday evening. And absolutely anyone can request to be put on our list for any reason. But they must request it of their own accord. And they stay on the list for two weeks. After that, they have to provide a progress report and request to remain on if they wish to continue. That's how we did it at Dick's. Would you all like to continue with that procedure?"

We all agreed, so Joe proceeded to explain the techniques of sending energy. "Everyone will have to develop their own technique. One of the most common is to envision a white light around the person. Or you can imagine yourself being there and doing hands-on healing. Or just meditate on their well-being, and picture them happy and healthy." Sue and John discussed other methods. I asked about Lawrence LeShan's technique of meditating on the person and trying to merge your consciousness with theirs (his "Type I" healing). Joe said that's one of the most effective approaches.

Later, we practiced meditating together and tried sending energy to Sue, who requested it. I told about my neck ache. Joe had me sit in a chair, and he put his hands on my neck. Then everyone stood in a line behind him, each one touching the person in front, and all focusing on sending energy to my neck. After a few minutes, the ache had gone completely.

I left feeling relaxed, and look forward to going back next week.

FRIDAY, APRIL 29, 1977

I'm developing a greater acceptance of my trance experiences. I'm still not convinced that I'm in touch with super-conscious knowledge, but becoming more relaxed with the process. Perhaps because of my greater relaxation, changes are occurring.

Our first session this month was on the 9th, the evening before my thirtieth birthday. We hadn't had a session in almost two weeks because of the move. Burt began by asking: "How is the trance this evening?"

The response was: "Tonight we have a trance sufficient for the purpose at hand. The long absence from trance states has somewhat impeded the development along these lines. This progress can still be achieved in coming sessions."

Next Burt asked about massage, which we're both interested in. I decided it was time to try sending my consciousness elsewhere. My arms and hands felt very heavy, almost paralyzed. Although I'm usually immobile in trance, this time I felt a tingling or warmth in my arms. I was uncomfortable, so I pictured myself strolling through the park. Suddenly I was on a cliff overlooking the ocean. A very developed, spiritual being appeared on my left. We sat on the rocks and conversed telepathically. Afterwards I had only a vague sense of the conversation; it was like a dream. Later I read what I had said about massage:

"Yes. This activity has importance on many levels. On the purely physical level, there is increased relaxation and receptivity to healing energies. There is energy transfer from the person giving the massage. It is important that this person have loving and healing intentions in this activity. There may be transfer of the higher or spiritual

237

energies during this process. It can be a very energizing experience under the proper circumstances. The masseur should meditate and pray before the massage and allow healing energies to enter the hands. During the massage the masseur should concentrate on the highest good of the person receiving the massage. This person should keep a clear mind empty of rambling thoughts and open to reception of positive thoughts and feelings. There may be telepathic transfer from the masseur to the person being massaged. This is one reason why the masseur must focus on loving and healing thoughts. This is a sophisticated technique, but it is in a primitive state of development on your plane."

When I came out of the trance, I had no feelings in my hands. I was still extremely relaxed, but mildly concerned, wondering if my hands would be numb for the rest of my life. But in a few minutes, they felt perfectly normal.

Our next trance session was on Sunday evening, the 17th. Again, I imagined myself to be strolling in the park. A great luminous figure in white appeared on my right and strolled with me. I had difficulty focusing my awareness in the park, and would periodically pop back to our study for a few moments.

Burt hadn't been feeling well lately and had been experiencing some discomfort that he thought was prostrate trouble. He asked for information regarding his health.

"This is a complex situation. There are karmic factors involved here. It is important to meditate. The body must be cared for well. It will be found that hot baths are very soothing for this body, especially with a small amount of bicarbonate of soda added to the water with a few grains of salt. Drinking fruit juices can be of help here, especially apple, cherry, and cranberry. Long walks also can be of help."

I was listening to this answer while also strolling in the park with the luminous being. I complained to him that a lot of nonsense was coming through for Burt on bathing. He smiled lovingly and encouraged me to focus my concentration in the park and forget what was happening to my body. I tried, but wasn't totally successful.

My voice changes were even more marked than usual, and Burt asked what they meant:

"This is a question of concern to Sandy also. It cannot be fully explained to your level of understanding. There are high energies flowing into the body and utilizing the body as a channel. As Sandy allows this energy to utilize the body, there is less conscious control over the body. The vocal cords are controlled by this energy more than by the conscious mind. This difference in source of control causes the change. It is normal under the circumstances and nothing to be concerned about. Now a great deal of energy has passed through and the body is fatigued. We will take our leave now and wish you both a good evening."

After coming out, I couldn't use my hands for a few minutes—they were so full of energy that I couldn't manipulate them physically. The energy drained into my little fingers and then disappeared. Burt commented on another change that had occurred during the session: my head kept moving from side to side. I didn't know why, and hadn't been consciously moving it, although I was aware of it.

The following week, I attended the Wednesday night healing group. I've been going to every meeting, and Burt is considering joining us soon. I'm getting to know the members better and like them all very much. I'm also becoming more comfortable with attempting to send energy. The group has been an enjoyable experience for me. But that week I was very uncomfortable with an experience I had.

As we were sending energy, I was extremely relaxed and "high," in an altered state of consciousness. Suddenly I was aware of a presence and energy in my arm as it shot up. A message was written in the air.

"Hi!"

"What am I in contact with?" I asked mentally.

"Kirk."

"Why?"

"To receive a message."

"For who?"

"The group. Someone is here who is on the pass-over list. She wants to say 'thank you' for your help. Her name is J."

That's all I received. I sat there feeling very uncomfortable. I knew everyone had their eyes closed, except for Sue who was reading the cards with the names on them. We always turned out the lights, and the reader sat near a candle to read. I wondered if Sue had seen my arm in the air and what she would think if she had. I understood the message. Every week, after the names are read for healing, a list is read of people who have died recently. We prayed for guidance for their souls, and pictured them being led towards a white light and being met by a guide. I knew there would be several names on the list that evening; they were the same ones that had been read the week before. But I couldn't consciously remember any of them. Possibly there's a woman whose name started with J. I struggled over whether or not to share the message with the group. Was it supposed to be shared? I didn't want to share it. I felt foolish. The group knew nothing about my work with Dick. How could I explain receiving a "message?" I still felt Kirk's presence, so mentally I asked if the message was to be shared.

"Yes," I received in reply, "it is for the group, and will in addition help your own growth to share it. But the decision is yours. Don't force yourself if you're extremely uncomfortable."

As I was debating with myself, I realized that Sue had moved on to the pass-over list. I listened closely to the names. There was a woman named Jean.

Soon we were finished. The lights were turned on and John brought out nuts, fruit and herb tea. After sending energy we usually discuss the experiences we had while meditating, and any experiences we've had during the week. On this evening, we spent a lot of time discussing our meditational experiences. I decided to take the plunge:

"I felt a presence. I sensed that a woman whose name started with 'J' wanted to say she appreciated our

240

prayers." No one seemed shocked or upset by my disclosure; it was received very calmly. I felt relieved. I reminded myself that this group was especially receptive and open-minded about psychic experiences of any kind. Several other members commented that they had felt a lot of energy when Jean's name was read and another member had felt a presence when we were concentrating on her. That helped me feel less weird.

I left feeling good, pleased with myself that I had been able to share my message. It seemed to be some kind of test or growth point for me. But I also had the disquieting feeling that I might have to face a similar experience again.

That weekend we did another trance session. In preparation, I meditated alone. It was a very deep meditation, and while doing it I felt a presence. But it wasn't just Kirk. It seemed to include Kirk's teacher or "supervisor" coming by to see how I was doing. I felt like they were checking to see if I were ready to be tested for a possible step in my development. They explained that they had to have my conscious consent. But I didn't get any information on what the test would involve. "Oh, well," I thought, "nothing's hurt me yet. I'll take a risk." So I gave my conscious consent. I thought that something unusual might happen in the following trance session, and warned Burt to be prepared for anything. But nothing out of the ordinary happened. I tried to focus on the park as usual, but was frequently pulled back into the study.

I was uncomfortable over a question Burt asked. He wanted more information on the advice from the previous week to drink fruit juices. He was told:

"This information was made available from spiritual channels for actualization on the physical plane. There are impurities in the body. These juices are helpful in attracting and washing away these impurities."

"What is the nature of these impurities?"

"This is difficult to explain in your terms. There are imbalances in the interactions of various chemicals. There is an effect from an ionization process that takes place in the body. The liver is involved here. There are exchanges

241

of molecular energies that are not complete in this case. The excess negative charges are attracted and washed away."

"How much juice would you recommend?"

"The ideal amount is six to eight glasses a day. This should be continued for three days, followed by one day of pure, distilled water. At that time, a normal diet should be resumed."

"On the fourth day, only distilled water?"

"No other liquids on the fourth day."

Then we proceeded to a reading. As the reading began, I felt great energy enter my body, my arms and hands became very heavy, immobile, and charged with energy. I was a bit uncomfortable with that energy, because I didn't understand it. I also wondered why my head continued to move from side to side.

After the reading Burt asked if there was any other information to be imparted, and was told:

"Yes. There is a need here to offer meaning to Sandy on the changes in this format. It must be understood that gradual change is taking place as we enter deeper levels. The body must learn to adjust to these levels. This adjustment causes unfamiliar bodily sensations. This is no cause for alarm. They will pass in time as the body adjusts to deeper levels."

I hoped that Burt would have sense enough not to try the diet suggested. It seemed absurd to me. I felt he should at least consult a doctor first. I assumed he would forget about the message.

Then several days later, I was alarmed to see him bring in a grocery bag with jars of cranberry juice and distilled water.

"Oh, Burt, you're not thinking of trying that juice diet, are you!" I exclaimed.

"Of course I am. Your source recommended it."

"My source could be my imagination! At least see a doctor first."

"For what? What harm could possibly come to me from drinking juice for several days? I'm going to try it."

I realized that there was no talking Burt out of his foolishness. He left for work the next morning with a large thermos of cranberry juice. I was restless at work all day wondering how Burt was faring. I was very upset when I got home that night to find that he had been feeling badly all day and was irritable and jumpy. He thought he was being affected by the excess fructose, since he also follows a low blood sugar diet.

"Well, I hope you'll give up this diet immediately," I said.

"Of course not. I want to have a session tonight, and ask the source why I'm feeling so bad."

I entered the trance very uneasily, hoping that the source would advise Burt to stop the diet. I found myself in the park again and a highly-developed entity—not Kirk—came to talk with me. It was unusally hard to focus in the park since I was so concerned about the material coming out. When Burt asked if the source had any suggestions to alleviate his irritability and jumpiness, I had an incredible battle going on inside of me. I was begging my source to tell Burt to stop the diet. I listened helplessly as these words came out:

"Yes. It must be understood that this process is important in ridding the body of impurities. It can help to eat large amounts of pure protein. Drink small quantities of the juice at a time—one-half glass is sufficient each time. Six glasses total is sufficient for one day. These effects will pass. The body will react more strongly to smoking at this time."

The part of my consciousness that was in the park cried to the developed entity about the words coming out of my mouth. I feared that in some deep part of myself, unrecognized, was a desire to hurt Burt.

The entity was very reassuring. He pointed to many other entities who were there with us in the park, and said they were all there to help. He stayed with me until the end of the session.

I was very worried about Burt for the next few days. But he's finally through with the diet. He says he feels fantastic, hasn't had any prostate pain since he finished it, and hasn't had to get up at night to urinate. I feel tremendously relieved.

Despite all my experiences with the trance communication and all of Dick's assurances, I still worry about hurting people with a psychic force. My fear carries over into work, where I worry about saying the wrong thing or doing the wrong thing with clients. I've been wondering lately if I need more past life work to get over this. I've never gone back to the life in which I was involved in the black arts, or misused psychic forces in some way. In the Amsterdam life, I was a fraudulent medium, but not evil; I didn't hurt people. But according to Dick's impression, according to the Solomon reading, and according to my own feelings, there was a life back there where I did a pretty heavy number on some people. Could I be feeling some residual guilt from that? Could the guilt be slowing down my progress now? I see Dick next week, so I think I'll ask his advice on doing another past-life session.

THURSDAY, MAY 12, 1977

I saw Dick two weeks ago for a routine session to go over notes on my dreams, trance sessions, and the other experiences I've had. I also made an appointment for a regression session later this month. The Foundation has recently moved to West Haven. It is now located in a rest home which utilizes many non-traditional approaches, including a nutritional testing program, which I don't fully understand. It involves doing a saliva and urine analysis to determine the body's chemistry, and then prescribing a special diet and distilled water to rid the body of toxins. The arrangement seems ideal: the Foundation has real patients that can benefit from its holistic healing approaches, and the rest home has use of the theories and approaches that Prana can bring in. The new location is also very peaceful, being right across from the beach.

I had so much material to cover in that session, that we only got through half of it—up to mid-March in my journal. So I scheduled another appointment in two weeks.

That evening, I went to the healing group, as usual. The experience was enjoyable, but I left feeling uneasy. I had sensed presences around again, and sensed that there was some message to be relayed to the group. I did my best to tune all that out and focus on the sending of energy. I didn't share my experience with the group, but left feeling that those experiences might become more intense in the near future. I was troubled, and decided I would discuss it with Dick in our next session.

The next evening, Thursday, Burt and I held a trance session. He asked: "Please comment on the importance of

Sandy's mood or state of mind before a session." The answer was:

"This is more important than is realized. There must be willingness on the conscious level for the success of these sessions. The resistance must be at a minimal level. The body must be relaxed and the mind at peace."

In the middle of the answer, my voice became very husky and my head began moving from side to side. Burt continued: "How can we best prepare for a session?"

"This must be done on emotional and physical levels. There must be harmony between the two of you. There must be peace and relaxation. There should be meditation beforehand by both of you. This is important. There should be a schedule but should not be enforced rigidly."

As soon as Burt asked his first question, I pictured myself in the park and immediately felt Kirk on my right. We sat and "talked," and this time I remembered most of what was said.

"How do I know if all this is my imagination?" I asked him.

He smiled and answered, "How do you know if your whole life is imagination?"

"Well, I can touch and see my everyday reality."

"You know this reality, also. The only reason you are more confident of the other is that everyone agrees on it. Most people do not agree on this reality so you must find more assurances inside."

"It's hard to focus in the park."

"You must try. It is very important at this point to get your attention away from what is happening to the body."

"What is the future of these sessions, Kirk? How will this ability develop?"

"This remains to be seen. You were asked recently if you're ready to move ahead and you consented. This means you will be tested as to your readiness to develop this ability further. You haven't even begun to explore the potential. There are many possibilities open for the future."

"What can I best do at this time to further my spiritual growth?"

"Meditate. This is extremely important." Then Kirk's

energy faded and I was again focused in my body. I was told the session must end.

As before, my consciousness had actually moved back and forth, sometimes being with Kirk and sometimes being with Burt. I was aware of what my body was saying and doing, but most of the time wasn't focusing on it. It was like watching a TV show while someone in the same room is on the telephone. It's possible to be so engrossed in the show, that you're not listening to the phone conversation, although you're aware of it. At times, you may tune into the phone conversation for a while, then focus again on the TV show. That's what my experiences in the park have been like.

On Sunday afternoon, we held another session. My head was again moving from side to side throughout the session, so Burt asked: "Why is Sandy shaking her head 'no'?"

"This is not understood. This is not a 'no'; this is a sign of the adjustment of the body to high energy fields. This will pass in time."

Burt next asked: "Is laetrile beneficial in treating cancer, and, if so, when will this be generally recognized?"

"Yes. There is benefit here; however, there is much to be understood about cancer that is not yet appreciated. There are many stresses and chemicals in your environment that lead to this ailment. The most important aspect of cure is state of mind, belief, diet, and relaxation. Laetrile can have positive physical effects but of greater importance are the psychological effects of those who believe in its efficacy. There is a long fight ahead for recognition. This fight may prove to be irrelevant before its conclusion. There are researchers on the verge of a more beneficial cure; especially from a small laboratory in California."

When Burt asked if there were anything more for tonight, he was told:

"No. We have no further messages to impart for tonight. It is important for Sandy to remember her conversations and lessons with her spirit guide during this time."

Our group met again last night. The energy was very

247

high, and I slipped into a pretty deep trance state. I very strongly felt Kirk's presence, and sensed that if I only allowed it, that creaky voice would come out of my mouth with a message for the group. I struggled against an extremely strong impulse to allow it. I felt that I had no right to allow it to come through without receiving the group's permission in advance. It would be very startling to suddenly have a raspy voice bellowing through the room in the middle of our meditation. I would be acutely embarrassed. And I wasn't sure that I had enough confidence in what I was doing to share it with others. For all those reasons, I refused permission for the energy to enter. But I also realized that I would have to deal with this problem in some way. I couldn't continue to enjoy the group and concentrate on sending energy if I were engaged in an internal struggle to block out communications that I felt such a strong urge to channel.

I need to talk with Dick about this. I'd like to talk with Joe, too. He's a regular group member and also knows about the work I've been doing with Dick. I feel really torn, between giving in to this urge to channel information in the group and my desire to keep that part of my life secret and hidden so that I can't hurt others with it or embarrass myself.

TUESDAY, MAY 17, 1977

I'm still in conflict over whether to share my experiences
with the group tomorrow night.

On Sunday afternoon, Burt and I held our usual
session. I had him ask about the advisability of my
channeling information during the healing group. The
answer was:

"We have here possibilities to increase the development of the channel and to augment the spiritual growth
of others. We see here reluctance on the part of the
channel to proceed along these lines. This will pass as the
self-confidence grows. This is a fruitful path to pursue at
this time."

Again, my consciousness moved in and out of the park
during these messages. Kirk and I had a long "talk" about
various spiritual matters. We laughed together about how
creaky my voice sounded, and I said it sounded like one
possessed. Kirk replied that I probably wouldn't want to
hear his response, but that in a way I was possessed—or
rather my voice was. But it wasn't possession by a spirit,
but rather by high energies. I didn't especially understand
his answer, but it didn't bother me either. He added that I
had no idea of how extremely well protected I was. Many
people are being trained now, he said, to be able to do this
kind of work in the hard times that lie ahead before we
evolve into a more spiritual future.

Since that session I've been doing a lot of thinking
about the Wednesday group. A part of me recognizes that
it's time to share my channeling experiences. Another
part of me is very frightened about doing so. It's been a
very private experience that Burt and I share. I talk about
it with Dick. A few others around the Foundation, like

Joe and Pat, know what I'm doing but we seldom talk about it. Judy and Jan know about it, and so does my Mom. And that's it. I've never tried to channel information with anyone but Burt or Dick present. Would I be able to do it with anyone else there? Would my voice terrify anyone else? Would I be laughed at or called crazy?

I already have an appointment with Dick scheduled for Wednesday morning, so I just called Joe and arranged to have lunch with him afterwards. After talking with them both, I'll decide if I'm going to share this experience with the group tomorrow night. Burt has already decided to come along to the group and give me moral support.

THURSDAY, MAY 19, 1977

Yesterday was a very profound emotional experience for me. I began the day at 10 a.m. in Dick's office for a two hour session. We covered the past month of entries in my journal. I pointed out, "A lot of my dreams lately have been about you. You're saying 'good-bye' to me or that there's not much more you have to teach me; I just need to assimilate what I've already learned."

Dick nodded. "What do you think those dreams mean?"

"That our work together is drawing to a close. I think that soon I'll be moving on. Perhaps to someone else; perhaps taking a course or two in this area; maybe just working on my own. But I feel an end drawing near. It makes me sad."

"I can understand the sadness, but it's not an end. Our relationship will continue, but on a different level. You'll still be around Prana a lot. We'll be friends, equals. It'll be a different relationship, but not an end."

I know Dick is right, but I still feel the sadness. I've been through so much in that big green chair.

Next I told Dick what I've been experiencing in the healing group, and my fears of sharing those experiences with the others.

"That's an ideal place to share it. I know all the members of that group; their heads are on straight. No one there is going to flip out or think you're a freak. In fact, they'll probably be delighted to have this opportunity. And it'll be a chance for you to grow and develop with their support. Many people who channel information do so for a group; it's a very common practice and can be mutually very rewarding."

"I know all that, but I'm still up-tight about it. I've never done it before in a group. It's really taking a big step and entering a new stage; from a very private experience to a shared one."

"I think you should tell the group the kind of work you're doing with me and discuss with them what might happen while in a trance state. I think they'll be very supportive. I know Joe will be."

"I'm going to have lunch with him right after I leave here. I need to talk with him before talking with the group."

"Fine," Dick said smiling, "but we both know what he's going to say."

I drove on to Milford eager to talk with Joe. I've always found him easy to talk to, with peaceful calming vibes. We sat in a secluded corner of a dimly-lit restaurant. The air-conditioning was a pleasant contrast to the intense humidity outside as a spring storm prepared to hit.

I repeated to Joe my experiences in the group and my concerns. He smiled as I finished my story. "I know that you already know what I'm going to say. There's got to be a reason. If you're having such strong impressions in that group, there's a reason for them. And we both feel that the reason is that they're to be shared with the group."

"I know. I think I've already made the decision that it must be done. But I'm afraid to do it. I'm really here for support."

"What are you afraid of?"

"Ridicule, being thought I'm crazy."

"Not in that group. No way. They're all into this stuff and have a lot of respect for it."

"Then there's the opposite extreme. They could accept without question anything that comes out of my mouth during trance."

"OK, look, you're going to have to educate the group. You've been working with Dick for a long time and have learned a lot from him. Now it's your turn to teach. Teach the group about this information, about how to deal with it and evaluate it. They'll be receptive."

I had a lot to think about as I left Joe to put in some

time at the office. I had little time to think, however, because we had several emergencies that afternoon, and I was busy every minute with clients.

It was fortunate that I didn't have more time to think, because I was very nervous. I couldn't eat any dinner. I just wanted to get the whole thing over with as quickly as possible. I was taking a big step, and it was so frightening. I wished I didn't have to go through with it, but I knew it had to be faced. Time dragged by until 7:30, when Burt and I left for the meeting.

As the group members filtered in, I got more and more tense. I just couldn't go through with it, and decided to postpone it indefinitely. Then I realized that the agony I was feeling would continue until I got it over with. So I sighed and took the plunge.

"I have something I'd like to talk about before we begin sending this evening." I rather hoped no one would hear me, but the room became hushed, as the other six members turned to me. I took a deep breath and began. "I've been experiencing some things here the past few weeks that I haven't shared. But I feel very strongly that they're meant to be shared, and I've been feeling troubled about keeping them to myself, so I'd like to tell you about them. I've been feeling presences in the room; guides. You see, I started seeing Dick over a year ago because I was depressed. Part of the reason was that I was sensing presences and hearing tappings. Dick taught me that these were nothing to fear and taught me how to use prayer and white light for protection. After awhile, I started doing auto-writing. I had messages that purported to be from a spirit guide and were of a spiritual nature. In time, I found that I was getting messages telepathically while I meditated, so we got the idea to turn on the tape recorder so I could verbalize messages while I received them. Then, more recently, things have changed a bit again. Instead of repeating telepathic messages, my vocal cords are supposedly controlled by very high energies, and a deep, raspy voice comes through with spiritual messages. Burt and I do this together a couple times a week. I'm still working with Dick trying to determine the authenticity. Some encouraging things have come through, but we don't have any hard evidence that I'm in touch with super-conscious knowledge. It could be subconcious, or imagination. Does everyone follow me?" There was a chorus of intrigued, affirmative responses. "Well, anyway, I get into fairly deep trances when we send energy, because the vibes are so high in here. And I've been feeling the urge to channel information for this group at the end of our healing. But it's got to be something that everyone wants and feels comfortable with."

I hoped that some people would say they were too uncomfortable to allow it, but the response was enthusiastic. Cindy expressed some nervousness, and the group said they'd white-light her at the time. I was relieved to have that part over with, and hoped the rest of the evening would go fast.

So the lights were turned out and we began. Soon after Joe began reading names, I found my consciousness projected to a beach. There was a man dressed in white standing next to me. He looked friendly, but he didn't have the glow and vibes of a spirit guide. And he certainly wasn't Kirk. I felt uneasy about this stranger, and jumped back to the room. I was there only for a moment, when I found myself back on the beach again. That man was still there.

"Who are you?" I demanded.

"A friend," he answered with a smile. I wasn't convinced.

A moment later, Kirk appeared. He put an arm around each of us. "I hope the two of you will become friends. I'm going to leave you together this evening to get acquainted."

"But, Kirk," I protested, "aren't you going to be with me during this process? I'm scared, and I need you."

"Your group needs me even more tonight. You'll manage just fine." Then he vanished.

I was disappointed, but was glad at least that this fellow was approved by Kirk.

"You seem like a George to me," I said turning to him.

"Actually, I'm Rick, but I don't mind if you call me George."

"You're not a spirit guide," I accused.

"No, I'm a soul with a body. And I'm struggling with many of the same things you are. Kirk is my spirit guide, too. And he thought we could be of help to each other."

I decided that I liked this man, and we continued a casual and friendly conversation while I simultaneously sent healing energies to the names on our list.

We soon finished the list. I felt myself go deeper into trance as my head began moving rapidly back and forth. I could sense Kirk and other guides in the room. I was also very aware of great love and support from the other group members. I relaxed. I heard Joe's voice.

"I'm getting a very strong impression right now to turn to Sandy and see if she wishes to channel information. Is there any information to be channeled from Sandy for us tonight?"

There was a long pause, then the voice began. It was weaker than usual. "Yes." Another long pause as the trance deepened. "We have here much energy and much love in this room. There are many spirit guides interested in the welfare of this group who are here to help. The work you are doing here is more important than you realize. The thought forms you send out are received as love and healing energies. Love radiates outward from this group to many other souls. And the love is also projected inward to each individual here." The voice was slower and softer than usual. Rick took my hand as the channeling began, and we strolled on the beach together. I was aware of both scenes simultaneously. The voice continued: "We are open now to a question if anyone wishes to ask."

I heard a female voice from the group. "I feel very gratified that you feel the work we are doing is important and helpful." It was Cindy's voice! It sounded relaxed and pleased; there was no fear. I relaxed even more.

"I have a question." It was Joe's voice. "Is there anything we can do as a group to increase our ability to send energy?"

"Yes. At the beginning of your sessions, stand in a

circle holding hands. Pray together. This will increase the vibrations faster. A group feeling of love is very important in this work. Thank you for this opportunity to share with you this evening." The voice faded out and stopped. My head stopped rolling and slumped onto my shoulder. The beach and Rick vanished as I found myself totally focused in the room.

I could hear Joe's soft voice. "Now, Sandy, just relax and let yourself very slowly come back to a normal state of consciousness. Everyone else, too, do the same. Very gradually bring yourselves out. Don't rush."

Very slowly my eyes opened and I could move my body again. The room was dark except for the candle. I was grateful for that, for my first feeling was one of embarrassment. I had spoken in such a strange voice, what would they all think of me? There was a great sense of peace in the room. The vibrations were still very high, higher than I can ever remember them. I felt one with the group. We went around the room sharing our feelings and impressions. Cindy, John, Sue and Joe had all experienced REM just as the voice was beginning. It was the first time Sue and Cindy had had such an experience. Sue, Cindy and Wil, our newest member, had been nervous at the beginning but then, as the voice got going, felt a great peace and love surround them. "Ah," I thought. "That sounds like Kirk's work. That's what he was doing here all that time." Burt, for the first time, had been able to enjoy the vibes and the message without taking notes.

For a long time we sat in stillness and darkness sharing reactions. We realized that we felt a strong sense of group purpose. The members felt inspired that our work was considered so important. Some members were intrigued by the new "group guide" and began suggesting questions to ask next time.

I sat back with Burt's arm around me, feeling drained but peaceful. I had been so tense, and had found the experience very deeply moving. I couldn't believe that I was listening to a room full of people discussing my messages with such confidence about them. There was agreement that holding hands in a circle would be of benefit to the group and that our new group feeling would help us in generating energy.

It was 11:00 before Burt and I left. I couldn't remember our group ever lasting so late.

I forgot to give myself a standard suggestion before coming out of trance: that the high energies I had experienced would not interfere with my sleep. I couldn't sleep for hours last night; I was too energized.

I woke up early this morning and took a walk before work. Something is very different in my life. My trance sessions are no longer a secret. They are no longer something Burt and I do in private. I know that before I was not ready to share this process. But now I am. Now, I must share it for it to continue to have meaning.

While I was walking, it occurred to me that Solomon did his reading for me one year ago tomorrow. This is an anniversary of sorts.

As an anniversary present, I think I'm beginning to understand some things. Last night was a profound experience for me because I saw people utilizing a piece of information I had channeled and evaluating the message itself. No one asked me to prove that the message wasn't my imagination. No one seemed to care. As we discussed the message, a lot of positive things happened. It increased our feelings of being a group; gave us a greater rapport and harmony. We discussed a technique that could improve our sending abilities. My channeling process produced positive results! It really hadn't hurt anyone! And it hadn't mattered what the source was; all that mattered was the message itself. Perhaps it really doesn't matter where the information comes from as long as it's helpful to others.

That thought sounds vaguely familiar; like maybe Dick's said that several hundred times.

I think I'm reaching a point where I'll be ending this book. At one time I thought that I wouldn't end it until I had definite proof either that my messages were from the superconscious, or that they were imagination. Now I'm thinking that I'll never ever reach that point. A more appropriate ending is to understand that it doesn't matter.

THURSDAY, MAY 26, 1977

We had a session on Sunday and Burt asked: "Do you have any comments on Sandy's work with the Wednesday group?"

"Yes. We have here many opportunities for development of the channel and for growth of the group members and increased effectiveness of the group. These mutual opportunities have been arranged and provide opportunity for many to grow."

Then Burt read a question I had written out in advance: "Please provide any information that will help Sandy understand the experiences she has while channeling information during trance states. Is she actually projecting her consciousness or only imagining it?"

"Yes. There is much to be understood here. It is possible to project the consciousness outside the body. This takes much practice. This soul is learning the basic techniques involved. There is still much to learn. This question cannot be answered in your terms. To imagine a projection of consciousness is to take the beginning steps of projection. It is part of the same process."

As usual, my consciousness was in the park talking with Kirk. Burt then gave me a name for a reading. As the information flow began, I felt an incredible surge of energy. It was so overwhelming that I wanted to scream, and couldn't. But I wasn't frightened.

Burt and I went to the group meeting last night. We were late, because we were helping Judy move to a new apartment. A new person had come, out of curiosity, to see what the group was like. Before we began, I went into the kitchen for a drink of water, and Sue joined me.

"We're not going to have you do your thing tonight,

258

Sandy. The new member may not be comfortable with it, and Cindy's been a little up-tight since last week. We need to talk about it later."

I felt relieved. I had been feeling tense about going through the channeling experience again; I still wasn't comfortable with doing it in a group. The energy, while we sent, seemed low.

After the sending, the new member left early, and the rest of us had a long talk. Cindy said that, although she had left feeling good the previous week, she became frightened later. She was feeling presences around and was afraid of having psychic experiences of her own before being ready for them and that voice *had* been rather scary. We agreed that as a group we weren't ready for that kind of communication.

I felt down. Had I hurt someone after all with the channeling? Had I made the wrong decision in sharing it? Would it still be possible to share my experiences? Should they just be kept between Burt and me?

Then John said that he had something he wished to share, but felt a bit uneasy and embarrassed about it. I told him that I could understand exactly how he felt, and we all encouraged him to continue. He said that he had been very moved by the strong vibrations and the intense energy the previous week. He wanted to find a way to symbolize what the experience had meant to him. Then, while meditating, a symbol had appeared. Since he's a jeweler, he produced the symbol in gold. He showed it to us: a wheel, with seven spokes, representing the seven regular members of the group. A small diamond was in the middle.

"I want to make one of these for each of us in the group, if you'll accept them as a gift from me. Sandy, I'd like you to have this first one," he said. I was extremely touched. I gave him a hug and a kiss. I asked if he would help me select a gold chain from his store, so that I could wear it around my neck. He added that he would make one a week until we each had our own.

I left with mixed feelings. I was very touched by John's

gift, but also feared that I had hurt Cindy. I wanted to give up the psychic work. Again.

I have a session scheduled with Dick on Friday to do another past life regression. I want to get to the bottom of my fear of hurting people.

MONDAY, MAY 30, 1977

Burt has to work today even though it's a holiday, so I'll catch up on my journal this morning. This afternoon, Judy's coming over so that we can sunbathe in the back yard.

I saw Dick Friday. I told him about my fears of having hurt the group by sharing the channeling process. I told him I was especially concerned that the energy seemed so low Wednesday.

We then began the hypnosis. I slipped into it easily, and Dick began asking questions:

"You can hear me clearly and will continue to hear me clearly. What do you see?"

"I see the sky. And the sun. And a road. There's a dirt road. I'm walking down the road."

"What is your name?"

"Gestaulf. I'm a big man. I'm walking home. I live in a shack in the country. Nobody like me very well. I live away from the others. By myself."

"Where do you live?"

"In a shack."

"In what town; in what country?"

"Mesopotamia. People are afraid of me. I'm very lonely. But I—I have my friends. I talk with them at night. They help me. I just sit back and relax and I call my friends. They come and we talk." My breathing became heavy, and my body was tense.

"What are you experiencing?"

"My friends are coming. They come and talk to me and help me."

"How did you learn to contact those spirits?"

"I just know. I just know how. I've always known."

"Do they do your bidding?"

"They teach me. They teach me how to get what I want. When I was a child I used to go off in the woods. And they would come. We would laugh. If my father punished me, I would go to the woods, and my friends would come. And they would tell me how to play tricks on my father to punish him. I would come and tell them how it worked, and we would all laugh. They would tell me about herbs in the forest. I would put the herbs in his drinks, and he would feel strange things, and never know they were from me. I just always knew about my friends. I just always knew. They come at night. They can haunt a house. There's a man in the village who's been cruel to me, and I told my friends and now he thinks his house is haunted. He's frightened. My friends laughed." Again my breathing became heavy. My voice was very emotional. "If people aren't nice to me, I tell my friends."

"How long did this continue?"

"All my life."

"How long did you live in that time period?"

"Oh, I lived—" I paused, confused. My speech became very slow and agonized. "I can feel my friends, I can feel their heaviness. I feel their energy in my body. My chest feels very heavy. They're coming into my body!"

"Have they gained your confidence?"

"Yes—"

"Are they trying to control you?"

"Yes, they do. They come into my body. I used to control them, but now they control me," I whimpered. "I'm frightened! I don't have any control any more! I don't know how this happened! How did it happen? I don't understand. I don't have control of my body!"

"Did this cause your demise in that lifetime? How did your life end?"

"They took over my body! I thought they were my friends, but they have my body!" I started sobbing.

"Relax. Relax now. Just relax." Dick's voice was very soft and gentle. "I want you to view it objectively now. How long ago did this happen?"

Gradually my sobbings ceased and a year came to mind, one digit at a time. "One. Two. Nine. Two."

"1292?"

"Yes. My body is dead."

"Yes, you paid very dearly for that lifetime."

"I thought they were my friends."

"But you learned. What did you learn from that life cycle?"

"I thought they were my friends, and they hurt me. I don't ever again want to talk to those friends. They're not my friends. Never again. They're so powerful. Never again."

"What's to prevent it from happening again?"

"All the lessons. All the lessons!" I sounded weary of them. "So many lessons before this lifetime! Over and over again. They kept telling me over and over again so it wouldn't happen again. All the lessons. At night, the lessons go on."

"Do you feel confident that you've learned?"

My voice left no doubt. "Oh, yes."

"Is there any logical reason why you should carry those fears from then to now?"

"Because it's part of the lesson. If I didn't have the fears, I might forget."

"But what if you were to have the memory and the respect?"

"I'm afraid of doing it again without the fears."

"Is it essential that you keep those fears or is the memory sufficient?"

"No. I have to pass the fears. I can't grow unless I pass the fears. They hold me back to the past. I'm afraid to trust the energies that are working with me now. I have to get over the fears or I can't trust them. And if I can't trust them, I can't grow."

"What evidence do you need to have faith and confidence in those energies that are now working with you?"

There was a long pause before I said, "I need to experience the good in the energy. I need to experience and understand the good that they bring. They're here to help. To really help me this time."

"Who's here to help you this time?"

"There's so many."

"Are they the same friends you had before?"

"Oh, no! These are real friends. They're here to help me. I have to learn the right way. After that life, I never again wanted to talk to anybody outside of myself. Never again. They told me that I have to. I have to learn how to do it the right way. I have to get over the fear and I have to learn the right lessons. They keep telling me I have to learn that the fear holds me back."

"Relax your mind. Relax your body. Return to the white light. Feel its protective vibration. Feel the security that it offers. Let go, and allow yourself to meet your new friends. Feeling very secure, because I will remain with you. Tell me who is with you now."

"I see the white light. I feel the pure energy. There are many here to help me."

"Does Sandy understand the importance of that life cycle she just reviewed?"

"She does now. She didn't before."

"Didn't she pay very dearly for her mistakes in that life?"

"Yes. There was much suffering. Much suffering. It produced many fears. The fears were necessary for a long time, so that the same mistakes would not be repeated. And now the time has come when the fears must be left behind, because they prevent the soul from growing. The same mistakes will not be made again. The soul has learned the necessary lessons. It's time to let the fear go, so there will be growth."

"Do you understand that we will continue to challenge this source of information?"

"Yes. The challenge is good. The searching is good. The questions are good. But the fear is not good."

"Does she understand the philosophy offered today, that she must have recall of the past life, but must develop respect rather than fear for the experience?"

"Yes, she is starting to understand. It will take time to absorb this knowledge."

"Explain what happened last Wednesday night. Why were the vibrations so low at prayer group?"

The answer began in my usual soft hypnotic voice, but after a sentence, it had progressed to the deep, husky trance voice.

"Sandy does not understand that she projects fears outward to others and in that group there is strong rapport and other group members are reacting to her fears. They are sensing her own insecurities, and they are reacting to them. Sandy hopes that this group support will help her over her own fears. She does not understand that she must develop confidence herself so she can project that confidence to the others in the group. It is necessary for her to work with this group and help them understand and overcome their fears. This will be a good experience for Sandy and will help her in working through her own fears."

"Who is speaking through her now?"

"This is high energy focused in the body by her spirit guide known as Kirk."

"Is this communication coming from within Sandy now, extraneously guided?"

"Yes."

"OK. Is this why she allows this form of communication?"

"Yes."

"She has more confidence with it?"

"Yes. She is not able to allow any other form but we are working on projecting the consciousness outside the body which lessens the interference of the ego. Much progress has been made here."

"Are you offering this information verbally for Sandy's sake?"

"Yes. It is very important for her to listen to this tape very carefully to understand the message."

Afterward, I felt relieved that the session was over. But then later I became depressed. There was no logical reason for it, but something was gnawing at me from that session.

On Thursday, I had an urge to contact Kirk and ask why I was feeling depressed. I didn't want to bother with the regular format, but decided to try a telepathic contact. I meditated until I felt his presence and sensed that we were in telepathic rapport.

"Are there any advantages to using this method?" I asked mentally.

I sensed amusement in the reply. "Not really. You're going back to a more primitive technique. But if you're more comfortable with it, fine."

"Why am I so depressed?"

"Soul memories. Past life memories are coming into consciousness. Your experience with the Wednesday group triggered past life memories. The depression must be worked through. It's a sign of something that needs to be resolved for growth."

"Will I be using channeling techniques again in that group?"

"In all probability, yes. Although free will could alter this. This experience has been arranged for the growth of all concerned. But you are projecting your fears to the group and then receiving them back. You must work this out and grow as a group. This is part of the test or lesson involved—all must grow together for anyone to benefit from this experience. I and others were present at the first session, but your fears were projected subconsciously to others and emerged later."

"I'm still wondering where this information comes from, and what role you play during trances. Could you try to explain it again?"

"You and I are in telepathic rapport. Occasionally I am here in the astral and you are in communication with an 'outside entity.' More often, our super-conscious minds or souls are in telepathic rapport. Messages go from my superconscious to yours and then are filtered by you up to consciousness. It is not telepathy from one conscious mind to another—therefore it technically comes from your soul—from you."

"Is my voice controlled by high energies? Do these energies come from inside or outside?"

"It's the same thing. In a trance state, you reach rapport with Universal Energy—or all souls. This energy

266

is you, and also is more than you. But it's not something different from you or apart from you. You have great potential to advance much further than you are now, but it will take much time and patience. Obviously, an unconscious medium is the best instrument and you may or may not reach that point in this lifetime—you understand your fears on this that arise from past lives. But you can certainly reach much higher levels and obtain far more detailed material."

I felt much better after this. Yesterday we did our Sunday session. Burt asked for more material on drugs.

"Yes. It is important to understand that early in earth times, souls did not need drugs for the body. Healing was done on the astral level. In time this knowledge became buried within the soul as man became concerned only with the physical. It was believed that illness began in the physical and had to be treated there.

"Drugs were discovered at this time. Drugs were substances with physical properties that could alter the chemical balance of the body. At times this change could heal the physical, while the astral was healing itself.

"Drugs have been refined and now produced chemically, but they still have the same purpose. As knowledge of healing is released from the souls on earth, drugs will cease to be needed."

Again, I went to the park with Kirk. We talked about my past life work, and he emphasized its importance to me. He then said that I was getting better at projection, and we could consider another location besides the park. He suggested our home planet. I was startled at the idea, but Kirk said that we would build up to it slowly. When I was ready, we would spend only an instant there before returning, until I became accustomed to the procedure.

I'm still feeling depressed about my past life session. I think there must be more material there I didn't get in touch with. Usually, I feel great after one of those sessions. I'm going to call Dick and schedule another appointment.

THURSDAY, JUNE 9, 1977

I discovered another past life yesterday in Dick's office. I had dreaded the session. As I pushed back the big chair preparing to go into a hypnotic state, I thought, "This is about as much fun as going to the doctor's for a shot." But we got into it quickly.

As I started feeling relaxed, I saw a long dark tunnel. Mentally, I was told that I was almost at the end of that tunnel but I now needed to complete the process to come out on the other side into the light. I remembered the night over a year ago, before I began my past life work, when I also saw a tunnel. I was told I had to pass through it. Perhaps my past life work had moved me almost to the end of the tunnel.

I immediately started breathing heavily.

"Let it out, Sandy. You've got to let it out." I cried for awhile, feeling great pain. "Relax, now. Just relax. Look at it objectively. What do you see?"

"I don't know. I'm running."

"What are you running from?"

"I'm very frightened!"

"What caused you to be frightened?"

"Those things I saw."

"Where did you see them?"

"Back—back in the woods."

"What did you see in the woods?"

"I was calling—calling on forces. I had a fire. And I was calling on forces to help me, and they turned on me. I'm so frightened. I don't understand what happened. Everything exploded and the air was filled with energy. I was so frightened. I couldn't see. I was just surrounded by this awful fear. I'm so afraid. I'm just trying to run and get away from it. I don't understand. I've used it before, and I always had control. I don't understand what happened."

"I want your soul and your subconscious mind to collectively help you understand that lifetime. Continue to look at it objectively."

"I can see the soul after it passed out of the body in that life. It's in great pain. It realizes that forces were misused again. It takes so long to learn. I feel like such a failure to have wasted another lifetime using the forces for selfish gain. I feel like it's hopeless. I don't even want to try again. I keep trying. I keep blowing it each time. I've hurt so many people. I understand between lifetimes, but when I go down to try it, I make the same mistakes over and over."

"You don't seem to understand karma. It's a self-induced method of learning. We, as individuals, choose our karma. Others serve as tools to help us fulfill our karma. When you talk in terms of hurting people, you must remember that when they chose to learn the lessons they become connected with you. You must look at it objectively, and realize that you were used as a tool, not only for your own growth, but for the growth of those who chose to serve with you. Look at that lifetime as long as necessary to place it in context. Relive it over and over if necessary until you understand it and the purpose of this life cycle."

"I can see myself as a man who is very involved in the black arts, with knowledge gained from many other lifetimes. I was very skilled. People would come to me and pay me to cast a spell or to make a formula to hurt somebody else. I was very selfish. Before, in the other lifetime, I was very lonely, but now I'm just selfish. I want to use this knowledge that I have to become rich. People fear me because they know what I can do. I thought that I would have a lot of power and people would look up to me. But I'm not happy with the power. I am very skilled but nobody will be my friend, because they're afraid of me. They're afraid of my power. I thought that this power would bring me happiness. But it didn't. I was alone in that life. Just like in the other life I was alone. I'm alone with my money and with my power. I think that if I get more power, some more money, then I'll be happy. And I'll have friends. I keep trying to work out herbs that are more and more powerful. And people come to me, and they pay me to destroy their enemies. I think that making the people happy will make me happy. But when I destroy their enemies, it doesn't make people happy. So I'm going to have a ceremony in the forest. And I'm going to call on the forces. And I'm going to demand—I'm going to *demand*—that they bring me happiness." I paused and then my voice became slower and full of emotion. "I use everything that I know. I build a huge fire. And there's an explosion. And I'm surrounded! Everything's out of control! It's dark, and I'm so frightened! Those forces are running after me! And then I stumble, I hit my head on a rock!" My voice became quiet. "It's a relief to pass out of that body, and to end that life. And then the pain comes. Because I realize what I did. How far I wandered. I feel so miserable! I don't want to go on living. But I'm already dead! I feel like such a failure as a soul. I don't think I'll ever learn the lessons!"

"If it's permissible, I want your soul to bring to consciousness how you were helped, and guided, and loved immediately after that lifetime."

"Not at first. At first, I wouldn't let anybody come near. I was so miserable. I just wanted to be alone. And then gradually, I realized that others were around. And they talked to me. They'd tell me I needed to understand that I didn't have to feel the guilt. I needed to learn love. No soul is ever helpless. I needed to open myself to their love and the lessons. I find that hard to believe. They tell me I have to learn to love myself. I have to forgive myself. They say there are many more lifetimes and many more chances to learn. I can feel their love, but I don't feel worthy of it. I've had many lifetimes of lessons, and learning comes so slow. It's the same teacher back there! It's Kirk! He's the one telling me all that! He's the same teacher who's been with me through all those lifetimes."

"Do you feel that he's lied to you at any time?"

"Oh, no. He couldn't lie."

"He *could* lie, but he hasn't. That's very important. Is there any reason why you should doubt any of the information he's offered to you in any time period?"

"No. There's no reason; just the old guilts. And the feelings of being unworthy of the love. The old fears that I'll mess it up again. Lack of trust in myself. Not a lack of trust in him; it's in myself. I want to grow, but I'm so afraid I'll blow it again like I have so many times before. Again and again I've had the opportunities and I've misused them!" I was still speaking as the soul from the past life who just passed out of body. But I was aware that remnants of that attitude were with me in the present. "I lack confidence in myself that I can use them properly."

"Don't you feel that you've been given sufficient protection in this lifetime to prevent that?"

"Yes."

"But you doubt it?"

"I doubt myself."

"You must have faith in the guidance you've been given, and work with it; not against it. You must have faith in your own instincts, knowing always on a conscious level, that you are safe; you are protected. And you are being guided."

"I can feel all those forces and all those experiences from the past. I can feel them inside of me. I think that they're starting to become a part of me instead of something that I keep fighting and resisting, trying to forget. I can feel them merging into me! And I think that I'm starting to feel whole, because I can understand and accept those parts of me that I didn't want to look at before."

"Do you remember Solomon's definition of God?"

"No."

"God is a being able to see good without reference to evil. You are able to see your lifetimes as growing experiences. You have an opportunity to cleanse yourself of negative thoughts and feelings, by feeling the reality of the information you've received. And you have been serving. And you are fulfilling your chosen karma, by sharing with and loving those who are brought to you, the knowledge you've received. Is there anything else Sandy needs to understand at this time?"

"No. The understanding is there. What is happening now is the integration of the past into the present. What was resistance is now becoming understanding."

I left feeling that I had finally allowed myself to see and accept all of me, instead of hiding the painful portions from consciousness. I feel like a whole person.

It was undoubtedly the most emotionally-charged past life session I've had, because full understanding seeped into consciousness. I understand now that much of my fear and reluctance is based on the fact that I've felt like a failure for misusing psychic abilities so often in the past. The awareness has brought me the confidence that it won't happen again.

I went for a long walk in the park late this afternoon. I suddenly felt Kirk's presence, and we established telepathic rapport. It was a new experience to walk through the park in body while conversing with Kirk.

"You've completed something very important, my friend. You've completed the preliminaries. We're ready to get to work."

"The preliminaries! I thought I *was* working!"

Kirk chuckled. "You have been working, but it's been introductory. Mostly we've been overcoming the resistance. Now you're ready to really begin to develop this ability." He continued to tell me that at the end of this life, I will have earned the right to return to my home planet for future lives, if I chose. But he advised me to choose another life on earth to solidify the growth I've made. "You will make much more progress in this lifetime. But you may always have some resistance, some doubts from your past experiences. Another life here will enable you to approach the psychic with confidence; casually and naturally from early in the life. You can fully solidify the gains from your present life before returning to your home planet. You can also use such a life to experience an aspect of earthly existence that you've had very little experience with: motherhood." As he spoke, I could see images of this possible future life. It seemed to be in

England, far in the future. I could see myself living in a rural area; possibly a farm. I was a woman, and there were children around. I wasn't certain if they were my children, or if I took care of them. I seemed to be quite psychic and was involved very naturally with the occult from childhood. I saw myself holding discussion groups and trance sessions for neighbors. However, I saw myself having no recollections of past lives. I wouldn't need them then as I do now. It looked like a quiet, secluded life. It seemed free of the doubts and insecurities that beset me now. Kirk continued, "When you return to your home planet, much hard work will begin in earnest to train you. You have chosen a future path of teaching. That's why your work here is so important—not just for your own growth, but for the help your experiences are in understanding others. In time, you'll play a role for others similar to the role I play for you.

"One more word, although I hate to add such a serious warning to a day that is bringing you such joy. You must remember that you have been given important opportunities for growth. You've seen past lives; you have conscious communication with advanced guides. These opportunities entail great responsibility to use them properly. I know that your growth will continue. But you must never forget the responsibility you have assumed."

I understood exactly what he meant. If I blow it now, the repercussions will be far more serious than they've ever been before. Before, I really didn't know any better. Now, I do. I've been given every opportunity to succeed. If I fail, it will take hundreds of lifetimes to recreate the same opportunities for growth.

There's another reason why yesterday was such a joyful occasion. It was our seventh anniversary. It was also group night, so we brought wine and carrot cake for refreshments.

While sending, I felt I was being contacted. I blocked it. "Look," I explained mentally, "we've decided as a group that we're not ready for this. So go away until such time as we may be ready."

I felt a very strong answer. "There's a message here for

the group. And it's very important. And it's important for you to play a role in delivering this message." I was surprised that the tone was so strong.

"I'll think about it. Maybe next week."

I decided not to share the experience with the group. I needed to think about it by myself for awhile.

Afterwards, we had a wonderful party. I feel very close to everyone in the group. Burt's coming regularly now, and the seven of us are developing a real group spirit.

This evening, I decided to make a list of the essential lifetimes I've received information on. I put them in order as best I could. The one I contacted yesterday with Dick was, I think, in Europe around the 1400's. But Dick didn't ask the year so that's just an impression.

EARLY LIFETIMES: Another planet, very developed spiritually. I was rebellious and not interested in learning. In my last lifetime there, I took an aircraft for a flight, although I was advised against it. I crashed on an enemy planet, and was tortured in an attempt to obtain information about my planet, which I didn't have. I was then left to die in the scorching sun. After passing out of my body, I realized how immature I was. I was advised to undergo a series of lifetimes on the planet Earth to learn maturity. For perhaps the first time, I took advice.

MESOPOTAMIA, 1200's: I was lonely, not fully understanding my new planet. I turned to the most natural way for me of making friends; contacting spirit entities—an ability that was natural on my home planet. I used the spirits selfishly to punish those who shunned me. I was not really trying to hurt others, however, but was trying to make friends and gain acceptance on this new planet. My spirit friends turned on me and I became possessed.

EUROPE, 1400's (?): I became heavily involved in the black arts, to gain power and money. I thought they would bring happiness and friends. When they didn't, I again called on forces beyond demanding happiness. Again, they turned on me. In running away from them in the forest, I stumbled and died by hitting my head on a rock. In passing out of body, I felt like a failure for having

274

misused the abilities in yet another lifetime.

SPAIN, 1500's: I was a young woman of noble birth in love with Burt, a young prince. During our engagement, there was an argument and I was pushed off a castle wall to my death.

AMSTERDAM, 1600's: I was a fraudulent medium, who claimed to contact the spirit world. Eventually, I became curious as to whether I might actually have such abilities. I called upon forces beyond, and was possessed. I was then burned to death by other villagers. This possession was supposedly a karmic lesson.

ENGLAND, 1800's: Burt and I were in love; he as Sylvia and me as Edward. I was a frivolous playboy, and rejected Sylvia's love.

FUTURE LIVES:

ON EARTH: Supposedly I am being advised to have one more life on the earth where I will be involved with children and again with the psychic, but on a very comfortable basis. This will solidify the growth I obtained from the other earth lives.

ON MY HOME PLANET: I supposedly have already made the choice to return to my home planet at this point for advanced training and further personal development. I will then work with others as a spiritual teacher, perhaps playing a role similar to Kirk's. This might also involve future lives on less-developed planets (such as Earth) to help others grow spiritually.

THURSDAY, JUNE 30, 1977

Since I'm approaching the end of my book, I decided recently to ask some questions from earlier portions of the manuscript that were never explained. First, Burt read, "Why was 'Joey' the first name given to Sandy for contact? Was Kirk actually born as her brother?"

"It is important here to understand many complex factors. The name 'Joey' was known to Sandy and was the best name at the time for initiating the contact. Kirk as a total entity was not born in this body, but a fragment of the total personality was selected for this earth to make an earthly contact for the later developments."

I don't really understand that answer, but it reminds me of the teachings of Seth in Jane Robert's books.

Then Burt asked: "What happened last May when Sandy was given a message about possession? Was she actually in contact with Kirk?" This question referred to the experience that led me to decide to give up auto-writing, and caused Dick to ask Solomon for a reading on me.

"No. This was the one occasion in which contact was allowed with lower forces. This was designed to allow familiarity with this difference in contacts and to propel the course of action which was so valuable in the development."

"Any other messages today?"

"Yes. It is important for Sandy to continue these trance sessions on a regular basis. The preliminary work is over now, and it is important to work hard and seriously on developing the abilities within. Every few days there should be a session. This continuity cannot be stressed enough. We no longer need to be so concerned with a positive attitude before a session, because the negativity is gone. We now need a regular schedule and serious devotion to development of this ability if its potential is to be fulfilled in this life. That is sufficient for today."

So that's what Kirk means when he says it's time to get to work. I guess the days of "only do this when you feel in the mood" are over. Kirk gave me a lecture in the park. He said my trance was lighter than usual because we hadn't held a session in awhile. He emphasized working on a regular schedule. I'll try, but Kirk's schedule certainly seems more flexible than ours.

I decided to leave myself open to receiving communication in the group. I think the group was uncomfortable about the voice, not about the message itself. I decided if I were contacted, then I would receive any message telepathically. If it were long and complex, I'd write it down. Then I'd share it with the group, and see if they wanted me to continue to allow such contacts.

I was contacted the next Wednesday night. It was in the middle of the sending of energy, when the room was dark except for candle light, and all eyes were closed except for Cindy's, who was reading. I could tell at once that the message was long and would have to be written. I felt uncomfortable about disturbing others while writing, and tried to be as quiet as possible. This message came through:

"There is a white light within us all. This light is a source of energy and protection. When you call upon energies as a group you draw on this source of energy within each of us. You also connect with each other and with universal forms of energy. That is why your work as a group is so important—you are able to connect with universal sources of energy."

I was disappointed in the message, and felt embarrassed about sharing it. It didn't say anything evidential of high-level communication. I could have sat down and made it up. I was considering not sharing it, when Cindy asked: "Were you writing, Sandy?" I nodded, and the others encouraged me to read the message.

Surprisingly, the group found the message meaningful.

Sue suggested we use it each week as a prayer to read while we hold hands. Everyone was comfortable with the message, and encouraged me to write down and share any future message I received.

I think I'm beginning to understand the importance of the group process. When we tried voice communication, none of us were ready for it. I was very tense, and it was a very new experience for the group. But the telepathic messages are very easy and natural for me. We're growing together as a group with this process.

On Friday evening, Burt and I held another trance session. I've been struggling with an important professional decision. I've completed the first year of the three-year training program in family therapy, and have a strong urge to drop out. I'm not learning anything that's useful in my work. I had Burt ask for any information that would help me in making the decision.

"We have information that should be considered at this time. It should be recognized that there is still resistance to fulfilling the chosen path. It is time to select the experiences which will directly benefit this one in the chosen path. This is a crucial time. This decision has greater importance than is realized. This one can choose a path of traditional professional training or can choose a path that is less traditional and will greater benefit the growth of the soul and fulfill the chosen mission. The former path will lead to professional security. The latter path will bring greater personal satisfaction. The soul must choose the path desired at this time."

That message was unusually straightforward. I sent my letter of resignation in to the program.

The following Wednesday in the group I again kept paper and pencil nearby in case of contact. Again, it came. I wrote:

"We have here many souls working who are working with your group to help in its growth and for sending energy. You are being guided and protected as a group. You may at times feel the energies or presences from these advanced guides. You may wish to have a name for reference: Kirin. In your terms this is the soul-name of the guide working with this group. Others are also present. There is much love here. You are striving for a group spirit. This is very important. Keep up this work. Continue to meditate as individuals and as a group. This will maintain your contact with the higher energies which are within and will facilitate your abilities to send this energy in love. Good night."

I felt my old reluctance about sharing the message. The idea of a group spirit guide seemed gimmicky. Was I imagining all this? After sending, we decided to move outside to the picnic table before sharing our experiences. John and I lagged behind.

"Did you write again, Sandy?" he asked me.

"Well, yes, I did. But I feel silly about sharing it."

"The messages are helpful and relevant to our group process. I don't care where they come from. I believe in them. I believe in them for what they have to say."

When I started receiving messages in the group I had the idea that I would need to educate the group about them. In actuality, though, the group is educating me.

I've been having some interesting experiences in the office. Barbara, a new counselor who started working a few months ago, is very interested in psychic phenomena. I told her a little about the past life work I've done with Dick, and she was fascinated, so I let her read my journal. She found it interesting, but also commented that it needed editing. I knew that but I hadn't found anyone with the interest, time, and ability to do the job. Barbara volunteered. She's edited other manuscripts and is very talented with words. I'm really pleased.

I've felt badly, though that I couldn't pay her for doing it. Then one day recently she commented that she had a neck ache and asked me if I'd give her a neck massage. Afterwards she said it was one of the best massages she's ever had. So I asked her if she'd like massages in exchange for editing. She was pleased with the idea.*

Things have been rather slow around the office the past

---

*When Barbara read this line in the draft version, she wrote in the margin: "Pleased? It was a fantasy come true!!!"

few weeks, so Barbara's been working on the manuscript and we've turned a corner of the counseling room into a temporary massage parlor. Barbara's really been enjoying the massages, and I enjoy giving them. It's such a pleasant experience for me to utilize energy in a way that helps someone. Occasionally, I try sending energy or doing hands-on-healing instead of massage.

Yesterday, Barbara was feeling poorly because of a stomach ache. I sat next to her and meditated. I imagined that I could actually see her stomach. It was in turmoil. I had a strong impulse to send it orange, so did so. I pictured the stomach bathed in orange, and could "see" it calm down. Barbara reported afterwards that she felt much better. I was pleased, but was left with a problem: *my* stomach hurt all day!

I'm becoming more interested in massage. I'm especially intrigued by the comment I made in a trance state that massage is a form of healing. I'd like to learn more. Recently, I was examining a list of workshops offered this summer by a local growth center, and saw one on massage. It will deal with such techniques as Esalen and psychic massage. *Psychic massage?* I did a double-take when I read that. I've never heard of it, but it sounds just up my alley. The instructor is a psychic healer, masseuse and psychotherapist in private practice in New York. Naturally, I signed up for the workshop. I'll be taking it in a couple of weeks.

Now that I've decided to drop out of my family therapy training program, I've been feeling more insecure about my professional future. I'm still receiving professional supervision to learn basic counseling techniques, but I imagine my future as a counselor to be involved in some way with meditation, hypnosis, and past lives. That makes me feel very isolated professionally. Dick and Joe are the only ones I know who use these approaches.

And the future is already happening. I often teach my clients meditation to help them relax. And, strangely enough, I'm finding that many clients want to discuss the occult with me. I never bring up the subject myself, but, increasingly, clients are telling me about their own psychic experiences. These experiences are becoming more common, and I often wonder how best to handle them in a therapeutically useful manner. There are few guidelines in this area.

But I've recently learned that there's a new branch of psychology called "transpersonal psychology." There's a journal devoted to it, which presents articles on altered states of consciousness, spiritual awareness, peak experiences, paranormal events, and similar subjects.

I'm starting to feel less isolated. I am a part of a group every Wednesday night, where I can be open about my experiences and have them accepted very naturally. I'm starting to realize that there are other people around the country besides Dick who are interested in a new kind of psychotherapy.

My graduate work in education, my past training in family therapy, and my present supervision are all giving me solid background in traditional therapeutic approaches, and I'm absorbing the best of the traditional for my own work. My own eighteen months of therapy with Dick, my incessant reading about the occult, meditation, hypnosis, healing and world religions, and my own experiences give me a background in the nontraditional. I think that my greatest challenge in the coming years will be a professional integration of these approaches.

FRIDAY, JULY 29, 1977

It's with mixed feelings that I sit down to write today. This will be the final journal entry in my book. I'm relieved to be completing the project; it's consumed a great deal of my time and energy. But I also feel sad about drawing to a close such a dramatic and intense period of my life. I don't know who future readers of this material will be, but I feel that we have established a relationship through these pages, and that I am now saying good-by to a friend.

This month has been one of completion. I took a train to D.C. last week for the oral examination on my dissertation. I passed, so, after making some final revisions, I'll graduate next month with my Ph.D.

I also had my terminating session with Dick this month. I always wondered when and how I would terminate my relationship with him. I used to wonder how I would know when it was time to end it. But, like with everything else in my life, when the time was right, I just knew. It wasn't easy to face my final session. I found myself adding more and more questions to my list and wondering if it would be possible for Dick to answer them all in one session. As I prepared my questions, I found myself becoming angry with Dick. I felt I could anticipate the answers I would receive, and, as usual, they would be openended rather than definitive. I remembered the many months of sessions, when I had been disappointed that Dick encouraged my own ability to find answers rather than giving answers to me.

As I thought about my anger, I began to understand it. I still wanted someone to explain in words to me things that can only be grasped intuitively. I wanted someone to answer questions for me that may not be answerable in earth terms. I wanted someone to explain infinity and the nature of the universe and the meaning of the psychic. It's very difficult to accept that such answers may have to be obtained from inside. Dick, I realized, had explained these concepts to me many times before in many ways, but I would never be fully satisfied until I found my own answers inside myself. And for that, I didn't need Dick. Or anyone. After touching this root of my anger, the anger dissipated. I understood that Dick had been preparing me for this realization since our first session.

That first session was exactly 18 months ago today. It was January 29, 1976, that I first arrived at Dick's office and began this journal. I showed up at his office again earlier this month for my final session, carrying notebook, tape recorder, and a list of unanswerable questions.

"I feel like I'm ending what I started when I came here eighteen months ago," I began. "I've worked through the basic needs I had then. This is a terminating session. It's possible that I might want another session sometime if I'm really discouraged, or perhaps I'll want some professional advice on a client. But basically, I feel this session ends what I started."

"I can buy that."

"That last session really tied everything together for me."

"It was like the last piece of the puzzle?"

"Exactly. I feel through with past life work now; I know what I need to know. Maybe in ten years there'll be need for additional work, but I doubt it. I think I've done what needs to be done."

"I agree. I think you know what you need to know, even though it may not all be on a conscious level. There's a word for that: *dharma*. It's when an individual intuitively knows his path—he knows what must be done, even though he may not be able to explain it in words. It's understanding that you are a tool and that you will be guided throughout your life. It's understanding that it really doesn't matter what you were or what you did in past lives—it was all part of soul growth. That's where

283

you are now. So I would say, if nothing else, you may need a short rap session with me at a Foundation tag sale. Or we'll B.S. over a cup of coffee. You may stop in to chat. But I doubt that you'll need any more formal sessions. Of course, the door's open to you if you do. But I doubt that they'll be needed."

"Just like I felt I *had* to have help eighteen months ago, I've felt I had to write my book. I don't know if it'll ever be published, but I just had to put my experiences down on paper."

"I'm sure it's helpful for your own sake to be able to read it."

"No question about it. I can't even relate to the beginning portions of the manuscript now; it doesn't seem like me—it's like reading someone else's story. If it weren't written down, I'd consciously forget a lot of it. And I need to remember it."

"As mortals, we take our growth for granted, and it's easy to forget the pain. Your approach is also an ideal one for sharing an experience with others. And the accuracy doesn't matter. All your past lives, all your experiences fit a very definite sequential pattern, which makes their reality highly probable. But like I said before, it really doesn't matter if you imagined those past lives or really lived them. The end result is all that counts—you're getting yourself together now. I could care less about proving if you were a particular person at a particular time."

"I've been rereading the early portions of the manuscript, and you talk a lot there about how you have techniques for verifying auto-writing. But I'm not sure that it's clear what those techniques are. Could you elaborate on that?"

"Sure. If the arm is totally taken over, the handwriting will totally change—there will not be any characteristics of 'you' in it. Now, we're not talking about an 'Exorcist'-type possession—there are many types of 'possession.' Your handwriting never changed enough to say you were 'possessed.' There was always a part of you in it. If it had totally changed, we would have taken even more precautions, moved even more slowly to make certain there was not a low-level entity working through you. It may take a long time—it may take another book," Dick added with a chuckle, "before you can totally give up conscious interference. And by that time you may be totally telepathic, and not need to rely on any tools like auto-writing."

"If someone does auto-writing and the handwriting doesn't change at all, does that mean that it's not authentic auto-writing?"

"It could mean that. They may be tapping their sub-conscious mind and relying on material they read and learned through the years. Now there's nothing wrong with this at all if the information is helpful. But if I felt this were the case, I would explain what was happening so that they would not delude themselves. The most important thing is to critique the information. Is it logical? Is it helpful? Is there tangible, verifiable, information? Does anything offensive come through? This is extremely important, and I look very closely for it."

I threw out a few other questions, like asking Dick to please explain the nature of time to me, but as usual I remained confused. I left feeling pleased that I had stuck with this therapy to its completion.

The following weekend, the workshop I had signed up for in psychic massage was held. I arrived eagerly with a large towel and lunch to share. As I waited for the instructor to arrive, I considered how much my attitude had changed. Eighteen months ago I was very frightened of learning any skill related to energies or the psychic. Now I was eager to learn. And I felt very strongly that it was time for me to learn as much as possible from as many people as possible.

I immediately liked Jackie Lapa, the woman who taught the workshop. She believes that massage is a form of channeling energy for healing. She emphasized working intuitively on a body rather than mechanically using specific strokes. She talked about various types of psychic healing, and I told her about my experience of sending orange to Barbara's stomach, and how I had a stomach ache afterwards.

"Yes, that really can happen, Sandy," she responded.

"It takes a certain amount of expereince to learn not to absorb the ailment of the healee."

"Can you give me any advice?"

"Yes, it's good to start by white-lighting yourself. Do you know how to do that?" I assured her that I had indeed heard about white lighting. "Then you may want to say an affirmation or prayer. Basically, the technique is learning not to open yourself up too much to the other person."

"I always think about my love for the person I'm trying to channel for. I feel healing can only be done from an attitude of love."

"That's true, but there's a dividing line. It's like counseling. An experienced counselor can be warm and caring, but doesn't take the client's problems home. You have to be objective, and leave the client's problems with the client. An inexperienced counselor might become depressed because the client is depressed. With experience, you learn how to help without absorbing the feelings. It's the same with healing. You've got to discover that line between loving and absorbing, and learn to stay on the loving side."

Of course, during the month, I've continued my unending search for Knowledge and Truth by reading voraciously. I'm presently reading several of Jane Robert's books. She's a medium, but has no interest in cups flying across the room or in dead souls delivering proof of their continued existence to loved ones. In fact, she does not consider the source of information to be an outside entity, but rather in some respect an aspect of herself. I'm beginning to understand this theory better through her book *Adventures in Consciousness: An Introduction to Aspect Psychology*. When I saw a summary of this book, I immediately ordered it. The book ties together a great deal of what I've been struggling with these past months. I'm not saying it provides The Answer, but it does suggest a possible interpretation.

We have, of course, been continuing our trance sessions this month. During our regular Sunday session on the 3rd, I had Burt ask about my book: "Please provide any information on Sandy's book. Any suggestions on revisions? Should she pursue trying to have it published?" This answer came through:

"Yes. It is important to complete this work as soon as possible. Its completion will enable the soul to move to further development.

"It is important to continue along the lines being pursued at present. This work provides growth for Sandy and allows the experience to be shared.

"The plans to attempt to publish the material should definitely be pursued."

(Of course, I couldn't understand why my source didn't just give the name and address of a publisher!)

I also had Burt ask about a subject that's been on my mind a lot this month: "Please provide further information on the meaning of time—especially the concept that all lives are lived at once. How does karma operate given this condition?"

"Yes. We have here a question that we could spend years answering. Years in your framework which do not exist in ours. This question is extremely difficult and possibly impossible to answer in your framework. However, we shall begin with some introductory comments this evening.

"First, please try to orient yourselves outside of your everyday reality. You see yourselves as moving through time, with yesterday gone and tomorrow yet to happen. In reality, however, all must happen at once.

"Your lives are structured by clocks and calendars. Without this structure you would be very confused. This structure enables you to function properly and orient yourselves on the physical plane.

"However, when one moves beyond the physical plane, these concepts of time become restrictive.

"At this point one is able to begin the process of learning the true nature of time. This learning is greatly impeded while you remain in your bodies. You can, however, grasp some of the elementary concepts.

"There is much to learn here, and we shall continue our

discussion in the next session. Please read carefully this material and prepare any questions on what has been presented at this point."

While this information was coming through, I projected my consciousness to the park with Kirk. He said that today would be relaxing; it was a transition between old tasks (e.g. the book) and new tasks. I had to complete the old tasks before I was fully able to move ahead. I told him how joyful I've been feeling lately. He commented that this is the real purpose of life—to discover inner joy *in spite of* any earthly restrictions. Once this is fully discovered, one is ready to move beyond the earth plane. The joy radiates outward and improves one's life situations.

We held another session the following Friday evening. I was becoming increasingly uncomfortable over the fact that some of our friends have been referring to me as a "medium." I don't like the word "medium." Burt asked why I had such a reluctance to accept this term.

"Yes. We see this reluctance. The soul does not wish to be associated with this term. There are past life forces at work here. There is also an association of the term with its older or traditional usage. The concept of contacting the higher energies within the self is very important. Everyone has this ability and should be engaged in this process. Each person's ability will develop in different directions and at different rates and levels. However, each person is capable of posing questions to the highest within the self and can with practice learn to interpret the answers. It is hoped that the experiences shared by Sandy in the book will help others learn to engage in this process for themselves.

"No channel, no medium, no source of information by itself should be relied upon to the exclusion of the self. The higher self always should be consulted to evaluate any information that comes from any other source. It is an important message, we wish to impart to readers of Sandy's book. If you visit a psychic or obtain any information from any source outside the self, evaluate it very carefully in light of the inner vibrations.

"Never allow an outside source to take away the process of looking inward. An outside source can be very helpful in providing guidelines and information that has not yet been retrieved inside the self. However, the inner self must be the ultimate source for each person. Learn to trust this source in yourself and never ever abandon this inner voice in favor of an outside source."

In the middle of this long narration, Burt became increasingly frustrated at taking notes. We no longer use the tape recorder since it takes so long to transcribe from it. Instead, Burt takes notes verbatim during the session utilizing his own short-hand system. The voice usually starts out very slowly, and there's no trouble in writing. However, it often speeds up later and taking notes can be very difficult. During this speech, Burt reached a point where he couldn't keep up, and shouted in frustration: "Stop!" The shock was so great that I was almost forced out of the trance state. But I calmed down, and in a few moments the narration continued, at a slower pace. After its completion, these words were added:

"We now wish to advise Burt on the importance of speaking gently while we are communicating here. A sudden loud voice can impair the trance depth."

Burt was in no mood for this gentle chiding. He said resentfully, "I wish to advise The Source on the importance of speaking *slowly*. It's very difficult for me to keep up with your speed. If you know so much, you should know when you're going too fast for me!"

The strong feeling in Burt's voice was rather startling, and I almost brought myself out of the trance. But Kirk encouraged me to relax and allow the session to continue. My voice responded gently to Burt:

"It is important for you to inform us each time we speak fast. A gentle request is sufficient."

"OK," Burt responded. "It's a deal."

During this session, I was again with Kirk in the park. He said I needed to learn how to focus my concentration much better than I was doing. To help me focus in the park, a line suddenly appeared on the sidewalk with a red light at the end. Kirk encouraged me to concentrate very hard on walking along the line while staring at the light. I found I had to concentrate hard to do so, and it made it more difficult to be aware of what was happening with my body. Later, I asked Kirk for some help in working out some personal problems. He told me there was no right or wrong answer, but the growth and challenge came from my efforts to work out a satisfactory solution for myself.

We didn't have time for a session that Sunday, so held one the following Tuesday evening, the 12th. Burt asked for a continuation of the explanation on the nature of time.

"We have here a subject that is very confusing. We can only relay the most elementary aspects because of your framework and because of the limitations of the channel.

"You have heard that time does not exist. This is accurate, but can be very misleading because of your understanding of that concept. It may be easier to grasp if you think in terms of everything happening at once. Think in terms of space. Just as you live your life in your apartment, your neighbors simultaneously live their lives next door. By the same token, your lifetimes are neighbors living next door to each other. All exist now in your framework.

"Yesterday no longer exists. In another framework, however, all exist. Nothing is ever lost or destroyed. Likewise tomorrow already exists in another dimension. But this in no way alters the free will of today.

"We shall continue this discussion in another session."

As I was entering the trance for this session, my body stiffened and I felt a bolt of energy. This process was repeated each time Burt asked a question. My entire body was swaying during much of the session, just as my head used to move from side to side.

Kirk and I strolled through the park and chatted. I was in one of my "this is all imagination and bullshit" moods and Kirk largely ignored my loud complaints about the lack of specifics. When I stopped complaining, he gave me a lecture about how I'd always have doubts and must learn to continue with this work *in spite of* them, especially since other people were being helped by my messages.

During our next session, I had my most unusual experience with Kirk to date. He seemed to have given up on lines and lights to attract my concentration, and devised something a bit more dramatic. We began in the park with a short stroll and discussion. Suddenly, I found myself in a hospital room. A man was being operated on, and he was on the verge of death. I became aware that his spirit was with us, and Kirk was speaking with him. Kirk reviewed his life with him and asked him if he was ready to pass on. He thought about it, and then said no; he chose to continue life. His spirit returned to a point just above his body where it remained throughout the operation.

Before I had time to ask Kirk about that experience, I realized that we were both flying through the air. Suddenly we landed on a dusty country road. Kirk said we were in Indiana and the year was 1942. I saw people wandering out from a fair. No one could see us, however, exept for a small boy who kept staring at us. He sensed that there was no point in sharing his experience with the adults, since they would laugh at him.

I was just adjusting to that scene, when I found us both in outer space. We were observing the earth from afar. I was captivated by the breathtaking beauty, by the splendor of the stars, and by the dark and quiet.

I must admit that it was a bit difficult to think about my voice while these scenes were going on.

Burt and I have continued attending the holistic healing group on Wednesday evenings this month. I brought a pad of paper and a pen to the group each meeting, just in case I felt the urge to write. On the 6th, after we finished sending, I sensed a presence, and wrote as fast as words came into my mind:

"Greetings, my friends—

"We are here with you this evening with love and energy to share. The message we wish to leave with you this evening is: Peace! Let us consider the process by which our messages are received. It may appear to you that one person is serving as a channel or medium for this information. In actuality, all play a role. We utilize the energies and vibrations of each person in this room to create the necessary conditions for this transmission.

"As we proceed in the coming weeks, you will each begin to sense your own impressions and receive messages of love during your group time. This process is to help in your growth as a group and in your individual spiritual development. In time, messages can be relayed to all as a group and be received by all as a group. This will take time."

Then an answer was provided on a question Joe had posed earlier: "Should we each have an individual technique, or all use the same one for sending?"

"As individuals, your techniques will vary. Follow that which is most natural. *Remember*—far more important than any technique is love. Focus on your love for the person in question. It is not necessary to use any other 'technique'. Love is the essential."

Then a question that Cindy had posed was answered: "Is Sri Chinmoy a good guru?"

"For Cindy's question—remember that all serve a purpose. This guide has helped many, but is not appropriate for all. Each must find an individual path and are attracted to those teachers they most need. A street cleaner may be a more effective teacher for some than any 'guru.' Seek your own teachers. Follow your inner voice.

"Love and peace to all—Kirin."

Last Wednesday the group met at John's, as usual, and we were all present except for Cindy. It seemed to be a very low-keyed evening and I was tired, so I decided I wouldn't even bother to do any writing. No one said anything about it or suggested any questions, so I decided that perhaps we all needed a break. And my own energy was still low after the drain of my D.C. trip and orals. I didn't even put a tablet and pen by my chair.

It was a relief not to be consciously preparing myself for writing, so I drifted easily and comfortably into a very restful state. I felt a lot of energy flowing through me, and felt I was really making contact with some of the people on our list.

Shortly into the list, I felt my consciousness drawn outside of the room to the front lawn. Kirk was there.

"Hello!" I greeted him. "What are you doing here?"

"To take you for a stroll. Isn't it much pleasanter out here than in that stuffy room?"

"Well, it is pleasant out here, but if I'm talking to you, I can't concentrate on sending energy. And that's what I'm here for."

"Don't worry about it. Your body is still serving as a channel, even though your consciousness may not be focused on the process."

"I still don't understand why you're here tonight. You must have more in mind than a stroll through the streets of Milford."

"Yes, you're being prepared to do voice communication again with this group. You've got to become more relaxed and be able to forget about what's happening in the room. This is an exercise in putting your concentration elsewhere."

We had a pleasant stroll, but then I brought myself back to the room as the list was concluded. I was preparing to bring myself back to a normal state since Joe had just finished reading. Then I was aware that Joe was speaking to me.

"Sandy, I have a few questions I'd like to ask tonight, if you feel into channeling information. Do you feel able to do so?"

"Yes," I muttered without thinking. Then I realized that I didn't have paper and pen nearby, so couldn't write. Suddenly I sensed Kirk's presence again and realized that Joe was asking for voice channeling. Mentally, I tried to refuse. I didn't feel comfortable doing it unless every member of the group agreed to it. Otherwise, I'd be imposing on them. But as I tried to refuse, I felt my body preparing for the channeling. My breathing was heavy and my head was moving from side to side. And my awareness was suddenly outside with Kirk. I knew that I didn't have the energy to resist the process underway in my body, and assumed that on some level I had granted permission for it. So, rather glumly, I went for a stroll with Kirk.

"I've been tricked," I complained. "Just when did I agree to this? I don't know where the others in the group are at on this. I may be imposing this process on them."

"No, you're not imposing it on them," Kirk responded. "But you are transmitting your feelings to them. They still feel uneasy about it because *you* feel uneasy about it."

A few questions were posed by the group and, as usual, general answers were provided.

Joe gave me the suggestion that I would sleep very well that night and helped me to gradually come back to a normal consciousness. Then he brought me a glass of water. I drank it gratefully, feeling embarrassed and uncomfortable. I shared my feelings and what the experience had been like for me. Others discussed their reactions. Sue said she was no longer uneasy about it. After reading the manuscript, she felt she had experienced it hundreds of times before. Others said that the voice change was easier to accept this time. Pat, who hadn't been a group member during the previous voice session, said that the change was startling for her at first, but she was comfortable after a couple of minutes. She thought she had experienced REM for the first time.

I emphasized how important it was for me to be certain that the process was acceptable for everyone, so each person discussed their feelings. Everyone expressed willingness to utilize the process again, so I think we will. I also think other group members will soon begin receiving messages of their own.

On the way home Burt told me he was feeling down.

"I'm really discouraged," he said as he drove down the expressway. "I'm thinking of quitting the group."

"Whatever for?"

"Everyone else has experiences to discuss after we send energy, but I never do. I never seem to feel anything or experience anything."

"Don't you feel relaxed and in a pleasant frame of mind, and energized?"

"Yes."

"Then you're experiencing something."

"But nothing dramatic. Others seem to experience so much more. It makes me wonder what's wrong with me."

Neither of us said much more the rest of the way home.

I was feeling down, both for Burt's sake and because I was concerned that my channeling may have brought the feelings on—(the old "I might-hurt-someone" paranoia), although Burt said that it was primarily because of the messages I've been receiving that he's continued to come.

I remember that another group member who had come only for a few weeks a long time back had dropped out for the same reason. I suspected that it may be common not to be able to sense energies. As I sat thinking about the subject, a lot of ideas rushed into mind.

First, I suspected that Burt *was* experiencing the same thing as everyone else, but didn't realize he was experiencing it. It's like smoking marijuana. The effects of being "high" are very subtle, and inexperienced smokers often don't feel anything. Only after one ceases to expect the world to change, and instead focuses on the very subtle changes in the body and the environment do they enjoy the "high."

Perhaps the energy "high" is the same thing. Perhaps one has to learn to interpret the very subtle changes that occur when energy is passing through. For a long time, one of my biggest problems in exploring trance states and automatic writing was that the changes were so subtle, I wasn't sure they were occurring at all. I was extremely relaxed and in a very pleasant frame of mind, but is that a trance state? The changes in my arm and the words in my mind all appeared so gently that I refused to consider them anything but imagination at first.

The same thing is true now. If Burt could experience exactly what I experience in a trance state, he would probably be very disappointed and claim that he hadn't felt much of anything. We would experience the same thing, but I would be more aware of the subtlety of those changes and would *interpret* them as changes. Burt would probably dismiss them as imagination.

That is especially true of my projections of consciousness with Kirk. I don't know if I "really" am in the park or not.

Anyone can experience this dilemma. Relax, close your eyes, and imagine that you are in front of your home.

Imagine very vividly all the detail of your house or apartment as you look at it. Notice the street, the sidewalk. Are there cars parked there? Are there pedestrians passing? If you stop to question if you're really experiencing this, you'll blow the whole thing. You've got to just experience it. Imagine it as vividly as you can. Sure, it was "imagination," but it was a pleasant experience. So repeat it again tomorrow. And the next day. In time, your ability to "imagine" the details will become much more vivid. And your experience of "actually" being there will be far more real. In time, you'll no longer be certain if you're imagining it or if it's reality.

This is basically what I experience in trance states when I take strolls and trips with Kirk. When I first started having these experiences, I asked if they were real or imagination. I was told that the question can't be answered in these terms. To "imagine" the experience is the first step to creating the experience.

I think our conception of reality is very shallow, that we may create our reality in ways that we don't yet understand. And I think that our conception of "imagination" is also very shallow. Where, after all, does imagination come from? It comes from the self, and often from very deep levels of the self.

I suspect that, to a large extent, the ability to experience the psychic dimension of life is the ability to suspend judgment about a "reality-imagination" duality. To insist on categorizing all experiences into one of these two boxes will probably limit psychic awareness more than anything else. To allow the mind complete freedom to experience without judgement, however, may be the most important factor in such experience.

I explained this theory to Burt when we arrived home. "There are a lot of people who feel the way you do for the same reasons. I was caught in the same dilemma for a long time, and still get caught in it periodically. But I think you'll start to experience energy, and many other psychic phenomena when you let yourself imagine and fantasize. You always need your intellect, but use it *after* you've had an experience. Use all the categories you want after an experience. But to evaluate it while you're having it will inhibit your psychic self."

My theory on reality and imagination helps me understand my own experiences better. When I started this journal, I assumed that I was searching to understand if my experiences were real or imagination. I figured that I'd end the book when I had a definite answer. Instead, I've come to see the question as irrelevant and unanswerable. Our terms "reality" and "imagination" are too misunderstood and shallow to serve as categories for such a search. I think it's more useful to examine the experiences for the role they play in my life, for their usefulness to me and others, for the feelings I have about them.

The past few days, I've felt that I've finally come to grasp a very important concept, and that now it's time to end the book.

This afternoon, Burt and I had a trance session. I was aware that it would be the last session included in the book. Kirk and I discussed that as we walked in the park. He said he felt I was ready to attempt a visit to his (and my) home planet, and that it would be a fitting experience at the end of the book, since he's been preparing me for it for a long time. However, he said the experience would only last for an instant, because it would take a long time to accustom myself to it. He said we would visit a garden, and that I should be prepared for the colors to be far more varied and intense than they are on earth. Then, in an instant, we were standing in a luminous garden. The light was blinding, and we were back in the park again. Kirk explained that it was not the sunlight, but rather the colors from the plants that had been so intense.

While I was having this experience, Burt asked, "Is there any further information to be channeled as a message to readers of the book?"

The answer that came through was long, and I think provides a fitting close to this book. I'll let these trance words end the experience I have shared with my readers:

"Yes. We have several points we wish to impart. We hope that this book has been a personal experience for the

297

reader. We hope that it inspires the reader to embark on his own journey into the Self. You have not yet begun to understand the nature of the mind or to explore its potential.

"Life is an opportunity for exploration and discovery. It is important to use these opportunities for the growth of the soul. We wish to encourage the reader to explore the depths of the soul, to understand the self and life's path.

"Please understand that there are many sources of help for each, sources within and also from the guides and energies surrounding the self. By embarking on a sincere effort to learn and by opening the self to the lessons, there will be many answers available. These answers may not appear as a specific spirit guide. They may not be evidenced through automatic writing or through channeling of the voice. But the answers will be felt in their own way for each individual.

"It is important to follow that flow within. This point has been made many times, and it cannot be stressed too much. We have here the story of a person who attempted to resist the flow of development in the life and now has found greater harmony through attempting to live within the flow.

"This is true for each reader of the book, but we must emphasize that the flow for each will be individual.

"Do not attempt to imitate the path of another. Rather, search for your own path. Your path may not include the necessity to study past life cycles or do automatic writing. Or these may be important in your path. You must follow that voice that is within yourself.

"We wish here to express our appreciation to the readers of this book. Just as you may benefit from Sandy's experiences, she will benefit from your reading this material.

"This may be a difficult concept to grasp, but in a universal sense, all growth is conducive to all souls. If one soul grows, all souls are able to benefit from the experience.

"There is a kind of union and sharing among all who read this material. A kind of common bond where paths have crossed, even though there may be no conscious awareness of this.

"We wish to encourage continued search inside the self, even though this may be difficult and discouraging at times. But the rewards are there.

"Thank you for your attention throughout this book."

ABOUT THE AUTHOR

Wilma Wake is a 36-year-old woman residing in a rural area of New Hampshire with her husband, a clinical psychologist. She obtained a B.A. degree in Social Studies Education in 1969 from the University of Illinois and then taught high school for one year. In 1971 she received an M.Ed. degree in History and Philosophy of Education from the University of Illinois, followed in 1977 with a Ph.D. in Social Foundations of Education from the University of Maryland.

She worked from 1976-78 as administrative director and counselor at a drug counseling agency. From 1978-80 she was head of the Prana Foundation, a holistic counseling center in Connecticut. The experiences she had there are described in her second book, *Beyond the Mind*.

At present, she maintains a part-time private practice in holistic psychotherapy and is also working on a Master of Divinity degree at a seminary in Boston.

SUGGESTIONS FOR FURTHER READING

Thomas Sugrue, *There Is A River: The Story of Edgar Cayce*. Dell Books, 1945. An excellent biography of the life and work of medium Edgar Cayce.

Jane Roberts—Medium Jane Roberts has produced volumes of material dictated by her trance personality, "Seth." They're all readable, yet profound.

> *The Seth Material*. Prentice-Hall, 1970.
> *Seth Speaks*. Prentice-Hall, 1972.
> *The Nature of Personal Reality:* A Seth Book. Prentice-Hall, 1974.
> *Adventures in Consciousness: An Introduction to Aspect Psychology*. Prentice-Hall, 1975. In this book, Ms. Roberts explores altered states of consciousness and the meaning of reality.

Sally Hammond, *We Are All Healers*. Ballantine, 1974. A good introduction to healing.

Jess Stearn, *Yoga, Youth, and Reincarnation*. Bantam Books, 1965. A highly readable introduction to hatha yoga and concepts of reincarnation.

Lawrence LeShan, *How to Meditate: A Guide to Self Discovery*. Bantam Books, 1975. Very good introduction to meditation with specific techniques suggested.

> *The Medium, the Mystic, and the Physicist*. Ballantine/Viking, 1974. Examines similarities in the reality described by mediums, mystics, and physicists.

Dick Sutphen, *You Were Born Again To Be Together*. Pocket Books, 1976. A hypnotist who has regressed thousands of people to past lives discusses his work, presenting real case studies.

Excerpts from the Paul Solomon Tapes. Fellowship of the Inner Light, 620 14th St., Virginia Beach, VA 23451. Fascinating information channeled through Paul Solomon.

Marion Weinstein, *Positive Magic: Occult Self-Help*. Pocket Books, 1978. An excellent guide on developing your own psychic powers.

Eklal Kueshana, *The Ultimate Frontier*, The Stelle Group, (Box 75, Quinlan, TX 75474), 1963. A readable account of the spiritual guidance provided by the great white Brotherhoods.

ORGANIZATIONS

Association for Research and Enlightenment (continues the work of Edgar Cayce)
P.O. Box 595
Virginia Beach, Virginia 23451

The Theosophical Society in America
P.O. Box 270
Wheaton, Ill. 60187

Connecticut Tri-Counseling Center* (Director: Dick
   Smith)
221 Broad St.
Milford, Ct. 06460 (ph. (203) 878-5022)

Spiritual Frontiers Fellowship, Inc.
Executive Plaza—10715Winner Rd.
Independence, Missouri 64052 (ph. (816) 254-8585)